Pandemic Crossings

US–CHINA RELATIONS IN THE AGE OF GLOBALIZATION

This series publishes the best, cutting-edge work tackling the opportunities and dilemmas of relations between the United States and China in the age of globalization. Books published in the series encompass both historical studies and contemporary analyses, and include both single-authored monographs and edited collections. Our books are comparative, offering in-depth communication-based analyses of how United States and Chinese officials, scholars, artists, and activists configure each other, portray the relations between the two nations, and depict their shared and competing interests. They are interdisciplinary, featuring scholarship that works in and across communication studies, rhetoric, literary criticism, film studies, cultural studies, international studies, and more. And they are international, situating their analyses at the crossroads of international communication and the nuances, complications, and opportunities of globalization as it has unfolded since World War II.

SERIES EDITOR
Stephen J. Hartnett, *University of Colorado Denver*

EDITORIAL BOARD
Rya Butterfield, *Nicholls State University*
Hsin-I Cheng, *Santa Clara University*
Patrick Shaou-Whea Dodge, *International College Beijing*
Qingwen Dong, *University of the Pacific*
Mohan Dutta, *Massey University, New Zealand*
John Erni, *Hong Kong Baptist University*
Xiaohong Gao, *Communication University of China*
G. Thomas Goodnight, *University of Southern California*
Robert Hariman, *Northwestern University*
Rolien Hoyng, *Chinese University of Hong Kong*
Dongjing Kang, *Florida Gulf Coast University*
Lisa Keränen, *University of Colorado Denver*
Zhi Li, *Communication University of China*
Jingfang Liu, *Fudan University*
Xing Lu, *DePaul University*
Trevor Parry-Giles, *National Communication Association*
Phaedra C. Pezzullo, *University of Colorado Boulder*
Todd Sandel, *University of Macau*
Zhiwei Wang, *University of Zhengzhou*
Guobin Yang, *University of Pennsylvania*
Yufang Zhang, *University of Shanghai*

Pandemic Crossings

Digital Technology, Everyday Experience, and Governance in the COVID-19 Crisis

Edited by Guobin Yang, Bingchun Meng, and Elaine J. Yuan

MICHIGAN STATE UNIVERSITY PRESS | *East Lansing*

Copyright © 2024 by Michigan State University

Michigan State University Press
East Lansing, Michigan 48823-5245

Library of Congress Cataloging-in-Publication Data
Names: Yang, Guobin, editor. | Meng, Bingchun, editor. | Yuan, Elaine J., 1974– editor.
Title: Pandemic crossings : digital technology, everyday experience, and governance in the COVID-19 crisis /
edited by Guobin Yang, Bingchun Meng, Elaine J. Yuan.
Description: East Lansing, Michigan : Michigan State University Press, [2024] |
Series: US–China relations in the age of globalization | Includes bibliographical references.
Identifiers: LCCN 2023032397 | ISBN 9781611864922 (paperback) | ISBN 9781609177614
Subjects: LCSH: COVID-19 Pandemic, 2020—China. | COVID-19 Pandemic, 2020–, in mass media.
Classification: LCC RA644.C67 P35995 2024 | DDC 362.1962/414400951--dc23/eng/20230731
LC record available at https://lccn.loc.gov/2023032397

Cover design by Erin Kirk
Cover photo: abstract colorful city background,
digital glitch art, generative ai, by Loks, Adobe Stock.

Visit Michigan State University Press at *www.msupress.org*

ON THE INTERSECTION OF EDGE BALL AND COURTESY:
NOTES ON SCHOLARSHIP IN THE AGE OF GLOBALIZATION

Like America or France or Brazil, China is a nation-state riven with fault-lines along region and race, ethnicity and education, linguistics and libido, gender and more general divisions. Media in the United States tend to portray Chinese society as monolithic—billions of citizens censored into silence, its activists and dissidents fearful of retribution. The "reeducation" camps in Xinjiang, the "black prisons" that dot the landscape, and the Great Firewall prove this belief partially true. At the same time, there are more dissidents on the Chinese web than there are living Americans, and rallies, marches, strikes, and protests unfold in China each week. The nation is seething with action, much of it politically radical. What makes this political action so complicated and so difficult to comprehend is that no one knows how the state will respond on any given day. In his magnificent Age of Ambition, Evan Osnos notes that "Divining how far any individual [can] go in Chinese creative life [is] akin to carving a line in the sand at low tide in the dark." His tide metaphor is telling, for throughout Chinese history waves of what Deng Xiaoping called "opening and reform" have given way to repression, which can then swing back to what Chairman Mao once called "letting a hundred flowers bloom"—China thus offers a perpetually changing landscape, in which nothing is certain. For this reason, our Chinese colleagues and collaborators are taking great risks by participating in this book series. Authors in the "west" fear their books and articles will fail to find an audience; authors in China live in fear of a midnight knock at the door.

    This series therefore strives to practice what Qingwen Dong calls "edge ball": Getting as close as possible to the boundary of what is sayable without crossing the line into being offensive. The image is borrowed from table tennis and depicts a shot that barely touches the line before ricocheting off the table; it counts as a point and is within the rules, yet the trajectory of the ball makes it almost impossible to hit a return shot. In the realm of scholarship and politics, playing "edge ball" means speaking truth to power while not provoking arrest—this is a murky game full of gray zones, allusions, puns, and sly references. What this means for our series is clear: Our authors do not censor themselves, but they do speak respectfully and cordially, showcasing research-based perspectives from their standpoints and their worldviews, thereby putting multiple vantage points into conversation. As our authors practice "edge ball," we hope our readers will savor these books with a similar sense of sophisticated and international generosity.

—Stephen J. Hartnett

Contents

ix   PREFACE, *Bingchun Meng, Guobin Yang, and Elaine J. Yuan*
xxv ACKNOWLEDGMENTS

PART 1. Governing with Digital Tools

3   Infrastructures for the Public: The Institutional Contexts of the Applications of Digital Technology in the U.S. during the COVID-19 Pandemic, *Elaine J. Yuan*

25 Pandemic Infrastructure, Mediated Mobility, and Urban Governance in China, *Yang Zhan*

45 DingTalk and Chinese Digital Workplace Surveillance in Pandemic Times, *Yizhou Xu*

67 Access as Method: Hopes, Friction, and Mediated Communication in a Remote Disability Reading Group, *Zihao Lin*

PART 2. Making Sense of the Pandemic

93 Chinese Students and Narratives of Freedom before and during COVID-19, *Yingyi Ma and Ning Zhan*

115 Cosmopolitan Imperative or Nationalist Sentiment? Mediated Experiences of the COVID-19 Pandemic among Chinese Overseas Students, *Bingchun Meng, Zifeng Chen, and Veronica Jingyi Wang*

137   Contesting for Consensus: Social Sentiment toward Fellow Citizens' COVID-Related Behavior in China, *Yan Wang and Yuxi Zhang*

PART 3. Contesting over Narratives

167   Narrating the Nation during the Global Pandemic: The "K-Quarantine" and Biopolitical Nationalism in the Era of COVID-19, *Ji-Hyun Ahn*

189   What Motivated the Sharing of Disinformation about China and COVID-19? A Study of Social Media Users in Kenya and South Africa, *Herman Wasserman and Dani Madrid-Morales*

213   China's Twitter Diplomacy: Crafting Narratives of COVID-19, *Wendy Leutert and Nicholas Atkinson*

241   CONTRIBUTORS

247   INDEX

Preface

Bingchun Meng, Guobin Yang, and Elaine J. Yuan

AS OF OCTOBER 4, 2023, THE COVID-19 PANDEMIC HAS CLAIMED MORE THAN 1.1 million lives in the U.S. and more than 6.9 million worldwide.[1] Ravaging through communities and disrupting lives and economies everywhere, the pandemic is not only the largest public health crisis since the early twentieth century, but has also led to unprecedented crises of public communication, social trust, and political legitimacy. Disinformation seems to always travel faster than official messages from public health authorities. People located on different ends of the political spectrum in different parts of the world do not even agree on the origin and the ontological nature of the virus, let alone the appropriate measures in dealing with it. Digital technologies promise effective contact tracing and instant connection, but often also become agents of harsh control and stringent exclusion. Secondary disasters of the pandemic have occurred frequently along the fault lines of social inequality. In China, for a long period before its zero-COVID policy ended in late 2022, there was widespread stigmatization and discrimination of COVID patients,[2] while those who are on the lower rung of the social-economic ladder suffered the most from strict lockdowns, such as happened in Shanghai in April and May of 2022. In the United States, COVID-related hate speech and racially motivated violence are rampant.[3] In both countries (and around the world), social groups that are already marginalized in society, such as the poor and racial, ethnic, and gender minorities, have the least capacity to cope with the harms caused by the pandemic.

One of the most significant episodes in the last wave of the COVID-19 pandemic took place at the end of 2022 in China, when the country abruptly lifted its zero-tolerance policy and the lockdowns. An estimated 250 million people got infected in the first three weeks of December.[4] Local governments, public health organizations, and other related social institutions were left overwhelmed by their lack of preparation while people struggled with the chaos caused by medical shortages and hospital rush. The glorious image of the success in fending off the pandemic under the central party leadership in mobilizing the country in the people's war against the virus dimmed. During the COVID pandemic, infections seemed to have already significantly abated with the widely available vaccines, and there was a significant reduction of fatalities. Yet the repercussions of the pandemic continue. The hope of a quick recovery of global mobility and economies has been impeded by the Ukraine war and its political-economic consequences. A post-pandemic order seems elusive.

The compounded crisis of the COVID-19 pandemic poses many challenges for researchers and academic communities. Besides the often-asked question of whether we can continue to do research "as usual," the pandemic raises the fundamental question of why we do research and publish in the first place. Conventional social science prioritizes theory, conceptualization, and methods. These are all important, of course, even in pandemic times.[5] But how urgent are they for tackling a raging pandemic and its profound social and political ramifications? We believe this historical conjuncture calls on scholars to be more oriented to social and political action. Indeed, the question is not so much whether scholarship should be more action-oriented, but what forms of action scholars can take.

Admittedly, the academic communities are themselves stratified, and individual researchers face very different personal and professional circumstances that affect how they do research. The contributors to this volume, for example, are at different stages of their career and were located in different parts of the world at the time of writing, including in China, Europe, North America, and Africa. Yet they all responded enthusiastically to a call for abstracts posted in July 2020, when many of them were still living under pandemic lockdowns. They all decided to research a public health crisis they were themselves experiencing. About half a year later, in March 2021, they convened on Zoom to share and discuss their research with a global audience. Their scholarship was a form of political action, because through it they enhanced public understanding of the pandemic experiences of people in different parts of the world, contributed to public discourse about the pandemic, such as by countering anti-Asian racism and violence, and revealed how governments in different countries responded to the pandemic. Conducting research on an ongoing pandemic was itself an accomplishment. It took courage for anyone to not only face but to reflect upon the traumatic experiences they were suffering from.

The contributions of our authors are a form of action in another sense: they document a historical event from diverse perspectives. Through data collection and analysis, their scholarship helps to preserve and understand the histories and memories of the pandemic. The data collected and analyzed in these studies consist of qualitative interviews, online ethnography, participant observation, and surveys of large volumes of social media posts. Social media can be ephemeral. Saving large quantities of social media posts related to the COVID-19 pandemic is itself an act of historical preservation. Data collected through online ethnography and participant observation, such as those in Zihao Lin's chapter, often concern the intimate experiences of small groups of people. These experiences are not readily accessible to the public. The Zoom meetings Lin organized, observed, and studied have come and gone. Yet by collecting, analyzing, and presenting these quantitative and qualitative data, our contributors have produced more than the usual academic research, for their work documents the history of the pandemic.

It is always important to document history, but the COVID-19 pandemic in particular demands historical documentation as moral action.[6] First of all, people around the world have produced incredibly large volumes of personal stories about their pandemic experiences. Shared in diverse media forms such as video blogs, photography, and online diaries, these stories are invaluable records of people's lived experiences during the pandemic. And yet many of these stories have already disappeared, due both to government censorship and the ephemeral features of cyberculture.[7] Second, research on pandemics of the past shows that everywhere there are efforts to shape a master narrative of national crisis that tend to marginalize the experiences of ordinary people. In the wake of the influenza pandemic of 1918 in the United States, as historian Nancy Bristow shows, healthcare professionals produced an optimistic narrative that "focused only on the promise of the future and erased the dark days of their recent past."[8] To study and document the COVID-19 pandemic is a means of fighting amnesia. Moreover, this study counters the disinformation, fake news, and conspiracy theories that have plagued both legacy and social media during the COVID-19 pandemic.[9]

The study of epidemics and pandemics is not new, of course, and there is much we and our contributors have learned from previous studies. Some issues persist across public health crises in different times and places. For example, in her study of AIDS, Paula Treichler shows that AIDS is as much an "epidemic of signification" as a medical issue. As different social groups impose their own interpretations, there is a tendency to perpetuate stereotypes and social stigmas.[10] Similarly, in her wide-ranging study of communicable diseases throughout the twentieth century, Priscilla Wald identifies an "outbreak narrative" with features such as the waging of microbial warfare and the stigmatization of individuals, groups, and locales promulgated through the mass media.[11] These features not only persist in the COVID-19 pandemic, but are made doubly poignant by the simultaneous occurrence of an infodemic and widespread protests against racism and hate violence.[12]

The theme of the social construction of an epidemic highlighted in the influential works of Paula Treichler and Priscilla Wald also dominates studies of epidemic outbreaks that came afterward. A study of *New York Times* coverage of the 2013 avian flu outbreak, for example, finds that "China was turned into a new danger because of its teeming cities and different ideological system, and its veil of secrecy could be seen as being conducive for the emergence of pandemic threats."[13] Contributions to two scholarly volumes on the 2003 SARS (Severe Acute Respiratory Syndrome) epidemic show how different communities affected by the same epidemic tackled the illness by constructing their own distinctive approaches.[14] Huiling Ding's study finds the rhetoric of the people's war was often used for mobilization in Chinese official media, while Western media highlighted the failure of China's political system.[15] Similar discourses appeared in Chinese and Western media during the Wuhan lockdown in 2020.[16] Scholars of the SARS crisis in 2003 also find that hero narratives, which appeared in Singaporean media but not in Hong Kong's, can boost social morale.[17] Again, we see similar uses of hero stories in Chinese media during the COVID pandemic.[18] In their prescient volume entitled—appropriately in retrospect—*SARS in China: Prelude to Pandemic?*, Kleinman and Watson wrote: "SARS is probably best seen as a harbinger of future events that might be catastrophic for the global system as we know it today."[19] It seems as if the oracle has unfortunately come true, and here we are in the middle of the COVID-19 catastrophe.

Beyond the discursive realm, anthropologist Katherine Mason examined how SARS, "the first global health crisis of the twenty-first century transformed a Chinese public health apparatus—once famous for its grassroots, low-technology approach to improving health—into a professionalized, biomedicalized, and globalized technological machine that frequently failed to serve the Chinese people."[20] Her case study of SARS's effects on China's public health system fits well with the "emerging diseases worldview" that dominated the public health administration in the United States and Western Europe since the 1990s.[21] Given its close association with colonial-era ideologies about national security and international commerce, as Nicholas B. King succinctly pointed out in his historical review of such a worldview, contemporary public health governance is characterized by three patterns: 1) A hierarchical spatial and territorial order, in which disease is portrayed as spreading from the undeveloped periphery to the developed center; 2) An emphasis on information and commodity exchange networks, which in turn overlap with surveillance and information management, biomedical and biotechnological research, and the development and dissemination of pharmaceutical products; and 3) The transition from colonial metaphors of a "civilizing mission" to a neoliberal discourse based on the assumed integration of developing nations into world markets.[22] The effects of such a worldview are reflected upon, explicitly or implicitly, in many of the chapters of this volume.

Indeed, contributors to our volume present case studies of the COVID-19 crisis in diverse regions around the world, from the USA to South Korea, South Africa, Kenya, the U.K., and the People's Republic of China. As scholars examine the COVID crisis across borders, they reveal the paradoxical co-existence of global crossings and severe limits to cross-border mobility. In addition to this tension between mobility and containment, the COVID-19 crisis has also given rise to tensions between individual bodies and the body politic, between unity and division, between personal stories and grand narratives, and between nationalism and globalism/cosmopolitanism. The issue of health governance and its mechanisms also recurs.[23] We refer to this bundle of crossings and tensions broadly as "pandemic crossings." Hence the title *Pandemic Crossings* for this volume.

Pandemic crossings encompass multiple forms of boundary-crossing, transgression, contact, and obstructions during the global COVID-19 crisis. These crossings and obstructions can be literal and symbolic. They incur intended or unintended consequences for both individuals and social groups even in ordinary times, but the consequences could easily go unnoticed in a pandemic if not for any conscious effort to record them. At the basic level, the COVID pandemic has crossed every imaginable boundary, real or symbolic. It moves from body to body, from city to city, and from country to country. It also moves from one discourse or ideological system to another, and in this process generates competing narratives not only about the virus and the pandemic, but also about science, technology, freedom, cultural values, political systems, race and racism, and more. In some cases, the pandemic becomes the alibi for differently motivated groups to advance their own agendas, thus exacerbating political polarization.[24] In other cases, the mediated experience of the pandemic provides a litmus test for those trying to formulate a coherent political view while grappling with different value systems (see the chapter by Bingchun Meng, Zifeng Chen, and Veronica Jingyi Wang).

Another type of crossing concerns digital technologies such as WeChat, Weibo, and Twitter. As infrastructures for everyday communication, they were immediately mobilized as technologies to manage the COVID pandemic.[25] As a result, these digital technologies reached deeper into everyday life than ever before. WeChat and smart phones, for example, were essential for citizens' basic needs in communication, work, and even in grocery shopping in China. They helped citizens overcome the limits of mobility during quarantines and lockdowns, but they were also deployed as tools of surveillance and control. In all parts of the world, contact tracing through health codes and QR codes is a double-edged technology that facilitates the control of both the virus and the population. The same technology, such as health codes, crosses over into multiple institutions but serves different purposes (see chapters by Yang Zhan and Elaine J. Yuan). Technology—in this case Zoom—also brings different social groups together to explore their shared aspiration (see Zihao Lin's chapter on hearing-impaired and non-disabled individuals). Likewise, while navigating the discipline of the labor regime at the workplace, citizens used their technical know-how to circumvent the control that was exercised through social media platforms such as DingTalk. As a result, a small social media application became an instrument of biopolitics par excellence (see Yizhou Xu's chapter).

A third, related form of crossing is nationalism, national belonging, and the meaning of China and being Chinese during the COVID pandemic. On the one hand, China became the center of global discourses about the pandemic, as whatever happened inside China or in Chinese cyberspace never failed to attract the scrutiny of international media and commentators. On the other hand, ethnic Chinese or Chinese nationals who happened to be sojourners outside China found themselves vulnerable to discrimination and racist violence during the pandemic. These Chinese expats, students, and international workers learned sobering lessons about the limits of the ideology of individual liberty during pandemic times. In short, even when China was not the center of analysis, it was still a felt presence. Ji-Hyun Ahn's chapter on biopolitical nationalism in South Korea, for example, considers the South Korean model as exemplary of a trend in East Asia, including China.[26] As media perceptions of China have turned more negative around the world, such as in Kenya and South Africa (as mapped in the chapter by Herman Wasserman and Dani Madrid-Morales), Chinese diplomats have taken to Twitter to produce their own narratives (as addressed in the chapter by Wendy Leutert and Nicholas Atkinson). Whether addressing public discourse in South Korea, the United States, or Kenya, these chapters demonstrate how global narratives about COVID-19 serve, in turn, to forward conflicting representations about China, its role in the world, and its possible roles as threat or ally.

In short, by analyzing the many forms of boundary-crossings during times of global contagion, the chapters in this volume capture the many ways in which citizens and states responded to a global pandemic. While nation-states asserted their power by closing or tightly controlling their borders, the passions to cross borders—and the symbolic clashes that resulted from them—seemed to have only grown in proportion to the intensity of border closures. These processes of boundary-crossings and obstructions, both within and across nation-state territories, were aided in no small measure by digital media technologies, despite the persistent inequality of digital access. Furthermore, these pandemic crossings had profound and often contradictory consequences on individual lives, national politics, and international relations. In this respect, China's health code serves as an iconic symbol of the complex meanings of pandemic crossings. The health code was used to both exclude and include. By tracking the itineraries of individual citizens, it serves as a technology of protection, but also one of surveillance. For better or worse, a small phone app like the health code has taken on a form of power not exercised (though completely imaginable) prior to the COVID-19 pandemic.

The Chapters

The chapters fall into three parts. Part 1 examines pandemic governance and the role of technology, part 2 focuses on pandemic practices and identities, and part 3 covers pandemic narratives.

Part 1 opens with Elaine J. Yuan's chapter on the role of digital technology as infrastructures during the pandemic. The systematic application of digital technologies such as mobile tracing apps rendered them crucial infrastructures of organization, mobility, and information. Moreover, digital infrastructures are often more flexible and scalable than traditional infrastructures. Their forms and functions are contingent on recursive interactions between technical capacities and deliverable services. For instance, China's health code system was based on an existing app and expanded rapidly from isolated regional applications to a national platform during the post-lockdown period. At the same time, Yuan notes that the development of digital infrastructures depends on common frameworks, goals, and standards "to provide information, mobilize resources and activate the public" to define and enable the needed services. Along this line, Yuan examines how digital infrastructures intersected with the institutions of public health, public administration, and public spheres in the U.S. during the pandemic. She shows that various infrastructures in the three realms were not only instruments enabling current practices but also embodied normative assumptions governing activities in these areas. At the center of the assumptions of all the three realms is the concept of the public as a fluid area of contestation subject to competing notions of governance. She argues that the tension between public values and neoliberal governance was the key to understanding the strategies and practices in the U.S. during the pandemic. At the same time, the success or failure of these infrastructures depended on whether they were capable of organizing or enabling "the public" during the pandemic.

Yang Zhan's chapter studies mobilities and urban governance in China. During the pandemic, China experimented with a variety of ways to contain the spread of the virus through mobility control. Zhan argues that these measures of mobility control did not mean simply the elimination of movements, but the reconfiguration of mobility by rendering movements traceable and/or outsourcing it to non-state actors such as the platform economy labor force and families. Zhan situates these reconfigured forms of mobility in the broader social-economic background, arguing that "Mobility matters as both the precondition as well as the response to the health crisis." Since China embarked on market reform and global integration of its economy in the 1980s, the flow of labor, capital, goods, and information has greatly accelerated. A growing "floating population," as well as urban infrastructure developments and the Belt and Road Initiative, were all anchored in mobility management. In this light, Zhan finds that the dominant media narratives, using an authoritarian framework to explain the Chinese approach (e.g., the people's war against the virus), fall in the old trap of the Cold War logic. Nonetheless, instead of a monolithic force, Zhan shows that China's state power manifested itself in unfolding and unfinished social processes, with effects and limits embedded in existing urban textures.

Yizhou (Joe) Xu's chapter studies social uses of DingTalk (or DingDing), a Zoom-like app of the Chinese tech giant Alibaba. With numerous productivity features, DingTalk evolved from a simple office collaboration tool into an all-in-one platform for work management during the pandemic. Xu depicts how the employees of an IT company in Guangzhou, one of the regional tech centers in southern China, navigated their work and lives during the pandemic. He notes that while they were subject to tightened technological surveillance, these IT knowledge workers, equipped with their own expertise in digital technology, were also skillful in circumventing and subverting such control. Xu discusses two social implications of the app. First, he argues that neo-Taylorism, contemporary modes of scientific management, transformed a supposedly qualitative labor process into a quantitative space in which labor precarity was disguised as productivity. This change conforms to the neoliberal logic of making work a responsibility of the individual while dressing it up as a liberating experience. Second, the app later provided the technological backbone for the health code system that China used to contain COVID-19 and manage mobility. Workplace surveillance, therefore, became intimately linked to the biopolitical governance of the Chinese state. The health code system was not simply a reaction to the pandemic, but rather took its particular form on the basis of existing socio-techno structures in Chinese life. Moving from workplace surveillance to biopolitical governmentality, Xu reveals the interplay between state, corporate, and platform-mediated forms of control, while also diagnosing how everyday users appropriated these same mechanisms of control to build new patterns of labor resistance.

Zihao Lin studies the Zoom experiences of a group of hearing-impaired and non-disabled individuals in the early months of the pandemic (July–September 2020). Lin finds that despite friction, frustrations, and broken access, group members persisted in finding ways to communicate with one another. He argues that by committing themselves to the aspiration of "barrier-free" communication, group members enabled different visions and interpretations of access, resulting in productive processes of negotiation and questioning of barrier-free communication. These very processes of negotiation and aspiring toward access helped to maintain people's remote co-presence. By foregrounding the question of barrier-free communication, the reading group members engaged in utopian thinking that both reveals the limits of the existing space and constructs alternatives. The group's work also urged people to consider and enact, at different scales, the institutional design of a better society and the ethical subjects and agents of such a society. In this light, challenges such as funding shortage, conflicts, frictions, frustration, and even anger became necessary reminders that the current reading group, far from being barrier-free, embodied the possibilities and promises of a much broader and ambitious reconstitution of society. These challenges also show that access is never achieved merely by a finished product or technical fix, but can only happen through negotiations, reflections, and recalibration. Using access as *a method* rather than *a goal* sustained the reading group and served as a moral glue that kept participants together.

Communication through Zoom and other online platforms became a norm in the COVID-19 pandemic. These virtual platforms presented many challenges as well as new possibilities for different groups of communicators. Part 2 begins with Yingyi Ma and Ning Zhan's chapter on Chinese international students' shifting narratives of freedom before and during the COVID-19 pandemic. Through in-depth interviews with two cohorts of Chinese international students who were studying in the U.S. before and after COVID-19 hit, they reveal the changing meanings of freedom and draw implications for understanding the nationalist sentiments of China's younger generation. Ma and Zhan's interview data reveal five thematic narratives about freedom for the two cohorts. For the cohort that studied in the U.S. before the pandemic, freedom means choices in universities, subject areas, and coursework. It also means respecting individuality in the educational setting, including one's sexuality. Students felt they had less restraint in expressing themselves in the classroom while studying in American universities. For those who were studying in the U.S. during the pandemic, however, freedom brought fear. Chinese students felt unsafe in an environment where many people disregarded public health regulations and dismissed scientific advice. They further attribute such attitude to selfishness resulting from the ideology of individual liberty. As a result of this experience, Chinese students started to develop a more critical view of individual freedom in America and more favorable opinions toward China's COVID policies. Ma and Zhan suggest that different evaluations of China's and the U.S.'s pandemic control strategies could give rise to stronger nationalistic sentiments among Chinese international students.

The chapter by Bingchun Meng, Zifeng Chen, and Veronica Jingyi Wang has two goals. First, the authors investigate how Chinese students studying in U.K. and U.S. universities have experienced the COVID-19 pandemic. Second, they explore how the mediated understanding of this global crisis has turned into a critical conjuncture that prompts an elite group of Chinese youth to reassess and reformulate their views of contemporary geopolitical order. The questions Meng, Chen, and Wang examine through interview data shed light on broader debates about how diasporic groups negotiate their national identities and political allegiance, and how individuals navigate incongruence and uncertainty by piecing together varied discursive resources in their efforts to articulate a coherent narrative. Their analysis of forty-five in-depth interviews yields three major findings. First, as much as living in a foreign land can be particularly distressing, the pandemic served as a prism through which overseas Chinese students reflected on a host of important issues, including race, class, national identity, and ideological affiliation. Second, although participants of their study belong to a relatively elite population with more resources to mitigate risks, they often felt powerless and vulnerable. Third, instead of witnessing the rise of "cosmopolitan imperatives," the authors identify the "exhaustion of consent" at the conjuncture of a profound crisis. Amid the failure of neoliberal globalization and the challenges to liberal democracy, research participants draw on a range of political vocabularies and ideological resources to articulate critiques of the hegemonic global order without being able to formulate coherent counter-hegemonic views.

COVID-19 has profoundly shifted how citizens interact. Private life is frequently displayed in public spaces, and individuals are held to account if their exercise of liberty increases the risks of COVID-19 transmission. Using a data set of four million COVID-19 related posts on Sina Weibo from January to December 2020, Yan Wang and Yuxi Zhang examine the evolving dynamics among fellow citizens, especially when and how individuals react to others' COVID-19-related behavior. They find that at the initial stage of the pandemic, the sudden and widespread risk of infection motivated an all-society solidarity as a surviving strategy. However, Chinese society entered a stage of "new normal" for the rest of 2020 with minimal increases in COVID-19 cases. The solidarity built at the beginning of 2020 was later undermined by the process of moralizing fellow citizens' COVID-related behavior via blaming, discriminating, and scapegoating. Not only COVID-related behavior but also people's daily routines and lifestyles were subject to public scrutiny under the pressure of zero-COVID policies. In the second part of their chapter, Wang and Zhang use two qualitative case studies to show that individual citizens were blamed, scapegoated, and discriminated against when they were perceived as risks while this kind of discriminatory behavior was also contested in online discussions.

Finally, chapters in part 3 study diverse pandemic narratives both within and outside China. Ji-Hyun Ahn focuses on "the K-quarantine" model, an initiative of the South Korean government to standardize the public health measures that were facilitated by digital technologies as a national brand and global standard during the pandemic. Examining the discursive space formed around the model, Ahn argues that within the K-quarantine model, biopolitical nationalism was formulated and reconfigured. She highlights the different variants in the "West versus East" narratives found in some mainstream Western media when explaining the early success of virus containment in East Asian countries. In comparison, domestic discourses in South Korea emphasized how the initial success of the K-quarantine model was primarily due to the "innovative use of the media and technology, openness and transparency, and civil engagement." This Korean model (echoing similar claims made about the Taiwanese model) represented the open and transparent use of such platforms to enhance public trust and safety in stark comparison to the heavy-handed technological surveillance and political domination allegedly found in "Asian cultures." More importantly, Ahn shows that the K-quarantine model became a means of promoting domestically produced biomedical products such as testing kits to the global market as well as branding South Korea as a world leader in biotechnology and the response to the pandemic. Ahn further argues that in the K-quarantine model, the ongoing public health crisis legitimizes "big government" solutions to containing the spread of the virus and protecting their citizens while everyday surveillance is increasingly normalized and rendered mundane.

At the peak of the first wave of the COVID-19 pandemic, social media outlets were inundated with disinformation about the virus and its origins, possible remedies and cures, and different government's responses to the outbreak. Much of the problematic disinformation circulating on social media was related to China. In their chapter, Herman Wasserman and Dani Madrid-Morales investigate how social media users in Kenya and South Africa engaged with disinformation about China and COVID-19. Both countries have seen in the last decade an increase in mediated engagements with China. During the first days of the pandemic, Chinese media, diplomats, and public information officers were active in their communication efforts toward African audiences with the goal of managing public opinion and reducing the criticism China was facing. Wasserman and Madrid-Morales use survey data to examine attitudes toward China and COVID-19 among Kenyan and South African social media users. They find that both Kenyans and South Africans had a more negative view of China than they did of the U.S. The authors explore respondents' views toward disinformation related to China during the first months of the pandemic. Survey results indicate that although most respondents in both countries did not assign much credence to China-related COVID disinformation, online hoaxes that were underpinned by perceived Chinese racism against African people were taken to be more believable. Finally, in examining social media users' motivations for sharing some widely circulated hoaxes about China and COVID-19, Wasserman and Madrid-Morales find that the strongest predictor of sharing was respondents' perceived accuracy of a social media post. Those who believed the post to be true were consistently more likely to say that they were sharing it as a "duty to warn," to "make a statement," or to "pass information along." On the other hand, lower levels of perceived accuracy of the posts were associated with users sharing a post to "warn it was fake" or to "spark discussion." While these observations about perceived truth or falseness correspond with what we know about why social media users like or forward posts, the chapter offers fresh insights into this discourse by showing how those perceptions about particular posts are inflected by larger belief patterns about the everyday consequences of China's foray into Africa.

A wave of Twitter debuts by Chinese ambassadors since 2019 reflects a concerted, deliberate effort by Chinese officials to shape global and domestic narratives about China and COVID-19. The volume ends with a chapter by Wendy Leutert and Nicholas Atkinson, which addresses China's Twitter messaging about COVID-19 by using quantitative and qualitative analysis of a dataset of Chinese ambassadors' tweets between June 2019 and July 2020. Building on an emerging genre of analysis addressing China's "soft" and "sharp" power,[27] the chapter finds that ambassadors used original posts and retweets to address topics including China's defeat of the virus, provision of medical supplies and other aid abroad, the importance of international cooperation, the World Health Organization, and other countries' pandemic responses. At the same time, however, ambassadors sharply criticized U.S. statements about China's and the U.S.' COVID-19 responses. By combining positive messaging with digital displays of anger, Chinese diplomats constructed narratives about COVID-19 that promoted China as a responsible international leader while fostering favorable public opinion at home. More broadly, Twitter diplomacy reflects the pluralization of global narratives on key issues involving China and its leaders' embrace of Western social media platforms to pursue discourse power on a global scale.

Taken together, the ten chapters in this volume contribute new insights into the role of digital technologies, everyday experiences, and state governance during the COVID-19 pandemic. They highlight multiple forms and consequences of pandemic crossings. In doing so, these studies open up new avenues of research not only on the COVID-19 pandemic, but also on global health crises more broadly. In this sense, this volume represents a collective endeavor by the contributors to intervene in an ongoing social and public health crisis through data collection, research, and writing—and to write as a form of historical documentation.

NOTES

1. See Centers for Disease Control and Prevention, "COVID Data Tracker," https://covid.cdc.gov; and the WHO COVID-19 dashboard at https://covid19.who.int/.
2. See Manya Koetse, "'Little Sheep People': The Stigmatization of Covid Patients in China," https://www.whatsonweibo.com; Caixin, "Put an End to Covid Discrimination," July 11, 2022, https://www.caixinglobal.com.
3. According to a report issued by Stop AAPI Hate, Asian Americans faced the dual challenges of COVID-19 and anti-Asian hate incidents during the pandemic. From March 2020 to December 2021, 10,905 hate incidents were reported to Stop AAPI Hate alone. Of these, 824 were reports of hate incidents against Asian American elders aged 60 and older. See Stop AAPI Hate, "Anti-Asian Hate, Social Isolation, and Mental Health among Asian American Elders during COVID-19," https://stopaapihate.org.
4. Dhruv Khullar, "The Dire Aftermath of China's Untenable 'Zero COVID' Policy," *New Yorker*, January 8, 2023, https://www.newyorker.com/magazine/2023/01/16/the-dire-aftermath-of-chinas-untenable-zero-covid-policy.
5. Paula A. Treichler, *How to Have Theory in an Epidemic: Cultural Chronicles of AIDS* (Durham: Duke University Press, 1999).
6. Guobin Yang and Adetobi Moses, "Building a Public Culture of Pandemic Storytelling," *Public Culture* 35, no 1 (2023): 9–19.
7. See, for example, Guobin Yang, *The Wuhan Lockdown* (New York: Columbia University Press, 2022), 187–210, and Yawen Li and Marius Meinhof, "Imagining Pandemic as a Failure: Writing, Memory, and Forgetting under COVID-19 in China," in *COVID-19 in International Media*, ed. John C. Pollock and Douglas A. Vakoch (London: Routledge, 2021), 83–92.
8. Nancy Bristow, *American Pandemic: The Lost Worlds of the 1918 Influenza Epidemic* (Oxford: Oxford University Press, 2017), 91.
9. Fabio Tagliabue, Luca Galassi, and Pierpaolo Mariani, "The 'Pandemic' of Disinformation in COVID-19," *SN Comprehensive Clinical Medicine* 2 (2020): 1287–1289. https://doi.org/10.1007/s42399-020-00439-1. Sander van der Linden, Jon Roozenbeek, and Josh Compton. "Inoculating Against Fake News About COVID-19." *Frontiers in Psychology* 11 (2020). https://doi.org/10.3389/fpsyg.2020.566790.

10. Treichler, *How to Have Theory in an Epidemic*.
11. Priscilla Wald, *Contagious: Cultures, Carriers, and the Outbreak Narrative* (Durham: Duke University Press, 2008).
12. Charlotte Lyn Bright, "The Two Pandemics," *Social Work Research* 44, no. 3 (September 1, 2020): 139–142; Cato T. Laurencin and Joanne M. Walker, "A Pandemic on a Pandemic: Racism and COVID-19 in Blacks," *Cell Systems* 11, no. 1 (2020): 9–10; Nelson A. Atehortua and Stella Patino, "COVID-19, a Tale of Two Pandemics: Novel Coronavirus and Fake News Messaging," *Health Promotion International* 36, no. 2 (April 1, 2021): 524–534.
13. Mika Aaltola, "Avian Flu and Embodied Global Imagery: A Study of Pandemic Geopolitics in the Media," *Globalizations* 9 (2012): 673. See also, Lisa B. Keränen, Kirsten N. Lindholm, and Jared Woolly, "Imagining the People's Risk: Projecting National Strength in China's English-Language News about Avian Influenza," in *Imagining China: Rhetorics of Nationalism in an Age of Globalization*, ed. Stephen J. Hartnett, Lisa B. Keränen, and Donovan Conley (East Lansing: Michigan University State Press, 2017), 271–300.
14. Deborah Davis and Helen Siu, eds., *SARS: Reception and Interpretation in Three Chinese Cities* (London: Routledge, 2007); John Powers and Xiaohui Xiao, eds., *The Social Construction of SARS: Studies of a Health Communication Crisis* (Philadelphia: Johns Benjamins Publishing, 2008).
15. Huiling Ding, *Rhetoric of Epidemic: Transcultural Communication about SARS* (Carbondale: Southern Illinois University Press, 2014), 177.
16. Guobin Yang, *The Wuhan Lockdown* (New York: Columbia University Press, 2022).
17. Xiaohui Xiao, "A Hero Story without Heroes: The Hong Kong Government's Narratives on SARS," in *The Social Construction of SARS. Studies of a Health Communication Crisis*, ed. John Powers and Xiaohui Xiao (Philadelphia: John Benjamins Publishing, 2008), 33–52.
18. See, for example, Jeroen de Kloet, Jian Lin, and Jueling Hu, "The Politics of Emotion during COVID-19: Turning Fear into Pride in China's WeChat Discourse," *China Information* 35, no. 3 (2021): 366–392, and Ralph Litzinger and Yanping Ni, "Inside the Wuhan Cabin Hospital: Contending Narratives during the COVID-19 Pandemic," *China Information* 35, no. 3 (2021): 346–365.
19. Arthur Kleinman and James L. Watson, eds., *SARS in China: Prelude to Pandemic?* (Palo Alto: Stanford University Press, 2005), 1.
20. Katherine Mason, *Infectious Change: Reinventing Chinese Public Health after an Epidemic* (Stanford: Stanford University Press, 2016), 3.
21. Nicholas B. King, "Security, Disease, Commerce: Ideologies of Postcolonial Global Health," *Social Studies of Science* 32, no. 5–6 (2002): 763–789.
22. King, "Security, Disease, Commerce."

23. We thank a reviewer for pointing out that these tensions characterize the COVID-19 pandemic across the globe.
24. Just to mention two examples, see P. Sol Hart, Sedona Chinn, and Stuart Soroka, "Politicization and Polarization in COVID-19 News Coverage," *Science Communication* 42, no. 5 (October 2020): 679–697; Julie Jiang et al., "Political Polarization Drives Online Conversations about COVID-19 in the United States," *Human Behavior and Emerging Technologies* 2, no. 3 (2020): 200–211.
25. For studies of social media platforms in China, see Hong Shen and Yujia He, "The Geopolitics of Infrastructuralized Platforms: The Case of Alibaba," *Information, Communication & Society* 25, no. 16 (2022): 2363–2380; Guobin Yang, "Social Media and State-Sponsored Platformization in China," in *Engaging Social Media in China: Platforms, Publics, and Production*, ed. Guobin Yang and Wei Wang (East Lansing: Michigan State University Press, 2021), xi–xxxi. For how one social media platform was used during the Wuhan lockdown, see Yue Qian and Amy Hanser, "How Did Wuhan Residents Cope with a 76-day Lockdown?," *Chinese Sociological Review* 53, no. 1 (2021): 55–86.
26. For a study of biopolitical nationalism, see Jeroen de Kloet, Jian Lin, and Yiu Fai Chow, "'We Are Doing Better': Biopolitical Nationalism and the Covid-19 Virus in East Asia," *European Journal of Cultural Studies* 23, no. 4 (2020): 635–640.
27. See, for example, Suzanne Xiao Yang, "Soft Power and the Strategic Context for China's 'Media Going Global' Policy," in *China's Media Go Global*, ed. Daya Kishan Thussu, Hugo De Burgh, and Anbin Shi (New York: Routledge, 2017); Maria Repnikovia, *Chinese Soft Power* (New York: Cambridge University Press, 2022).

Acknowledgments

WE ARE DEEPLY GRATEFUL TO SERIES EDITOR STEPHEN J. HARTNETT, ACQUISITION editor of the MSU Press Caitlin Tyler-Richards, and former MSU Press editor in chief Catherine Cocks for their thoughtful and thorough editorial work and their good-humored encouragement and support. Going above and beyond the call of duty as series editor, Stephen edited all the chapters in this volume with great patience and care. We also thank MSU project editor Amanda Frost for keeping this project on schedule and copyeditor Jill Twist for her careful and professional copyediting of the manuscript. We thank four reviewers for providing detailed comments on earlier drafts of these chapters. Most of the chapters are based on presentations given at the international symposium titled "Narratives of COVID-19 in China and the World: Technology, Society, and Nations," which was organized by the Center on Digital Culture and Society and co-sponsored by the Center for the Study of Contemporary China at the University of Pennsylvania. Held on Zoom in March 2021, the symposium was made possible through the funding support of the Dean's Office of the Annenberg School for Communication and the Penn China Research and Engagement Fund of the Office of the Provost, University of Pennsylvania. Natacha Yazbeck helped organize the symposium. Julie Sloane and Emma Fleming designed the symposium program and helped with publicity. Richard

Cardona and his IT team provided technology support. Trang Dang assisted with manuscript formatting. John L. Jackson Jr, then dean of the Annenberg School for Communication, provided support in more ways than we can mention here. To all, we give our sincere thanks.

PART 1

Governing with Digital Tools

Infrastructures for the Public

The Institutional Contexts of the Applications of Digital Technology in the U.S. during the COVID-19 Pandemic

Elaine J. Yuan

IN MARCH 2020, SHORTLY AFTER THE WORLD HEALTH ORGANIZATION (WHO) officially declared the COVID-19 virus a pandemic, an article published in *Science* demonstrated that immediate notifications through a contact-tracing mobile phone app could help efficient quarantine measures for containing the spreading of the virus among the population. If used by a sufficiently high proportion of the population, the scientists showed, such an app could help stop the pandemic without having to resort to stringent lockdowns.[1] Indeed, digital technologies for data collection and analysis as well as public communication played crucial roles in global infection prevention before vaccines were widely available.[2] The successful application of these technologies, however, depended on the public's trust in relevant institutions from public health organizations to governments on various levels.[3]

    Conceptualizing systematically interconnected digital technologies as infrastructures, this chapter argues that a digital infrastructure serves as a technical interface for information flows between public health surveillance, government leadership, and public communication. The chapter thus focuses on the historical and ethical factors that affect the development and application of digital infrastructures in the key areas of public health, public administration, and various public spheres during the early stage of the COVID-19 pandemic. Unlike traditional infrastructures defined by their stability, digital infrastructures often take shape in recursive interactions among technical capacities, institutional contexts, and deliverable services contingent on structural and situational conditions. Accordingly, they are highly flexible and scalable, capable of generating new relationships and processes.[4] For the same reason, digital infrastructures are inseparable from their institutional contexts.[5] The stability, functionality, and accessibility of digital infrastructures depend on common frameworks, regulations, and standards of the relevant institutional actors to provide information, mobilize resources, and activate the public to enable the needed services.

This chapter explores the institutional contexts of the applications of digital technology in the United States during the early stage of the COVID-19 pandemic. It looks into the historical and institutional considerations of public health, administration, and communication, which laid the foundation for the development and applications of digital infrastructures during the pandemic. Factors ranging from underinvestment in public health systems, administrative fragmentation, and polarization in the public sphere help explain how and why digital infrastructures evolve into certain forms with certain functions. Fundamentally contested, these digital infrastructures are the sites where competing conceptions of public health, the roles of government action, and collective identities evolve and clash in relevant institutional histories and contexts. The operation of digital infrastructures creates recursive movements in which the forms of the infrastructures generate effects that loop back upon society, organizations, and people, and reshape them.[6]

Digital Infrastructures in the COVID-19 Pandemic

Countries across the world harnessed a diverse range of digital technologies to support the comprehensive response necessary to contain COVID-19. Many key public health measures—including population surveillance, case identification, contact tracing, evaluation of interventions, and communication with the public—benefitted from the information processing power of digital technologies, especially during the early stage of the pandemic.[7] The adoption of some technologies, however, also provoked strong resistance from activists, who invoked privacy and civil liberty concerns. The adoption of mobile-tracing apps, for instance, encountered strong pushbacks from civil rights activists.[8] Privacy advocates emphasized that the apps, designed as a public health tool, should not be authorized for use in other settings or for non-public health purposes. Mandatory use or widespread deployment could be warranted, these critics argued, only if there was sufficient scientific evidence to assess public health efficacy against privacy and other concerns.[9] These concerns indicated that the application of technologies was always embedded in broader institutional contexts. Individual technologies were only components of digital infrastructures that linked ongoing public health measures to administrative management and public mobilization. Their successful implementation required coordinated policies, with collaboration between multiple agents of governments, decision-makers, private sectors, non-governmental organizations, and multiple publics.[10]

In this light, the digital infrastructures that emerged in the pandemic were different from traditional infrastructures, such as electricity and water utilities, which rely on "tight functional interlocking between the underlying technical capabilities, the service delivery model, and stable industry organization."[11] Digital infrastructures, in contrast, are often the results of the recursive alignment among their technical features or forms, services, or contents enabled and the institutional contexts involved. Consequently, digital infrastructures are highly scalable, flexible, and generative.[12] The various mobile-tracing apps used in different countries, for instance, are often emergent and are rarely built from top-down in an entirely planned and orderly fashion.

On the other hand, all infrastructures are dense social, material, and political formations wherein increased technical fluidity and flexibility co-evolve with social and regulatory arrangements.[13] In fact, social and institutional relations and contexts can be decisive in the configuration of digital infrastructures both in terms of the applications of information technologies and their organizational structures.[14] Instead of a fixed and predetermined entity, digital infrastructures can be best understood as a fluid assemblage of regulations, policies, and discourses. As articulations of technology with "institutional actors, legal regimes, policies, and knowledge practices" constantly evolve, digital infrastructures are formed with "the moralities and materials of the time and political moment in which they are situated. They have histories and 'grow' incrementally in a dynamic political environment."[15]

This chapter redirects the analysis of digital infrastructures, as anthropologist Brian Larkin advocates, "upstream, away from the social effects of infrastructure and toward practices of conceptualization that come before the construction of the systems themselves and which are engineered into them."[16] It looks into the set of political and cultural institutions that form the foundation for social activity and governance and enable (or constrain) the smooth operation of digital infrastructures. More importantly, this chapter shows that such digital infrastructures are more than simply instruments that we employ to solve real-world problems; rather, they also embody normative assumptions governing public health and communication activities by problematizing, assessing, and utilizing information flows. At the center of the assemblage is the concept of the public as an always-negotiated and contested entity subject to governance from above while also, at the grassroots level, appropriating and reconfiguring particular political rationalities and technologies in an age of digitalization. Beneath the narratives of technological progress, public health, and national security, the institutional history of such infrastructures reveals "tenuous relations between citizens, information, and the institutions that govern or provision them." In this light, infrastructure, as Nikhil Anand, Akhil Gupta, and Hannah Appel argue, is a productive location for examining the constitution, maintenance, and reproduction of political and economic life.[17] Looking into the related sites of public health, public administration, and the public sphere, this chapter discusses specific ideas and expectations that accompany the public in the context of the pandemic and its recovery to reveal how they laid the foundation for the digital infrastructures emerging in the U.S. during the early stage of the pandemic.

Public Health

The United States has been consistently ranked by Global Health Security Index as the best prepared country in the world to handle infectious disease emergencies.[18] The country's performance during the COVID-19 pandemic, however, indicated otherwise. As the Pulitzer Prize–winning health reporter Ed Yong noted in *The Atlantic*, 16 percent of global COVID deaths occurred in America, a country with just 4 percent of the global population. With more expenditures on medical care than any other wealthy country, its hospitals were nonetheless overwhelmed. It helped create vaccines in record time, yet lagged behind in the vaccination rate. In fact, America experienced the largest life-expectancy reduction of any wealthy country in 2020, and this expectancy continued declining in 2021.[19] These outcomes show that technological advancements alone were not sufficient in preparing the

U.S. health system for addressing the overlapping public health crises triggered by COVID.[20] The virus, in fact, laid bare pre-existing healthcare crises, which, in large part, stemmed from the ways the U.S. has slowly but steadily reconfigured notions of public health toward a model wherein individuals are responsible for their healthcare, hence transforming health from a public good into an individual's lifestyle or set of consumer choices.[21]

In his article, Yong disputed the idea that America's poor performance could be attributed solely to either the Trump or Biden administrations' inchoate responses, although both made grievous mistakes. Rather, he argued the coronavirus exploited the country's many failing public institutions: "its overstuffed prisons and understaffed nursing homes; its chronically underfunded public-health system; its reliance on convoluted supply chains and a just-in-time economy; its for-profit healthcare system, whose workers were already burned out; its decades-long project of unweaving social safety nets; and its legacy of racism and segregation that had already left Black and Indigenous communities and other communities of color disproportionately burdened with health problems."[22] Indeed, recent decades have witnessed the increasing privatization of healthcare systems and underinvestment in public health infrastructures in the U.S.[23] The persistent compromise of government programs in the country has seriously weakened the institutional capacity of public health service at both federal and state levels.[24] The U.S. public health system is historically fragmented in both organization and funding sources. While the federal government has systematically cut and underfunded the public health sector for the past two decades, local and state public health capabilities are nowadays often inadequate and vary widely.[25] According to statistics compiled recently by doctors, researchers, and journalists published across a wide range of media outlets, there is a $4.5 billion annual shortage in funding for "basic but essential activities such as disease surveillance, data gathering and reporting, sanitation, and immunization."[26] In the last ten years, funding for state and local health departments has fallen by 17 percent; the Centers for Disease Control and Prevention's public health emergency budget was cut in half, leaving its budget for global-disease-outbreak prevention, according to the *Washington Post*, down by 80 percent.[27] Its major disease-surveillance network as well as numerous centers and bureaus in the Department of Public Health have also been mired in shortages of staffing and resources.[28] Additionally, there is an estimated shortage of more than 250,000 public health workers.[29] These overall trends, scholars from Yale argue, are "emblematic of an American willingness to pay more later than invest upfront—of the 18% of the federal budget spent on health care, only 3% goes towards prevention and mitigating disease."[30]

Moreover, relying on for-profit healthcare systems exacerbated the pandemic situation in the U.S. As of 2018, about 28 million Americans, or 9 percent of the population in the country, did not have health insurance, and another 29 percent were underinsured; when COVID hit, these people were less likely to seek care.[31] Nationally, there is no uniform policy of paid medical leave, meaning many working-class citizens—a group traditionally lacking healthcare resources—were under pressure to work while sick.[32] Indeed, pro-business government officials, as Young pointed out in his report, often prioritized local economies over population health, consistently framing COVID as a matter of personal responsibility.[33] Both the federal government and that of many states delayed their responses to COVID at the early yet crucial stage. Internationally, the conservative governments of both Trump in the U.S. and Johnson in the U.K. were keen to protect the market against shutdown even at the cost of lives.[34] To avoid shutting down businesses, the U.K., for instance, even suggested the country take a behavioral science approach to flatten the curve, advocating to let the virus "run its course" to achieve herd immunity. Subsequently, the vast majority of people who died from the coronavirus, in the U.S. and elsewhere, were elderlies, minorities, and/or in poor health conditions.

Moreover, the U.S. focused mainly on hospital-based care rather than large-scale measures for infection prevention and population protection during the pandemic.[35] This focus reflects the changing perspective that defines the field of public health. The practices of public health are underpinned by the scientific, ethical, and social principles that delineate powers, rights, and responsibilities in the field.[36] These principles always evolve in response to dynamic factors ranging from outbreaks of new diseases and economic development to population growth and lifestyle trends. Historically, modern public health began in tandem with the development of industrial capitalism and the prototype welfare state in the late eighteenth century. During its early years, officials and scientists treated epidemics as social problems similar to poverty, lack of access to housing and sanitation, and unsafe working conditions.[37] To address these social problems, emerging industrial countries started to develop urban infrastructures such as water supply, sewage systems, and hospitals, as well as public health provisions and policies such as health insurance and healthcare systems. The principle of public health that emerged from this period emphasized that health was a public good and that government had a duty to provide it.[38]

Since the advent of germ theory in the late nineteenth century, however, a prevalent biomedical approach has emerged, treating diseases as battles between hosts and pathogens inside individual bodies. Instead of tackling social problems, scientists have turned to focus on fighting microscopic organisms with products of medical science and technology such as vaccines and medicines. In contemporary societies, such medical resources and cures, however, are often unequally distributed among the population, with marginalized communities left far behind. Hence, the damage of COVID has been most severe among blacks, women, the elderly, the economically deprived, and other minority communities—groups that are underrepresented in political-decision processes.[39] In fact, a broad scope of health inequities have existed in the U.S. for decades through many cycles of diseases and pandemics.[40]

The public health paradigm further evolved during the twentieth century, shifting its focus on the role of personal responsibility rather than broader social provisions by the state.[41] Most developed countries have effectively put many of the communicable diseases associated with poverty under control. Consequently, modern medical science prioritized medicine and clinic treatment to cure chronic and degenerative diseases—such as cardiovascular disease, cancer, stroke and diabetes, which are linked to lifestyle behavior and aging unhealthy diet, lack of exercise, and consumption of substances, among other factors. Instead of the social context of disease such as sanitation, the environment, and infrastructures, the new paradigm emphasizes issues of individual behavior and lifestyle, matters for the private sector and local communities.

Yong concluded his article with the dire premonition that the U.S. will continue to struggle against infectious diseases in the future. One main reason, Yong believed, was what he called "pandemic individualism," an antithesis to the concept of public health. As a long-held social value, individualism prioritizes individual freedom and self-reliance over government guidance and provision. According to this ethos, people are responsible for their own well-being, and social vulnerability results from personal weakness rather than policy failure.[42] With the historical tension between individual rights and actions and the pursuit of the common good, contemporary public health constantly struggles to define its core values.[43] While it is true that public health interventions must be culturally sensitive and consider a range of values on issues such as privacy, autonomy, liberty, and dignity, protecting the common good should stand at the core of public health practice. It therefore does not make sense, for example, to establish individual autonomy as a primary guiding principle for public health ethics, especially in the face of a deadly pandemic.[44]

Public Administration

Critics such as Daniel H. Xu and Rashmita Basu from the field of public administration linked the successful containment of the pandemic by the East Asian societies at the early stage to the pivotal role of their governments in public health planning and management.[45] Such an emphasis on centralization, however, often omitted the fact that the governments in these countries were able to mobilize and collaborate with local communities, non-profit social organizations, and the public in general.[46] While responding to such a large-scale crisis requires collaboration and coordination with non-profit organizations, non-profits often lack sufficient capacities and infrastructures to play an adequate role. The governments, therefore, need to step up their efforts to support and coordinate these organizations. Take Shanghai, a metropolis with more than twenty million people, for example. The city employed a hybrid of the government-grassroots collaborative system. According to the data released by the Shanghai Municipal Government Office in March, 2020, over 6,700 volunteer units and 200,000 volunteers participated in the fight against the pandemic.[47]

In contrast, the federalist system in the U.S. put the states in charge of the efforts to combat the pandemic while the federal government was supposed to provide guidance and resources. Although often effective for finding innovative solutions to problems specific to local conditions, such a federalist system is prone to causing delays and confusions during national crises.[48] During the early stage of the pandemic, public health measures and policies differed widely across the states and within some states. The states' policies were also different from the guidance of the CDC and the federal administration.[49] For instance, a range of different quarantine measures and the testing services were carried out by state and local governments in collaboration with private labs.[50] But as demonstrated by the experiences of other countries with the federal system, such as Canada and Germany, the system per se doesn't preclude efficient coordination by the government. Party polarization and federal gridlock in the U.S. greatly hindered the ability of the country to respond in a coherent manner during the pandemic.[51]

The issues of the public administrative system have their historical roots. Over the past half century, public administration theory and practice in the U.S. have evolved along the changing material and ideological environments.[52] Early traditions of public administration regarded government agencies as the primary deliverers of public services as well as the embodiment of public values. While elected officials determined the goals corresponding to political direction, citizens were viewed primarily as clients or constituents.[53] To address the increasing concerns with government failures, however, the dominant approach moved away from large, centralized government agencies toward privatization in the 1980s and 1990s. This second-generation public management model emphasized the efficiency of market competition and economic rationality for delivering government services. Private managers were considered "entrepreneurial" and result-oriented, whereas the public was treated as customers instead of citizens.[54]

This "neoliberal turn," with its an emphasis on the role of the market, transformed governance over the past decades.[55] The U.S. government was increasingly perceived to be "the problem." Public administration privileged market solutions and served private interests at the expense of the common good.[56] Critical scholars such as Matthew A. Crenson and Benjamin Ginsberg point outed that the market mechanism as the instrument of public policy was unlikely to mobilize the public because the market discouraged collective purposes and obscured accountability. "Decentralized, privatized, or atomized into thousands of market transactions," public policies and services were transformed into customer relations. The public became a mere aggregation of private customers rather than citizens.[57] This administrative regime encouraged the conception of citizens as customers who pursued individual interest and pleasure without concerns for community values or public interest.[58] Without coherent common interests, it's difficult for people to form a collective identity through collective political action.[59] It was also unlikely for people to cooperate in making difficult decisions or sacrifice during times of crisis.[60]

In efforts to contest the neoliberalist development, practitioners and researchers in the field of public administration recently turned to defend the public sector by grounding governance in the pursuit of public values.[61] The new "public value" paradigm emphasized that in an increasingly diverse and complex society, governments alone cannot effectively address all social issues. While government had a special role to play as a guarantor of public values, citizens as well as private sector and non-profit organizations were equally important as actors to solve public problems.[62] The rise of the so-called networked governance, where public managers were required to collaborate with non-profits, businesses, the media, and citizens to accomplish public purposes, was to overcome the limits of representative government in the new social context.

The paradigmatic change reflects a long historical shift in public authority from government to more collaborative, multisector modes of governance.[63] Critics such as Adam Dahl and Joe Soss, however, pointed out that the public-value model, while opposing laissez-faire efforts and trying to bring back the state, derived much of its logic from market templates.[64] This model tended to conceptualize public value as an analogue to shareholder value and democratic engagement in primarily instrumental terms. Moreover, public-value governance conceived the relations between state and market actors as purely collaborative while paying less attention to the desirable separation of powers and the importance of how one should check the other. Consequently, the distinction between market (the corporation, the shareholder) and political (the citizen) collapsed.[65]

As shown during the early stage of the COVID pandemic, the federalist government and the fragmented public health system made the collaborative network difficult. A growing urban-rural divide within the United States strained state-local (e.g. urban cities) dynamics. Frictions took place not only between federal government agents, states, and local governments, but also between the governments and the public regarding the appropriate balance of security and liberty, as evident in protests of state stay-at-home orders during the pandemic.[66] Local governments are traditionally the most under-resourced and least powerful in federal systems. It is, therefore, difficult for local authorities to manage large-scale crises without some outside assistance from states or the national government.[67]

Moreover, the U.S. government did not effectively activate its partnerships with community groups and other constituencies during the outbreak. Public-private partnerships were also not sufficiently engaged, as exemplified by the lack of engagement of the private sector to produce adequate amounts of personal protective equipment and testing kits.[68] And the states had to bid against each other in the market for this equipment and supplies. Most of the existing non-profit alliances were loose, making it difficult to pool resources and carry out joint actions that would generate a larger impact. Many human service non-profits had to cut back key services while demands for basic necessities increased as a result of the unfolding COVID crisis.[69]

Nevertheless, the new administrative model advocates that public value emerges from dialogue and deliberation among broadly inclusive social groups instead of the exclusive domain of the government. Lasting civic values are the result of self-organized, continuous efforts and are essential for solving common problems. During the process, citizens "move beyond their roles as voters, clients, constituents, customers, or poll responders to becoming problem solvers, co-creators, and governors actively engaged in producing what is valued by the public and good for the public."[70]

Consequently, the public-value model is premised on the public sphere. The public sphere comprises "the web of values, places, organization, rules, knowledge, and other cultural resources held in common by people through their everyday commitments and behaviors, and held in trust by government and public institutions."[71] Such a public sphere serves as the foundation of a shared sense of belonging, meaning, and purpose. The public in the new administrative model, therefore, is not given but must be constructed through a sustained process of dialogue. At the same time, citizens are seen as quite capable of engaging in deliberative problem solving that allows them to develop a public spiritedness.[72]

Public Sphere

New models of public administration are premised on an engaged citizenry and its political agency. In theory, the public is constituted in the public sphere through debates about the role of government, the way of public engagement and active citizenship, and the function of democratic institutions.[73] The public sphere, therefore, is a place where mere political subjects develop into political actors and mature citizens.[74] It itself is an important institution to facilitate self-government by an engaged citizenry.[75]

The public sphere, however, was plagued by disinformation and political polarization during the COVID-19 pandemic in the United States. This happened in news coverage in newspapers, televised network news, and social media discussions, among both the elites and the masses.[76] Political leaders and media outlets on the left and right sent divergent messages about the severity of the crisis, which not only impacted public sentiments toward government measures and the tendency to share health and prevention information but also the extent to which the public engaged in social distancing and other efforts to reduce infection.[77]

In the era of social media, the question is not simply how the framing of the pandemic influences trust in public communication. Discursive communities formed by policymakers, scientists, journalists, and local and national public health officials as the sources of circulated knowledge both informed and interacted with the wider public's outlook on the pandemic. Marked by division, fragmentation, and polarization, the discursive process, however, failed to produce a consistent ontology of the COVID-19 pandemic disease—its causes and sources, patterns and prospects, risks and consequences, and the appropriate methods of containing and curing the virus. Nor was there agreement on "the moral economy and historical narrative, explaining how and why we find ourselves in the situation that we do now, identifying villains and heroes, ascribing blame for failures and credit for triumphs."[78]

The polarization of the public sphere has been long in coming. Recent years have witnessed the significant change in the way and the context in which political actors are informed for participating in politics. Public trust in social institutions such as civic associations as well as in journalism has been declining. Emotions and affect prevail over factual evidence and rational analysis, eroding shared understandings of reality. This so-called epistemic crisis in public spheres threatens to undermine political agency.[79]

Some attributed the crisis to the new media environment brought about by digital technologies, especially social media.[80] The rise of digital technologies facilitated a "platformization" of media infrastructures, which became increasingly essential to our daily lives and further changed the power relations between the media and users.[81] Corporate entities such as Facebook and Google dominated information services accessible to the public. The algorithmic control of user preferences and behaviors belied transparency and accountability. Public information, communication, and expression were turned into business transactions within profit-driven corporate ecosystems. Users' agency and public discourse were expressed in the economic and algorithm characteristics of platforms instead of democratic intent.[82]

It is simplistic and inadequate, however, to only focus on the media side of the equation. Doing so risks a techno-deterministic interpretation. More importantly, it distracts us from paying critical action to the institutional arrangement of civil society itself.[83] Civic participation, for instance, is often premised on a pluralist model, where citizens organize to advocate their interests in the governmental marketplace. The public is manifest in the processes in which individuals with similar concerns come to form organic interest groups.[84] In practice though, such a model often favors elites and is stacked against less privileged citizens. There has been ample evidence that it is difficult for a general public will or a public concern to make itself heard if it is not economically or politically sponsored by a strong social group.[85]

The public sphere is also significantly susceptible to the recent rise of populism. Populist activists and politicians managed to mobilize an array of deep economic and cultural grievances against perceived systematic deception by the power elites in the past couple of decades. The "populist revolt" tried to establish discourses that set an abstract "us," that is "the people," against "them," that is the elites, among which liberal mainstream media were especially singled out as the cause of the problems. Taking advantage of the social media platforms, populist groups spent much political energy attacking the established media and journalistic practices.[86] Given the fact that Republicans are far more likely to distrust the mainstream media than are Democrats,[87] right-wing political groups are more likely to use tactics such as hate speeches, fake news, and disinformation, developing a right-wing counter-public sphere.[88]

More importantly, we need to reckon with the structural transformation and decline of the public sphere in the broader socioeconomic context. As American political theorist Wendy Brown pointed out, decades-long neoliberalist practices imposed a particular form of market rationality on the social, the subject, and the state. The shift to a market rationality in governance involved a specific and consequential organization of these spheres.[89] A focus on market mechanisms weakened social institutions and depoliticized "decisions about public welfare and the public good." Meanwhile, citizens were recast as consumers, and collective decisions were turned into questions of individual choice. The issue of the public sphere is more than a question of whether or not we can deliberate issues through a plural media representing the public interest. Rather, it is a question about whether the public realm is withering up altogether.[90]

Conclusion

The wide application of digital technologies during the fight against the COVID-19 pandemic was crucial to facilitate the collaboration between governments, medical experts, emergency managers, and the public. Large-scale crises such as the current pandemic call for integrated systems that link efficient public health measures to emergency administration and public communication.[91] Instead of isolated applications, digital technologies needed to operate in a system to provide a holistic response to the highly complex issues during the pandemic.

Digital technologies such as the mobile-tracing apps emerged as infrastructures enacting recursive relations among services, devices, networks, and social institutions. These infrastructures were flexible, scalable, and generative—capable of morphing into different assemblages of things, people, and practices.[92] Instead of a result of a planned, orderly, and mechanical process, the formation of such a digital infrastructure is often fluid, open to modification and maneuvering.[93]

At the same time, digital infrastructures are technology-based solutions in response to social, organizational, and cultural issues.[94] Rather than a distinct technological domain external to social and political domains, they are a mixture of political rationality, administrative techniques, and material systems. They are critical locations through which "sociality, governance and politics, accumulation and dispossession, and institutions and aspirations are formed, reformed, and performed."[95] Instead of the applications and the effects of digital infrastructures, this chapter focuses on what they reveal about how practices and conditions of public health, administrative, and communicative governance affect their adaptation and translation of the public.

As our experiences with the COVID-19 pandemic during the early stage showed, timely and accurate information about the spread of the virus was crucial for disease prevention. Infectious disease surveillance is a global public good in a pandemic. For this reason, the Institute of Medicine argued for the loosening of consent requirements for the use of individual health data in population-level research.[96] In 2005, WHO introduced *International Health Regulations*, putting some limitations to personal freedom to prioritize public security.[97]

Moreover, due to its focus on population and community as well as its interest in the structural conditions of health, public health generally involves direct or indirect state action.[98] The U.S. federal government's capacity to coordinate the efforts to contain the pandemic, however, was severely reduced because of the fragmentation of public health and administration systems, causing much delay and confusion. The failure was in a large part due to the historical development of neoliberalist models in public health and governance. During the thirty years of market fundamentalism, the role of the government was dismantled and society was reconceptualized as constituted of individual consumers rather than around common interests.[99] Market templates served as starting points for governance, whereas public managers operated as entrepreneurs with the mentalities of corporate managers.[100] The consequence was a political world in which citizens ceased to compose a public. As the public interest atrophied, it became very difficult for political leaders to frame policy arguments on behalf of the common good, let alone to complete the more complex tasks of facilitation.[101]

Moreover, neoliberalist developments in the recent decades severely eroded the boundary between state and market and advocated for cooperation among market, state, and civil society actors.[102] In practice, "civic infrastructural systems are increasingly managed by public authorities in partnership with private capital and shaped by a politics of decentralization that encourages the monetization of component networks in line with neoliberal agendas focusing on the out-sourcing of service provision."[103] Contrary to the powerful antigovernment rhetoric, the efforts to coordinate states, localities, and non-profit agencies depended on "government facilitation with investing in infrastructure, creating confidence among market participants, and helping them to coordinate the timing of their action."[104]

To address the challenge of neoliberalism, the new model of public administration aims to anchor public values in the public. It seeks to derive public values from intersubjectively held principles that define a society's "normative consensus" regarding the rights and benefits of citizens as well as the obligations that link state, citizen, and society.[105] Although typically contested, public values are often premised on a relative consensus that is discernible from constitutions, legislative mandates, policies, literature reviews, opinion polls, and other formal and informal sources.[106] To achieve the goal, it needs a healthy public sphere with supporting institutions and the processes necessary to forge agreement on and achieve public values in practice.

In the rapidly evolving media environment, however, the role of mainstream journalism as an arbiter of "the truth" and civic value has been profoundly diminished.[107] The platformization of the information environment has created a system that "refuses public accountability in the name of freedom while subjugating all areas of mediated activity to a market logic and competition through evermore commercialization, privatization and restructuring."[108] The political economy and the technological architecture of the platform has put an enormous amount of control in the hands of corporate actors and in various ways shaped the character of the information made available.[109]

Yet the media is only one aspect of the issue. The entire governmental system is endangered by entrenched power and political bias, fragmented government, intensely partisan politics, sharply divided public opinions on many issues, and competing organized interests. There are clashing conceptions of what public value might be in any situation.[110] The extent to which it is possible for dialogue and deliberation to take place in practice remains unclear.[111]

In conclusion, this chapter emphasizes that technological infrastructures are not simply a matter of a digitally enabled solution but also a technology of organization and politics. The boundaries between technical and social solutions are mobile in the realm of digital infrastructures.[112] They are dynamic technological forms that mediate social subjects and relations constituted in a socio-political system. In this light, a society, with its egoistic, disintegrative tendencies, may become the main impediment to achieving public health goals predicated on civic virtue.

NOTES

1. Luca Ferretti et al., "Quantifying SARS-CoV-2 Transmission Suggests Epidemic Control with Digital Contact Tracing," *Science* 368, no. 6491 (2020).
2. Jobie Budd et al., "Digital Technologies in the Public-Health Response to COVID-19," *Nature Medicine* 26, no. 8 (2020): 1183–1192; Wenwu Zhao et al., "A Systematic Approach Is Needed to Contain COVID-19 Globally," *Science Bulletin* (2020).
3. Wenhong Chen, Gejun Huang, and An Hu, "Red, Yellow, Green or Golden: The Post-Pandemic Future of China's Health Code Apps," *Information, Communication & Society* 25, no. 5 (2022): 618–633; Eszter Hargittai et al., "Americans' Willingness to Adopt a COVID-19 Tracking App," *First Monday* 25, no. 11 (2020).
4. David Tilson, Kalle Lyytinen, and Carsten Sørensen, "Research Commentary—Digital Infrastructures: The Missing Is Research Agenda," *Information Systems Research* 21, no. 4 (2010): 748–759.
5. Tilson, Lyytinen, and Sørensen, "Research Commentary," 748–759.
6. Penelope Harvey, Casper Bruun Jensen, and Atsuro Morita, eds., *Infrastructures and Social Complexity: A Companion* (London: Taylor & Francis, 2016).
7. Budd et al. "Digital Technologies," 1183–1192; World Health Organization, "COVID-19 and Digital Health: What Can Digital Health Offer for COVID-19?," https://www.who.int; Qing Ye, Jin Zhou, and Hong Wu, "Using Information Technology to Manage the COVID-19 Pandemic: Development of a Technical Framework Based on Practical Experience in China," *JMIR Medical Informatics* 8, no. 6 (2020): e19515.
8. Nadeem Ahmed et al., "A Survey of Covid-19 Contact Tracing Apps," *IEEE Access* 8; Glenn I. Cohen, Lawrence O. Gostin, and Daniel J. Weitzner, "Digital Smartphone Tracking for COVID-19: Public Health and Civil Liberties in Tension," *JAMA* (2020); Tanusree Sharma and Masooda Bashir, "Use of Apps in the COVID-19 Response and the Loss of Privacy Protection," *Nature Medicine* (2020): 1–2.
9. Cohen, Gostin, and Weitzner, "Digital Smartphone."
10. Budd et al., "Digital Technologies," 1183–1192.
11. Tilson, Lyytinen, and Sørensen, "Research Commentary," 3.
12. Tilson, Lyytinen, and Sørensen, "Research Commentary," 748–759.
13. Nikhil Anand, Akhil Gupta, and Hannah Appel, eds., *The Promise of Infrastructure* (Durham, NC: Duke University Press, 2018); Harvey, Jensen, and Morita, *Infrastructures*.
14. Tilson, Lyytinen, and Sørensen, "Research Commentary," 748–759.
15. Anand, Gupta, and Appel, *The Promise*, 18.
16. Brian Larkin, "The Politics and Poetics of Infrastructure," *Annual Review of Anthropology* 42 (2013): 332.

17. Anand, Gupta, and Appel, *The Promise*.
18. Ed Yong, "The Pandemic's Legacy Is Already Clear: All of This Will Happen Again," *The Atlantic*, September 30, 2022; https://www.theatlantic.com/health/archive/2022/01/for-covid-with-covid-hospitals-are-mess-either-way/621229/; Kate Tulenko and Dominique Vervoort, "Cracks in the System: The Effects of the Coronavirus Pandemic on Public Health Systems," *American Review of Public Administration* 50, no. 6–7 (2020): 455–466.
19. Yong, "The Pandemic's Legacy Is Already Clear: All of This Will Happen Again."
20. Tulenko and Vervoort, "Cracks," 455.
21. Yong, "The Pandemic's Legacy Is Already Clear: All of This Will Happen Again"; Carlo Caduff, "What Went Wrong: Corona and the World after the Full Stop," *Medical Anthropology Quarterly* 34, no. 4 (2020): 467–487; So Hyung Lim and Kristin Sziarto, "When the Illiberal and the Neoliberal Meet around Infectious Diseases: An Examination of the MERS Response in South Korea," *Territory, Politics, Governance* 8, no. 1 (2020): 60–76.
22. Yong, "The Pandemic's Legacy Is Already Clear: All of This Will Happen Again."
23. Caduff, "What Went Wrong," 2020; Nason Maani and Sandro Galea, "COVID-19 and Underinvestment in the Public Health Infrastructure of the United States," *Milbank Quarterly* 98, no. 2 (2020): 250.
24. Daniel H. Xu and Rashmita Basu, "How the United States Flunked the COVID-19 Test: Some Observations and Several Lessons," *American Review of Public Administration* 50, no. 6–7 (2020): 568–576.
25. Robin Taylor Wilson, Catherine L. Troisi, and Tiffany L. Gary-Webb, "A Deficit of More Than 250,000 Public Health Workers Is No Way To Fight Covid-19," *Stat* 5 (April 2020); Maani and Galea, "COVID-19," 250.
26. William Eger and Margaret House, "Confronting a Legacy of Scarcity: A Plan for Reinvesting in US Public Health," *Stat* 28 (June 2021); Xu and Basu, "How the United States," 568–576.
27. Eger and House, "Confronting a Legacy of Scarcity"; Lena H. Sun, "CDC to Cut by 80 Percent Efforts to Prevent Global Disease Outbreak," *Washington Post*, February 1, 2018.
28. Tulenko and Vervoort, "Cracks," 455–466; Xu and Basu, "How the United States," 568–576.
29. Taylor Wilson, Troisi, and Gary-Webb, "A Deficit."
30. Eger and House, "Confronting a Legacy of Scarcity."
31. Maani and Galea, "COVID-19," 250.
32. Mark J. Rozell and Clyde Wilcox, "Federalism in a Time of Plague: How Federal Systems Cope with Pandemic," *American Review of Public Administration* 50, no. 6–7 (2020): 519–525.

33. Yong, "The Pandemic's Legacy Is Already Clear: All of This Will Happen Again."
34. Stefan Ecks, "Coronashock Capitalism: The Unintended Consequences of Radical Biopolitics," *Medical Anthropology Quarterly* 30 (2020): 1–6.
35. Tulenko and Vervoort, "Cracks," 455–466.
36. Mark A. Rothstein, "Rethinking the Meaning of Public Health," *Journal of Law, Medicine & Ethics* 30, no. 2 (2002): 144–149.
37. Virginia Berridge, Martin Gorsky, and Alex Mold, *Public Health in History* (Maidenhead, UK: Open University Press, 2011).
38. Berridge, Gorsky, and Mold, *Public Health in History*.
39. Nason Maani and Sandro Galea, "COVID-19 and Underinvestment in the Health of the US Population," *Milbank Quarterly* 98, no. 2 (2020): 239.
40. Maani and Galea, "COVID-19 and Underinvestment in the Health of the US Population," 239.
41. Berridge, Gorsky, and Mold, *Public Health in History*.
42. Yong, "The Pandemic's Legacy Is Already Clear: All of This Will Happen Again."
43. Katherine Mason, *Infectious Change* (Redwood City, CA: Stanford University Press, 2020).
44. See Rothstein, "Rethinking," 144–149; and Mason, *Infectious Change*.
45. Xu and Basu, "How the United States," 568–576.
46. Fisher and Choe, "How South Korea Flattened the Curve," *New York Times*, March 23, 2020.
47. Shi-Hong Weng et al., "Responding to the Coronavirus Pandemic: A Tale of Two Cities," *American Review of Public Administration* 50, no. 6–7 (2020): 497–504.
48. Rozell and Wilcox, "Federalism," 519–525.
49. Daniel J. Mallinson, "Cooperation and Conflict in State and Local Innovation during COVID-19," *American Review of Public Administration* 50, no. 6–7 (2020): 543–550.
50. Xu and Basu, ""How the United States," 568–576.
51. Rozell and Wilcox, "Federalism," 519–525.
52. John M. Bryson, Barbara C. Crosby, and Laura Bloomberg, "Public Value Governance: Moving beyond Traditional Public Administration and the New Public Management," *Public Administration Review* 74, no. 4 (2014): 445–456; Nicholas Henry, "Paradigms of Public Administration," *Public Administration Review* (1975): 378–386.
53. Bryson, Crosby, and Bloomberg, "Public Value," 445–456; Henry, "Paradigms," 378–386.
54. Bryson, Crosby, and Bloomberg, "Public Value," 445–456.
55. George, H. Frederickson, "Toward a Theory of the Public for Public Administration," *Administration & Society* 22, no. 4 (1991): 395–417.
56. Adam Dahl and Joe Soss, "Neoliberalism for the Common Good? Public Value

Governance and the Downsizing of Democracy," *Public Administration Review* 74, no. 4 (2014): 496–504.

57. Matthew A. Crenson and Benjamin Ginsberg, *Downsizing Democracy: How America Sidelined Its Citizens and Privatized Its Public* (Baltimore: Johns Hopkins University Press, 2004), 202.
58. Frederickson, "Toward a Theory," 395–417.
59. Crenson and Ginsberg, *Downsizing Democracy*, 2004.
60. Frederickson, "Toward a Theory," 395–417.
61. Bryson, Crosby, and Bloomberg, "Public Value," 445–456; Dahl and Soss, "Neoliberalism," 496–504.
62. Bryson, Crosby, and Bloomberg, "Public Value," 445–456.
63. Dahl and Soss, "Neoliberalism," 496–504.
64. Dahl and Soss, "Neoliberalism," 496–504.
65. Dahl and Soss, "Neoliberalism," 496–504.
66. Mallinson, "Cooperation," 543–550; Rozell and Wilcox, "Federalism," 519–525.
67. Mallinson, "Cooperation," 543–550.
68. Tulenko, "Cracks," 455–466.
69. Qiang Dong and Jiahuan Lu, "In the Shadow of the Government: The Chinese Nonprofit Sector in the COVID-19 Crisis," *American Review of Public Administration* 50, no. 6–7 (2020): 784–789.
70. Bryson, Crosby, and Bloomberg, "Public Value," 447.
71. Bryson, Crosby, and Bloomberg, "Public Value," 450.
72. Bryson, Crosby, and Bloomberg, "Public Value," 445–456.
73. Bryson, Crosby, and Bloomberg, "Public Value," 453.
74. Crenson and Ginsberg, *Downsizing Democracy*, 2004.
75. Frederickson, "Toward a Theory," 395–417.
76. Sol P. Hart, Sedona Chinn, and Stuart Soroka, "Politicization and Polarization in COVID-19 News Coverage," *Science Communication* 42, no. 5 (2020): 679–697; Julie Jiang et al., "Political Polarization Drives Online Conversations about COVID-19 in the United States," *Human Behavior and Emerging Technologies* 2, no. 3 (2020): 200–211; Jon Green et al., "Elusive Consensus: Polarization in Elite Communication on the COVID-19 Pandemic," *Science Advances* 6, no. 28 (2020): eabc2717.
77. Hunt Allcott et al., "Polarization and Public Health: Partisan Differences in Social Distancing during the Coronavirus Pandemic," *NBER Working Paper* w26946 (2020); Green et al., "Elusive Consensus," eabc2717; Jiang et al. "Political Polarization," 200–211.
78. Nicholas B. King, "Security, Disease, Commerce: Ideologies of Postcolonial Global

Health," *Social Studies of Science* 32, no. 5–6 (2002): 767.
79. Peter Dahlgren, "Media, Knowledge and Trust: The Deepening Epistemic Crisis of Democracy," *Javnost–The Public* 25, no. 1–2 (2018): 20–27.
80. Dahlgren, "Media, Knowledge and Trust," 20–27.
81. Jean-Christophe Plantin et al., "Infrastructure Studies Meet Platform Studies in the Age of Google and Facebook," *New Media & Society* 20, no. 1 (2018): 293–310.
82. Jodi Dean, "Communicative Capitalism: Circulation and the Foreclosure of Politics," *Cultural Politics* 1, no. 1 (2005): 51–74; José Van Dijck, *The Culture of Connectivity: A Critical History of Social Media* (Oxford: Oxford University Press, 2013).
83. Natalie Fenton, "Fake Democracy: The Limits of Public Sphere Theory," *Javnost–The Public* 25, no. 1–2 (2018): 28–34.
84. Frederickson, "Toward a Theory," 395–417.
85. Frederickson, "Toward a Theory," 395–417.
86. Dahlgren, "Media, Knowledge and Trust," 24.
87. Rozell and Wilcox, "Federalism," 519–525.
88. Dahlgren, "Media, Knowledge and Trust," 20–27.
89. Wendy Brown, "American Nightmare: Neoliberalism, Neoconservatism, and De-democratization," *Political Theory* 34, no. 6 (2006): 690–714.
90. Fenton, "Fake Democracy," 30.
91. Budd et al., "Digital Technologies," 1183–1192.
92. Harvey, Jensen, and Morita, *Infrastructures*.
93. Anand, Gupta, and Appel, *The Promise*.
94. Paul N. Edwards et al., "Understanding Infrastructure: Dynamics, Tensions, and Design" (paper presented at Report, History and Theory of Infrastructure: Lessons for New Scientific Cyberinfrastructure Workshop, University of Michigan, Ann Arbor, 2007).
95. Anand, Gupta, and Appel, *The Promise*, 3.
96. Mason, *Infectious Change*.
97. Christina Vogel and Maia Funk, "Measles Quarantine—the Individual and the Public," *Journal of Travel Medicine* 15, no. 2 (2008): 65–67.
98. Mason, *Infectious Change*.
99. Brown, "American Nightmare."
100. Dahl and Soss, "Neoliberalism," 496–504.
101. Fred Block, "Swimming against the Current: The Rise of a Hidden Developmental State in the United States," *Politics & Society* 36, no. 2 (2008): 169–206.
102. Dahl and Soss, "Neoliberalism," 496–504.
103. Harvey, Jensen, and Morita, *Infrastructures*, 9.

104. Block, "Swimming against the Current."
105. Dahl and Soss, "Neoliberalism," 496–504.
106. Bryson, Crosby, and Bloomberg, "Public Value," 445–456.
107. Dahlgren, "Media, Knowledge and Trust," 20–27.
108. Fenton, "Fake Democracy," 33.
109. Dahlgren, "Media, Knowledge and Trust," 20–27.
110. Bryson, Crosby, and Bloomberg, "Public Value," 445–456.
111. Dahl and Soss, "Neoliberalism," 496–504.
112. Harvey, Jensen, and Morita, Infrastructures, 5.

Pandemic Infrastructure, Mediated Mobility, and Urban Governance in China

Yang Zhan

SINCE THE COVID-19 OUTBREAK IN LATE 2019, VARIOUS MEASURES AND TECHNOLOgies have been utilized across countries to regulate people's everyday mobility and to contain the virus.[1] As discussed by Noel B. Salazer, "existential and essential mobilities" have been reconfigured by the health crisis.[2] While mobility has been impacted globally, the control measures used to contain the virus have varied across the globe. For example, Singapore, South Korea, and Taiwan exemplified those nations that turned to vaccines for the answer. Some countries, including Japan and Thailand, relaxed border controls to boost their economies.[3] China, on the other hand, normalized its pandemic control over mobility, implementing its zero-COVID policy until popular protests in December 2022.[4] One of the major characteristics of the zero-COVID policy was the meticulous management of the everyday movement of people and goods, especially in places with dense populations and higher health risks.[5] The first lockdown was implemented on January 23, 2020, when the Chinese state shut down Wuhan, where the virus was first detected.[6] On January 7, 2021, one year after Wuhan's lockdown, new cases were reported. Lockdown measures were again implemented in Shijiazhuang and Xingtai, two cities in Hebei Province, near Beijing.[7] Then, in December 2021, there was another outbreak in Xi'an, in Northwest China, where 13 million citizens went into lockdown on December 22.[8] In April 2022, the lockdown in Shanghai, which lasted two months, sent shockwaves throughout the country.[9] There were also lockdowns in many smaller cities in Xinjiang and borderlands in Yunnan Province, which lasted for months and posed challenges to people trying to maintain their livelihoods.[10] Here cultural differences and incommensurability are worth noting. As the word "lockdown" connotes strict control in Western contexts, the Chinese term fengcheng (sealing the city) evokes "a more protective sealing off of a city" and is associated with "an ethics of care."[11]

Along with the city-based lockdowns noted above, China has experimented with regional mobility restrictions. For instance, following the outbreak in Wuhan in early 2020, public transit and outbound transportation were both suspended.[12] To mitigate health risks, China restricted movement across Hubei Province in sixteen cities and suspended intraprovince bus services to Beijing.[13] Later on, quarantine measurement became normalized across the country. Those who had to travel across international borders and those who had travel history in the highest-risk areas within China were required to quarantine in designated facilities.

Across these various lockdowns and restrictions, the Chinese state sought to control COVID by monitoring, limiting, and sometimes channeling the mobility of people, goods, and services. This process of controlling COVID-era mobilities is preconditioned on the formation of a "pandemic infrastructure." This chapter analyzes the pandemic infrastructure through the lens of mobility and investigates the question of how controlling mobility became thinkable to the state, manageable at the social level, and acceptable to ordinary people. It also demonstrates how making mobility highly mediated has become a feature of urban governance since the COVID-19 outbreak.

I argue the management of everyday mobility cannot be understood as a series of responses to crises, but rather, needs to be understood as evolving from infrastructure that both existed before the pandemic and evolved throughout it. As I demonstrate herein, the mediation of everyday movement in COVID-era China was achieved through three mechanisms. First, community was deployed as a key institution mediating everyday movement.[14] For instance, people who wanted to return to their hometowns were often required to get permission from their local communities. Second, the health-code and itinerary-code system was converted into a form of health-based political monitoring wherein everyday movement was tracked. Citizens had to obtain a health code and itinerary code in order to travel, to enter public spaces, and even to return to their own residential communities, turning a health-triggered imperative into a functional form of regulation with spatial-temporal features. Third, a range of digital platforms enabled many urbanites to outsource their labor and movement during the pandemic, leading to the evolution of new form of im/mobility.

My analysis demonstrates how these three layers, or modes, of pandemic infrastructure overlapped to create new forms of state control/care and citizen agency, and negotiated and contested forms of mobility. Indeed, it is important to emphasize how the pandemic infrastructures of mediated mobility are flexible. Through the infrastructure approach, it is clear that governance is no longer about whether people's movement is restricted, but rather about the mediation of everyday mobility. The pandemic infrastructure, then, is not simply about the technologies of control and repression but about evolving forms of political life, wherein each instance of enhanced control is matched by creative modes of citizen action.[15] Across this dialectic of control/care, however, one key fact is that regardless of where or how Chinese citizens interact with these new pandemic infrastructures, the state can no longer promise certainty. Those who decide to travel must travel with great unpredictability—mobility is now linked to risk.

Due to the COVID interruption, I was not able to conduct fieldwork in China until December 2021. Much of the materials used in this chapter are based on documentary research, as well as online interviews I conducted after the outbreak of COVID-19, from April 2020 to September 2020. Then, in December 2021, I went through a fourteen-day quarantine in Shenzhen and then a seven-day home observation in Chongqing in January 2022. In September 2022, I again went through a ten-day quarantine in Shenzhen and traveled in several provinces in China from September 2022 to October 2022. Therefore, I have incorporated my personal experiences and direct observations during these two trips into this chapter. Moreover, it would be problematic to assume a consistency in China's COVID-19 experiences, as the pandemic infrastructures I experienced on this trip were fundamentally different from the infrastructure I experienced in late 2021 and varied from city to city. The pandemic infrastructure, therefore, is not a monolith but a network of overlapping forms of governance, negotiation, and invention.

Pandemic Infrastructure and Mediated Mobility

To understand how mobility is regulated and human contact is managed to contain the coronavirus, we should first understand how urban life had been organized with regard to mobility before the outbreak. In this section, I sketch out the configuration of mobility in urban China during the Reform era.

Mobility and migration have been critical to China's market reform since the 1980s. As globalization unfolded, the flow of labor, capital, and information accelerated.[16] To insert itself into the global economy in the 1990s, the Chinese government implemented nationwide reforms to reduce friction in the movement of labor. In urban China, nationwide urban reforms untied laborers from socialist work units (*danwei*).[17] In rural China, the relaxed control of peasant movement enabled millions of rural workers to enter urban production or service sectors, where they became known as a "floating population."[18] By 2020, the population of rural migrants had reached 285 million.[19] Moreover, thanks to the nationwide education reform in the late 1990s, young people from smaller cities migrated to the so-called first-tier and second tier-cities for educational and employment opportunities.[20] The post-Mao period of "opening and reform" therefore triggered, in large part, a nationwide revolution in how Chinese citizens practiced mobility, with the nation's economic explosion enabled by relaxed rules around the movement of bodies, goods, services, and ideas.

Other than labor mobility, urban China also witnessed the proliferation of logistics, or *wuliu*, a term often translated as "the flow of goods." Prior to China's economic reforms, goods were distributed through China's "three-tier system," which paralleled administrative lines and city hierarchies. Tier-one distributors were in metropolitan cities including Beijing, Tianjin, Shanghai, and Guangzhou; tier-two distributors operated in the provincial capitals and medium-sized cities; and tier-three wholesalers operated in smaller cities and towns.[21] In the 1990s, the distribution system became more complex as private actors stepped in to build new logistics networks. The rapid expansion of e-commerce in the early 2000s was decisive in establishing even more sophisticated logistics infrastructure.[22] As a burgeoning middle class became more accustomed to online shopping, same-day delivery, and food delivery, companies in e-commerce and those in delivery established an extensive logistics network comprising warehousing facilities, telecommunications systems, and transportation.

State-led urban infrastructure development also contributed to the increased speed of the flow of people and goods in China. In 2008, when the global economic crisis hit, the Chinese central government injected four trillion RMB into urbanization and urban infrastructural projects.[23] Highways and high-speed trains were built all over the country, which resulted in "time–space shrinkages and mobility between cities."[24] This urban infrastructure development increased China's spatial connectedness and expedited the movement of people and goods nationwide. Whether we call it socialism, or Keynesianism, or Roosevelt-style New Dealism, this state-led infrastructure component is key: facilitating modern mobilities—of bodies, goods, services, and ideas—creates jobs, greases the wheels of economic growth, and leads to citizen satisfaction. In this sense, mobility is not something to be controlled or curtailed so much as managed and rendered productive.

This explains why Biao Xiang argues that China's economy has become so "hypermobile" that it has turned into a "gyro-like economy."[25] In fact, China's hypermobility extends to other parts of the world. For instance, in the 2000s, the transnational movement of people and goods accelerated after China joined the WTO and became an important trading partner on an international scale. Since 2013, China's One Belt One Road Initiative has further extended China's capital, workers, and goods to the Global South.[26] Pre-COVID, the Chinese state understood that vying for international prestige and power hinged, in part, on facilitating a wide range of mobilities on domestic, regional, and international levels.

COVID-19 broke out in the abovementioned contexts, where economic activities were increasingly relying on the mobility enabled by high speeds and large scale.[27] Since the COVID outbreak, this mobility has become increasingly mediated, thanks to a new pandemic infrastructure that seeks to control it. Two characteristics of the pandemic infrastructure should be noted. First, the pandemic infrastructure of mobility in urban China is not a result of governmental actions alone. Even though the movement of people and goods are the target of state regulations, such movement is enabled by existing social and technological infrastructure and market forces.[28] The platform economy and emergent pandemic economy in China have been particularly important in mediating the movement of people and goods. Therefore, the management of mobility is realized through the coordination of various actors during the health crisis. Second, while lockdowns, quarantines, and other related measurements to contain the coronavirus are restrictive, the overarching aim of the pandemic infrastructure of mobility is neither to alleviate nor to promote the everyday movement of people. Rather, the aim is producing a new governing infrastructure that renders people's everyday movements traceable, outsourceable, and sustainable. This infrastructure renders everyday mobility highly mediated, instead of spontaneous. Moreover, the infrastructure can regulate individuals' movement based on the given conditions and therefore generate a level of flexibility.

Go and Check with the *Shequ*: The Reterritorialization of Mobility Governance

Since the outbreak of the pandemic in China, spatial units, or *qu*, have become central to implementing anti-virus measures to eliminate the unwanted movement of people. By October 2021, when China's containment of coronavirus had become routinized, yet sporadic cases and outbreaks popped up from time to time, *qu* had further been categorized into three types based on the exposure and risks to the virus: Communities that have new cases are identified as *fengkongqu* (sealed and controlled zones), where the movement of people is restricted and surveilled. Residents are confined to their homes, while community workers deliver groceries and other daily necessities to their doors. The second category of *qu* is *guankongqu* (managed and controlled zones), where the risk is lower. *Guankongqu* residents can still leave their apartments, but they are restricted from leaving the *guankongqu*. The last category is called *fangkongqu*, where cases have not been reported, but the residents are advised not to gather. This categorization of urban spatial zones has become part of China's urban community governance during the pandemic. It ensures the flexibility and prevision of pandemic governance.

For anyone who remained in the risk zones, everyday mobility became subject to the zoning system and community-level governance. My experience in September and October 2022 was telling: I entered Futian District in Shenzhen. During my ten days of quarantine, five COVID cases were reported in the district, and several subdistricts and buildings were marked as high-risk. Anyone who had spent time in Futian District was restricted from visiting any other districts in Shenzhen, and I could not book hotels in other districts. I had to cancel my plan to stay in Nanshan District and left Shenzhen. Throughout my trips to other Chinese cities, I had to check the list of mid-to-high-risk zones, which was updated twice a day, to ensure that the cities I intended on visiting were not on it and my future travel plans were not affected.

Moreover, *shequ*, or communities, have become the main sites for coordinating their members' mobility during the pandemic. In the socialist era, the basic units of urban governance were employment-based work units, or *danwei*.[29] The *danwei* was not only the physical site of production, but also the employment-based social infrastructure providing social services. As urban reforms dismantled these work units in the 1990s, a "community building" (*shequ jianshe*) project was launched.[30] Beginning at the end of the 2000s, the government designated the "community" as the basic unit of urban social, political, and administrative organization. Since then, the Chinese government has continually promoted the conversion of residential units into basic units of governance. As a consequence, state control and care no longer reach people where they work, but rather where they live. "Community" has also begun to acquire both physical and institutional attributes: Community centers have been erected in urban residential compounds; community workers have been incorporated into the employment scheme with low, yet stable, salaries. According to statistical reports, as of this writing, there are 650,000 residence-based rural and urban communities in China, which formally hire about four million community workers. During the Wuhan lockdown, for example, community councils provided basic subsistence for people who were unable to obtain basic needs on their own.[31] Councils were responsible for promoting virus-mitigation tips, as well as delivering food and medicine to every household in the neighborhood so that unnecessary movement of people could be curbed. They also established close contact with residents during the home-quarantine period, monitoring while simultaneously providing assistance, so as to enable people to remain housebound.

Shequ and community-level coordination was critical for the implementation of the sealed management (*fengbishi guanli*). While widely used during lockdowns and quarantines, sealed management is not new. Before the health crisis, the state had tried out sealed management among its migrant population. In Beijing for example, in 2012, over five hundred urban villages implemented sealed management. The village gate would close every night and the village would be placed under curfew, barring entrance and exit from midnight to early morning.[32] These exercises before the pandemic built up the state's capacity to carry out its response to a sudden outbreak. Sealed management was widely implemented in Chinese urban communities, including, since February 2020, Beijing.[33] According to official documents, sealed management requires communities (urban residential units and rural villages) to set up roadblocks to restrict individuals from entering and exiting residential units; local residents need certificates to go in and out of their communities. Additionally, outside personnel and vehicles are barred from entering the communities/villages unless absolutely necessary. Landlords are also incorporated into the sealed management as active agents, as they are asked to report renters' information to community officials.

It is important to note that the capacity for communities to manage mobility in times of need was also strengthened by the commodification of urban housing. In the 1990s, China's urban-housing provision became privatized. Real estate development began to feature "sealed residential quarters."[34] Such gated communities are built to cater to the tastes of the middle class. Walls are built, and gates are often guarded in these sealed residential units, limiting the flow of outsiders.

High-tech surveillance equipment such as closed-circuit cameras and infrared alarm systems are often used at their borders. Most residential compounds offer some semi-public amenities within the gated walls; depending on the price range of the units, the amenities range from a mere central green space to a variety of extras such as playgrounds, a clubhouse, and even shops and swimming pools. Thus, residents can exercise without leaving their compounds. Therefore, communities, often in the form of residential compounds, become the basic administrative units of governance.

In addition, *shequ* have become central to urban China's grid management (*wanggehua guanli*), which was introduced in urban residential communities in 2004. China first experimented with grid management in Dongcheng District in Beijing, modeling it on London. Grid-style social management subdivides counties into smaller zones, and assigns each zone to a person who regularly reports to the local government. Community centers hire temporary grid workers (*wanggeyuan*) to collect information, which is later processed in grid computing centers. Thus, grid management is as much about constructing new forms of physical space as it is about building new forms of organization.[35] In 2015, grid management was promoted throughout China.

When pandemic governance over mobility was routinized during the pandemic in 2022, community workers became the most essential unit in mediating community members' everyday mobility. Those who visited a residential community would report their travel history and health status to the community workers. Those who have recently quarantined would report to the communities so that housebound health-monitoring measures could be implemented. It is important to note that *shequ* governance during the health crisis should not be understood merely as a form of control, as it also shoulders the responsibility of care. Zhiying Ma's analysis of the Chinese notion of *guan* in health governance is particularly telling.[36] Communities will also use the information they gather to distribute food and resources during lockdowns.

PCR Stations and Tracking Mechanism

Technologies and algorithms are indispensable to mediating mobility. They make people's everyday movements trackable. In the past, power operated territorially and was most effective within a certain radius—when people are within that radius, they can be monitored and watched, but when they are outside of it, they are no longer within the reach of regulative power. This model has become central to how we conceptualize nation-states, borders, and other spatial notions through which we understand how and where power operates. China's most well-known and well-studied tool of population control, the household registration system, also operates territorially: household registration is most effective when people remain in their places of origin. Once migrants leave their places of origin, they "escape" the household registration system, to an extent. This explains why rural migrants are asked to return to their hometowns for various forms of documentation, for example when they send their children to school or to purchase real estate in their adopted cities.[37] In addition to the household registration system, the most prevalent community surveillance technologies in contemporary urban China are also territorial. Cameras, for instance, can only capture images within their field of vision and cannot follow individuals around.

However, due to COVID-19, algorithms, digital technologies, and platforms have made it possible to trace people, documenting their everyday movements and turning quotidian practices and human contact into the core subject of health risk control.[38] The prototype of mobile power existed long before COVID-19, however. After the outbreak of SARS in 2003, China established health-control centers modeled on the CDC in the United States. While contact tracing has become crucial to dealing with contagious diseases—the World Health Organization's Michael Ryan has said the attempts to reopen a coronavirus-ravaged society without contact tracing would be like driving a car with your eyes closed—the procedure has long been routine in detecting and controlling contagious diseases in China. One Chinese contact tracer said COVID-19 had barely changed his work rhythm because his job had always been the same: tracing hundreds of people whenever a new case of a contagious disease is detected.

But rapid advances in digital technologies and algorithms have made it possible to expand contact tracing to the entire population in the COVID-19 era. The use of a country-wide "health code" (*jiankangma*) since February 2020 has been the most significant step.[39] On February 7, 2020, in response to a cluster of infections, Zhou Jiangyong, secretary of the Hangzhou Municipal Committee of the Communist Party of China, proposed the introduction of a citizen health code at a regular meeting on epidemic prevention.[40] Two days later, Tencent, China's most important technology company, launched its Health Code app in Shenzhen. By the end of April 2020, over one hundred Chinese cities were using the QR code system. By

2021, Health Code use was nationwide. Health Code users gave the app permission to gather information such as their name, ID number, health status, and location. People are also able to register with facial recognition and update their health status as needed. GPS and network carriers also determine whether users have visited high-risk regions and areas. Moreover, the Health Code app also relies on data recorded on apps such as Alipay and WeChat to determine whether users have had contact with potential carriers of the coronavirus.[41] The Health Code status is updated nightly at midnight.[42]

Health Code users are classified into three color-based categories: green, yellow, and red. The color code is based on factors like users' travel history, their time spent in risky areas, and their relationships to potential carriers. A user's green code will turn yellow or red if smartphone GPS data shows that the user has been to a risky area. A person with a green code can move around freely. Yellow or red codes restrict users from taking public transportation or entering public spaces such as shopping malls and restaurants because they indicate that these people have been exposed to medium or high risks and thus need to self-quarantine. In reality, many people with yellow codes are still able to move freely.

Other than the health-code system, itinerary codes were introduced in China in February 2020. The communication service providers identify the cities where the cell phone holders have stayed for at least four hours and record that information on the itinerary code for seven days. Whenever a person enters public spaces such as airports, train stations, or malls, he or she is asked to show both the health code and the itinerary code. Those who have been to cities in risk zones are restricted. Thanks to both codes, people's everyday movement becomes data that is traceable and trackable. Besides identifying close contact with the infected patients, the government also identifies "time-space companions" of those confirmed cases, however the term is defined.[43] According to reports, in the city of Chengdu, for instance, those who had shared a cell phone signal station for over ten minutes with someone with COVID within an eight hundred–meter radius are identified as time-space companions.

The use of these codes has changed over time. When I had just come out of quarantine and arrived in Chongqing in December 2021, I used my health code and itinerary code to enter the airport. After that, I rarely had to show my health code. My informants in Chongqing were able to take me to many places without any problem because no cases had been reported in Chongqing, and the monitoring of the health code and itinerary code was relaxed. But when I traveled in Shenzhen,

Shandong, and Jiangsu Provinces in 2022, the health-code system was impossible to ignore. Every time I exited the highway in a car, I had to get out and have my itinerary code and health code checked. Most cities and towns required a forty-eight-hour PCR test to enter. Therefore, the health code and itinerary code not only trace people's movements and gather relevant information, but also determine who is allowed freedom of movement.

The digital code restricted my movement in October 2022. Right after my quarantine in Shenzhen, I got a pop-up window (*dan chuang*) on the Beijing Health Code app because several cases had been reported in Shenzhen. Since I was just out of quarantine and had no travel history in so-called risk zones, either within or beyond the boundaries of Shenzhen, I hoped that the community workers in Beijing would remove the pop-up window for me and allow me to enter Beijing. However, the 12345 hotline cut me off.[44] The community workers in my parents' compound told me that they would be happy to lift the restriction once the 12345 center had passed my case to them. In the hope of entering Beijing, I would check the list of risk zones every few hours and avoid having a "risk zone" appear in my digital travel history. However, the situation was uncertain, and just as I arrived in Shandong Province, several cases were reported in the area. I had to accept that I could no longer travel to Beijing to visit my parents, friends, and informants, as planned.

Outsourcing Essential Movement

There are movements and forms of human contact that have not been able to be restricted or traced during the pandemic, much of which has been categorized as essential labor or care work. Unlike jobs in the production sector that can be suspended or turned remote, care work usually involves direct human contact and cannot be suspended, regardless of circumstances. After all, those who stay housebound during the pandemic must rely on logistical systems to sustain their everyday basic living. During the pandemic, families, communities and platform economies have been critical to the outsourcing of essential movement during lockdowns, or when everyday movement is restricted.

Before the pandemic, online shopping and delivery services had already become China's urban norm. People, especially young adults living in urban areas, rely on e-commerce companies such as Meituan, Tencent, and Alibaba, as well as on other platforms for grocery shopping, food takeaway, and delivery. During the pandemic, online shopping and delivery services have become not a lifestyle choice, but a necessity. Since everyday mobility is restricted, more people must rely on the platform economy to get the goods they need. Thus, online-shopping platforms and the logistics sector must move goods (for instance, masks) in response to the increased needs of people who are immobilized. In fact, to sustain normal life, more people than ever ordered food delivery through online platforms during the pandemic. Even when hotels were sending hot meals to the door for people in quarantine, people still relied on Meituan or Taobao for fruit and other everyday necessities. On my first stay in a quarantine hotel in Shenzhen in 2021, I ordered on Meituan two or three times per day for everyday items I needed.

This marks another important change during COVID-19, that is, the surge in what Biao Xiang has called the "redistribution of mobility," or outsourced movement.[45] And more importantly, the reduction of movement itself, as argued by Biao Xiang, has become the very condition for the emergence of other forms of mobility. While some movement is curbed and restricted, many people, especially those providing essential care work in and beyond families, have had to be more mobile so that others could remain at home and be less mobile. This condition has given rise to the outsourcing movement, as many people have had to stay housebound.

During the Wuhan lockdown, Meituan received nearly four million orders. Food and prescription drug orders both doubled. Likewise, China's major online-shopping platform, Jingdong, is also reporting huge profits during the pandemic. In the first quarter of 2020, Jingdong's revenue increased by 20.7 percent, reaching 170.7 billion RMB, which not even the company expected. Statistical reports have shown that China's online-takeaway market grew from an annual revenue of 577.9 billion RMB in 2019 to 650 billion RMB in 2020. It is not an exaggeration to say that big companies like Meituan and Jingdong are consolidating their power and securing their market shares. Meanwhile, e-commerce companies have attracted new customers to their platforms because of the pandemic. It has been reported that at least 25 million new users registered accounts on Jingdong in 2020, and at least 70 percent of new registered users were from third- or fourth-tier cities. Over 60 percent of the company's new orders were from smaller cities.

With growing demand for online shopping and the outsourcing of everyday mobility, companies specializing in logistics have also expanded their power. As few platform companies run their own logistics, delivery companies have also become crucial; demands on delivery service and pressure on delivery workers are immense. Shunfeng, China's biggest logistics company, saw a 77 percent increase in orders in the first quarter of 2020.⁴⁶ In the first half of 2020, Shunfeng's profit skyrocketed 42.05 percent. Shunfeng also experimented with new services in the middle of the lockdowns. For instance, according to one of the company's official reports, Shunfeng expanded its services to the delivery of fresh vegetables and meat, and errand-running for housebound individuals. As the pandemic has receded, Shunfeng has already expanded it network coverage in Chinese cites of various scales.⁴⁷

As the platform economy has gained power and become essential infrastructure mediating people's everyday movement, a new pattern of labor absorption in urban China has emerged along class lines. Given the rising demand for outsourcing everyday movement, and given the growing capacity of companies to mediate these needs through online platforms, more Chinese rural migrants are being incorporated into the platform economy.⁴⁸ From January 20 to March 18, 2020, 3,360,000 people registered accounts on Meituan's website and became new delivery workers. About 80 percent of them came from rural backgrounds. Among the newly recruited workers, 18.6 percent were from the manufacturing sectors, and 14.3 percent were from the service sectors.⁴⁹ It should be noted that this rise in mediated mobility indicates the advent of a new class politics. People who are unable or unwilling to move utilize online platforms to order food and services so they can outsource their everyday movement and offload health risks to others through the platform economy. Those privileged enough to rely on telecommuting to work have become even more dependent on working-class people, who have to be mobile to make a living. This means that the pandemic has facilitated a new type of class politics, with health risks being redistributed along class lines. Thus, lower-class migrants are becoming the population who face the greatest care burden and shoulder the most risk.

Coordination between platforms and communities is critical to mediating outsourced mobility. Before the pandemic, platforms directly interacted with customers. Yet, during the pandemic, as the coronavirus was understood to attach to persons and goods, delivery services were not welcome on community grounds or in personal living spaces. Therefore, logistical companies had to work closely with community workers to regulate and control outsourced movement. One of my interviewees, a Beijing resident, told me that delivery companies had set up their own stands in designated areas when delivery workers were not allowed to enter the communities. Residents would have to exit the communities and retrieve their goods at their own risk.

In the event of lockdowns, essential mobility can be outsourced to volunteers and mediated at the community level. For instance, during the Shanghai lockdown, many communities relied on *tuanzhang* to purchase everyday necessities.[50] *Tuanzhang* commonly refers to regimental commanders. But during the lockdown, people used the term to refer to those who coordinate with merchandise and delivery-service providers to ensure basic household needs in their communities. They would make connections with wholesale markets or other providers to secure fresh vegetables, rice, milk, meat, and other goods. Many *tuanzhang* were also in charge of the distribution of supplies. The group purchasing relies on delivery workers and logistical systems too. According to several reports on group purchasing during the pandemic, *tuanzhang* often lead a group of volunteers who are subdivided into groups in charge of tasks such as communication, purchasing, consulting, and distribution.[51] It has been reported that over 80 percent of the *tuanzhang* are women and that they form WeChat groups so that community members can voice their needs.

Discussion and Conclusion

In the above sections, I have discussed how everyday movement was reduced, traced, outsourced, and sustained during the lockdown in China through the pandemic infrastructure of mobility. I have shown how mobility has become increasingly mediated, thanks to a pandemic infrastructure involving communities, technologies of tracking, and platform economies. The infrastructure is not entirely new. Other than the health-code and itinerary-code system, the infrastructure had been in place before the pandemic. How mobility becomes increasingly mediated serves as the method through which we might make sense of the changing nature of Chinese urban governance. Unlike what has commonly been implied in the discussion of Chinese urban governance during COVID, the management of people should not be seen as solely the result of state action. Rather, the government, companies, the technology sector, and families together have enabled urban governance. Even though lockdowns and quarantine measures are often considered to be sudden and temporary responses to health crises, and many assume society will return to "normal" after the pandemic, the pandemic infrastructure of mobility may have long-term effects on the future of urban governance, as well as on socioeconomic conditions in general.

First, the community has become a significant unit in the making of pandemic infrastructure under the zero-COVID policy. Bureaucratic powers from the top down, the privatization of housing, and the prevalence of new technologies each contribute to community governance. Community governance shoulders the responsibilities of both control and care in response to the health crisis. While the community as a spatial unit moves to the center of urban governance, there has also been a rise in mobile power enabled by digital technologies during the COVID era. Compared to territorial power, which is exercised over a limited, physical radius, mobile power attaches to individuals, and the rise of mobile power during COVID-19 is significant for future urban governance.

Second, big companies in e-commerce and logistics have gained more power and are absorbing low-skilled workers without providing adequate protection during the health crisis. This new pattern of labor absorption might reconfigure the nature of labor precariousness in China. When I started my research on Chinese rural migrants a decade ago, many rural migrants left factories and entered the informal economies so they could have, in their own words, "more freedom." They were unhappy with their lives in factories and hoped that the informal economy would bring them more flexibility in work and a way to manage family life in the cities.

Third, the pandemic infrastructure of mobility is gendered. Much of the essential movement and service provision during the health crisis has relied on women. The pandemic has pushed women back to families to shoulder care responsibilities, while little is being done to systematically address the care crisis; the state has done little to restrain the platform-economy monopoly or to address the unfolding care crisis. If the pandemic illuminates the central role of social reproduction and how desperately we need a human-centered economy, then the responses so far tell us we still have a long way to go in achieving these goals.

NOTES

Biao Xiang has inspired me to think about the COVID pandemic through the lens of mobility with his work on migration and mobility. I also benefited from the "Keywords" workshop organized by Louisa Schein, Fan Yang, and Silvia Lindtner in 2020.
Conversations with Zhiying Ma, Yige Dong, Zhongjin Li, and Ying Chen also shaped this chapter. A previous version of this chapter was shared at a roundtable titled "Pathologies of Governance," which was organized by Critical China Scholars in January 2021, and

at a workshop titled "Community Governance or Governing Communities," which was organized by the China and Global Development Network at the Hong Kong Polytechnic University and the Paul Baerwald School of Social Work and Social Welfare at the Hebrew University of Jerusalem in January 2022. The fieldwork of this research is made possible by two General Research Grants from the Hong Kong Research Council (F-PP6V and B-Q91B).

1. Please see Xuefei Ren, "Pandemic and Lockdown: A Territorial Approach to COVID-19 in China, Italy and the United States," *Eurasian Geography and Economics* 61, no. 4–5 (2020): 423–434; Rajib Shaw, Yong-kyun Kim, and Jinling Hua, "Governance, Technology and Citizen Behavior in Pandemic: Lessons from COVID-19 in East Asia," *Progress in Disaster Science* 6 (2020).
2. Noel B. Salazar. "Existential vs. Essential Mobilities: Insights from before, during and after a Crisis," *Mobilities* (2021): 1–15.
3. Vijitra Duangdee, "After Reopening, Thailand's Battered Tourism Struggles to Rebuild," Al Jazeera, May 16, 2022.
4. Please see Owen Dyer, "Covid-19: Lockdowns Spread in China as Omicron Tests 'Zero Covid' Strategy," *British Medical Journal* 376 (March 31, 2022).
5. Some scholars have explored the mixed movement of things and people. Please see parts 1 and 2 of Do Dom Kim, "Mixed Movements: Virus, Things, Persons, and Signs," *Coronavirus and Mobility Forum* (blog), COMPAS, https://www.compas.ox.ac.uk/publications/blog/.
6. Please see Guobin Yang, *The Wuhan Lockdown* (New York: Columbia University Press, 2022).
7. Jane Cai and Ji Siqi, "Coronavirus: Chinese City in Lockdown as Hebei Province Has Biggest Outbreak in Months," *South China Morning Post*, January 6, 2021.
8. Vincent Ni, "China Imposes Covid Lockdown in Xi'an after Handful of Cases," *Guardian*, July 5, 2022.
9. Alan Taylor, "The End of Shanghai's Two-Month COVID Lockdown," *Atlantic*, May 21, 2022.
10. Bloomberg Businessweek, "Life Turned Upside Down in Ruili, China, the World's Strictest Zero-Covid City," *South China Morning Post*, October 23, 2022.
11. The incommensurability of lockdown and *fengcheng* can be seen in the discussion among scholars working on the Chinese–English Keywords Project. See Louisa Schein, Fan Yang, and Silvia Lindtner, "COVID Tech & China: After Surveillance? After Authoritarianism? After COVID?," Ethics, Society, and Computing, University of

Michigan, February 6, 2021–April 17, 2021, Zoom seminar, https://esc.umich.edu/covid-tech-china/. The discussion on the Chinese way of thinking of control and care can be seen in Zhiying Ma, "Promises and Perils of Guan," *Medicine Anthropology Theory* 7, no. 2 (2020): 150–174.

12. Anna Fifield and Lena H. Sun, "Travel Ban Goes into Effect in Chinese City of Wuhan as Authorities Try to Stop Coronavirus Spread," *Washington Post*, January 22, 2020.
13. Hamish Gibbs et al., "Changing Travel Patterns in China during the Early Stages of the COVID-19 Pandemic," *Nature Communications* 11 (2020).
14. The word "community," as I use it in this chapter, refers to the Chinese administrative unit *shequ*, which often consists of a neighborhood with mixed-use residential/commercial buildings.
15. Please see the similar observation and argument made by Patrick Shaou-Whea Dodge, "Imagining Dissent: Contesting the Façade of Harmony through Art and the Internet in China," *Imagining China: Rhetorics of Nationalism in the Age of Globalization* (2017): 311–338.
16. Arjun Appadurai, *Modernity at Large: Cultural Dimensions of Globalization*, vol. 1 (Minneapolis: University of Minnesota Press, 1996).
17. Please see Alan Smart and Josephine Smart, "Local Citizenship: Welfare Reform Urban/Rural Status, and Exclusion in China," *Environment and Planning A* 33, no. 10 (2001): 1853–1869.
18. Please see Zai Liang, Zhen Li, and Zhongdong Ma, "Changing Patterns of the Floating Population in China, 2000–2010," *Population and Development Review* 40, no. 4 (2014): 695–716; Zai Liang and Zhongdong Ma, "China's Floating Population: New Evidence from the 2000 Census," *Population and Development Review* 30, no. 3 (2004): 467–488.
19. National Bureau of Statistics, "2020 nian nongmingong jiance diaocha baogao [Annual Monitoring and Research Report of Rural Migrant Workers, 2020]," last updated April 5, 2021, http://www.stats.gov.cn/tjsj/zxfb/202004/t20200430_1742724.html.
20. In addition to rural to urban migration, China's entire population has become increasingly mobile as many people hop from job to job. As such, labor mobility has become a structural component of China's economic growth and social composition. Please see Biao Xiang. "The Gyroscope-like Economy: Hypermobility, Structural Imbalance and Pandemic Governance in China," *Inter-Asia Cultural Studies* 21, no. 4 (2020): 521–532.
21. Chia-Lin Chen, "Reshaping Chinese Space-Economy through High-Speed Trains: Opportunities and Challenges," *Journal of Transport Geography* 22, no. C (2012): 312–316; Bin Jiang and Edmund Prater, "Distribution and Logistics Development in China,"

International Journal of Physical Distribution & Logistics Management (2002).
22. Please see Mark Goh and Charlene Ling, "Logistics Development in China," *International Journal of Physical Distribution & Logistics Management* (2003): 23–56.
23. Hao Shi and Shaoqing Huang, "How Much Infrastructure Is Too Much? A New Approach and Evidence from China," *World Development* 56 (2014): 272–286; Yumei Zhang, Xinxin Wang, and Kevin Chen, "Growth and Distributive Effects of Public Infrastructure Investments in China," in *Infrastructure and Economic Growth in Asia*, ed. Cham Springer (Cham, Germany: Springer), 87–116.
24. Chen, "Reshaping Chinese Space-Economy through High-Speed Trains," 315.
25. Xiang, "The Gyroscope-like Economy"; Biao Xiang, "From Chain Reaction to Grid Reaction: Mobilities & Restrictions during SARS & Coronavirus," *University of Oxford* (March 2020).
26. Ching Kwan Lee, *The Specter of Global China: Politics, Labor, and Foreign Investment in Africa* (Chicago: University of Chicago Press, 2018).
27. It might well be that because a sudden halt to mobility had seemed unimaginable, many people tended to attribute the successful implementation of lockdowns to authoritarianism.
28. Zhongjin Li, Ying Chen, and Yang Zhan, "Building Community-centered Social Infrastructure: A Feminist Inquiry into China's COVID-19 Experiences," *Economia Politica* (2021): 1–19.
29. Vivienne Shue, *The Reach of the State: Sketches of the Chinese Body Politic* (Redwood City: Stanford University Press, 1990); David Bray, *Social Space and Governance in Urban China: The Danwei System from Origins to Reform* (Stanford: Stanford University Press, 2005).
30. Thomas Heberer and Christian Göbel. *The Politics of Community Building in Urban China* (London: Taylor & Francis, 2011).
31. Li, Chen, and Zhan, "Building Community-Centered Social Infrastructure."
32. Jane Hayward, "Building City Walls: Reordering the Population through Beijing's Upside-Down Villages," *Modern China* 48, no. 5 (2022): 1019–1049.
33. Please see COVID Prevention Leadership Office in Beijing, "Beijing fabu yiqing fangkong tonggao, yange juzhu xiaoqu fengbishi guanli [Beijing Announces the Notice of COVID Prevention, Strengthening the Sealed Management in Communities]," last updated February 10, 2020, http://politics.people.com.cn/BIG5/n1/2020/0210/c1001-31578622.html.
34. Pu Miao, "Deserted Streets in a Jammed Town: The Gated Community in Chinese Cities and Its Solution," *Journal of Urban Design* 8, no. 1 (2003): 45–66; Youqin Huang, Collectivism, Political Control, and Gating in Chinese Cities," *Urban Geography* 27, no.

6 (2006): 507–525; Karita Kan and Rebecca W. Y. Wong, "Gated Villages: Community Governance and Social Control in Peri-Urban China," in *Handbook on Urban Development in China*, ed. Ray Yep, Jun Wang, and Thomas R. Johnson (Cheltenham, U.K.: Edward Elgar Publishing, 2019).

35. To understand the grid-management system, please see Yujun Wei et al., "COVID-19 Prevention and Control in China: Grid Governance," *Journal of Public Health* 43, no. 1 (2021): 76–81; David Bray, "Garden Estates and Social Harmony: A Study into the Relationship between Residential Planning and Urban Governance in Contemporary China" (paper presented at the China Planning Network 3rd Annual Conference, Beijing, 2006).

36. To understand the notion of *guan*, please see Zhiying Ma, "Biopolitical Paternalism and Its Maternal Supplements: Kinship Correlates of Community Mental Health Governance in China," *Cultural Anthropology* 35, no. 2 (2020): 290–316, and Zhiying Ma, "Promises and Perils of Guan," *Medicine Anthropology Theory* 7, no. 2 (2020): 150–174.

37. Household registration has become less of a barrier for rural outmigration and more a tool of population differentiation in recent years.

38. Please see Chuncheng Liu and Ross Graham, "Making Sense of Algorithms: Relational Perception of Contact Tracing and Risk Assessment during COVID-19," *Big Data & Society* 8, no. 1 (2021).

39. Please see Fan Liang, "COVID-19 and Health Code: How Digital Platforms Tackle the Pandemic in China," *Social Media and Society* 6, no. 3 (2020).

40. Paul Mozur, Raymond Zhong, and Aaron Krolik, "In Coronavirus Fight, China Gives Citizens a Color Code, with Red Flags," *New York Times*, March 1, 2020.

41. Liang, "COVID-19 and Health Code."

42. On May 22, the Hangzhou Health Commission held a special meeting to normalize and routinize the use of the health-code system. It proposed integrating medical records, health checkups, and lifestyle-management data, linking users' health indicators and health-code colors to create a personal-health index ranking. Beyond China, it has been suggested that the use of tracing apps might become a normal practice in many other countries. Please see Liang, "COVID-19 and Health Code."

43. The Paper News, "duodi chutai chikongbansuizhe guanli fangfa, dingyi buyi, guanli cuoshi youbie [Several Places Announce the Time-Space Companions Management: Variations in Definition and Method]," last updated November 5, 2021, https://news.cctv.com/2021/11/05/ARTIN5pamaLUQyEDUxSqS4Yd211105.shtml.

44. Dialing the numbers 12345 connects people to a hotline for optimizing government service. During the COVID pandemic, many people reported their situation to the hotline

so they could get help and service.
45. Biao Xiang has discussed the redistribution of mobility. Please see Biao Xiang, "Remote Work, Social Inequality and the Redistribution Of Mobility," *International Migration* 60, no. 6 (2022): 280–282. Also see "MMC Interviews Biao Xiang: 'Covid as Catalyst,'" Mixed Migration Centre, December 3, 2020, http://www.mixedmigration.org/articles/mmc-interviews-biao-xiang-covid-as-catalyst/.
46. Shunfeng Express, "Shunfeng konggu gufen youxian gongsi niandu baogao 2020 [The Annual Report of Shunfeng 2020]," last updated 2020, https://www.sf-express.com/uploads/2021_03_18_002352_SZ_2020_e79355bd58.pdf.
47. Shunfeng Express, "Shunfeng konggu gufen youxian gongsi niandu baogao 2020 [The Annual Report of Shunfeng 2020]," last updated 2020, https://www.sf-express.com/uploads/2021_03_18_002352_SZ_2020_e79355bd58.pdf.
48. Lei Che, Haifeng Du, and Kam Wing Chan, "Unequal Pain: A Sketch of the Impact of the Covid-19 Pandemic on Migrants' Employment in China," *Eurasian Geography and Economics* 61, no. 4–5 (2020): 448–463.
49. "2019 zhi 2020 nian yiqing qijian meituan qishou jiuye baogao" [The employment report of delivery workers at meituan, 2019 to 2020], https://s3plus.meituan.net/v1/mss_531b5a3906864f438395a28a5baec011/official-website/ed3e2bb5-13dd-46ca-93ba-30808a1ca852, accessed January 15, 2023.
50. Hanzhi Lu, "Shanghai Jiulinghou tuanzhangmen, chongxin dingyi shequ tuangou [The *Tuangzhang* Who Were Born in the 1990s that Redefine Group Purchasing for the Communities in Shanghai]," last updated April 14, 2022, https://m.yicai.com/news/101380278.html.
51. Ruotong Yi, "shequ tuantou zhong, zhiyuanzhe yu jumin jian guanxi ruhe [In Group Purchasing in the Communities, What are the Relationships between Volunteers and Residents]," last updated June 9, 2022, https://news.xhby.net/zt/cmgc/202206/t20220609_7575462.shtml.

DingTalk and Chinese Digital Workplace Surveillance in Pandemic Times

Yizhou Xu

ON JANUARY 23, 2020, ON THE EVE OF THE CHINESE LUNAR NEW YEAR, I WAS SITTING in my cubicle on the twenty-fifth floor of a high-rise building in downtown Guangzhou when Chinese state media announced the lockdown in Wuhan, the epicenter of the COVID-19 pandemic.[1] The lockdown was soon extended across China due to the rapidly escalating situation in dealing with the spread of COVID-19. Working in the mobile tech industry as part of my dissertation project in China, I witnessed firsthand the impact of the pandemic on the lives of tech workers, especially when many were confined in their homes. Unable to travel, I was also isolated in my apartment and increasingly reliant on digital media to keep up to date with the outside world. This extended to my daily movements, which were also heavily monitored via mandatory contact-tracing apps in the form of the various "digital health codes" that were required for even a simple outing to get groceries.[2] In contrast to Huiling Ding's articulation of the use of communication technologies to challenge state narratives during the 2003 SARS outbreak, I argue the adoption of contact-tracing tools and mobile apps in China during the pandemic highlights the increasing co-optation of technological infrastructures for the purpose of state control.[3]

This increasing intrusion of software-mediated tools in governing everyday life in China informed me of the heightened precarity in the labor sector, which was upended by the pandemic, as companies scrambled to maintain productivity. Major Chinese tech companies, such as Tencent, Alibaba, and NetEase, all announced policies where laborers could remotely work from home.[4] As a result, corporations became wholly reliant on software and apps as the means to keep track of worker productivity outside the formal workplace setting. The various intrusive modes of workplace surveillance are nothing new, as measuring and maintaining employee efficiency and performance has long been the central aim of the neo-Taylorist corporate regime.[5] Nonetheless, the onset of a global pandemic created both obstacles and opportunities for evolving new methods of monitoring the workforce. On the one hand, the lockdown-imposed self-isolation at home made it increasingly difficult to track workers who were otherwise contained within organized spaces and tight cubicles. On the other hand, the pandemic provided an opportune time for the intrusion of digital surveillance software into the private domestic sphere, something that has long eluded total corporate control.

One such software, DingTalk (or DingDing) has taken center stage in facilitating, measuring, and governing the day-to-day operations of the Chinese workforce. Since its introduction in 2014, DingTalk, a product of the Chinese tech titan Alibaba, has evolved from a simple office collaboration tool similar to Slack into a one-stop platform for all work-related tasks. By late 2020, DingTalk had amassed over three hundred million users across fifteen million public and private organizations, hence achieving near ubiquitous adoption in the Chinese labor sector.[6] DingTalk represents the tendencies for Chinese software companies to make "all-in-one" apps that are bloated with features encompassing every function imaginable.[7] In addition to its main purpose of facilitating office communication, DingTalk enables file sharing, to-do lists, calendars, video calls, company wiki, and a dizzying array of mundane features, such as live-streaming, video classes, achievement badges, digital business cards, and even a fitness tracker that alerts you if you have been sitting for too long. During the pandemic, it became the de facto tool for many Chinese companies as it served as a repository for much of a given company's policies, employee guidelines, and work-related authorizations. DingTalk is also a multiplatform experience, as it is available as a mobile app (iOS and Android) and on various desktop clients (Windows and Mac), which in turn forces workers to have DingTalk installed on every device they carry, wherever they are, be it the office, home, or public spaces. Because of this stunning array of functions, DingTalk served pivotal roles during the pandemic, not just as the primary software that workers used to report their up-to-date status on a regular basis, but also, as this chapter will show, in providing the infrastructural foundations for the adoption of the health-code system for China's COVID-19 contact-tracing program. In other words, workplace surveillance is intimately linked to the oppressive regimes of Chinese state control, with the tech industry, and more specifically tech workers, being the experimental grounds for its instrumentalization.

Taking cues from a mix of ethnographic approaches, discursive interface analysis, and my own "insider" status working in the mobile game industry in China during COVID-19, this chapter centers on the lives of tech workers and asks how they navigated both their personal and professional lives, which are increasingly controlled and monitored via digital technologies. DingTalk thus serves as an important vantage point for unpacking the interplay between state, corporate, and platform-mediated forms of control, along with the often-conflicting motivations driving workers to contend with workplace software in their daily lives. To this end, I offer critical insights into two intervening developments related to digital workplace surveillance during COVID-19. First, I offer a discursive interface analysis of the core features of DingTalk, unravelling how several key monitoring features provide the building blocks of the wider digital surveillance apparatus that was used for contact tracing during the pandemic. Second, through extensive interviews with Chinese tech workers, I look at the various tactics and strategies used in order to circumvent and subvert digital-mediated forms of control on worker's personal and professional lives.

I argue the pandemic-imposed lockdown, while enabling the further means of digital surveillance through software such as DingTalk, also exposed potential vulnerabilities in the system, which workers can subvert and work against. In doing so, I dissect the various institutional and infrastructural limits imposed on productive tech labor via digital software while also mapping new ways of thinking about worker agency and means of resistance. Here, tech workers occupy a contradictory position wherein they are often the makers of the very oppressive surveillance technologies that regulate their lives. Indeed, tech workers, such as developers, IT specialists, backend operations, and designers, all possess the technical literacy to potentially exploit the system in ways other workers might not have the wherewithal to do. Centering this chapter within the context of the Chinese tech industry thus provides a unique vantage point for addressing the relationships at the intersections of state control, software-mediated surveillance, and worker agency.

This chapter is based on a ten-month-long, IRB-approved ethnographic fieldwork (October 2019–August 2020), where I worked as a localizer at a mobile game company in the Chinese city of Guangzhou. During this time, I experienced firsthand the initial wave of COVID-19 outbreak in China and spent the subsequent months under various forms of lockdown, all while working full-time. Doing fieldwork in the middle of a pandemic not only provided me opportunities to intimately research workplace oppression, but also allowed me to be an active participant during a time of crisis. My methodological approach draws from existing archives of corporate and organizational studies, which portray the possibilities of writing "insider ethnography."[8] This chapter fits that model, as I was actively employed within the tech industry. Drawing on dozens of interviews with co-workers and through extensive participant observation of work routines, I gained firsthand accounts into the quotidian working conditions of a typical Chinese tech company and formed close personal relationships with workers in the industry during a time of increasing precarity. Additionally, my research also integrates the method of "discursive interface analysis" to probe the design, interface, and affordances of DingTalk, thus addressing how its intended usage helps shape, and is simultaneously shaped by, the corporate workplace.[9] A discursive analysis of DingTalk's interface provides useful optics in understanding the norms, values, and power structures encoded in the functional designs of software that workers must contend with and against on a regular basis. When coupled with my on-the-ground interviews, this mixed-methods approach provides a survey of how different workers make sense of their digital working experiences.

Being an employee in a tech company also provided me with a corporate DingTalk account, which gave me access to additional features that a personal account does not possess, particularly features that deal with workplace monitoring and tracking. Unlike approaches such as the "walkthrough method,"[10] this chapter is not intended to provide a definitive overview of DingTalk and its myriad of features but, rather, focus on its specific affordances in dealing with surveillance and control. Likewise, because apps are transitory interfaces that are always connected and updated via cloud networks, and are thus always subjected to changes and updates,[11] I will only be looking at versions 4.7 to 5.0 (which were released between October 2019 and July 2020, the period that coincides with my fieldwork and the initial waves of the pandemic). Finally, I will augment these methods by using extensive archival analysis of DingTalk's corporate user manual and official company FAQs, along with news articles about DingTalk to dissect the formal and informal reception of the app and its impact on Chinese society in the backdrop of a global pandemic.

Contextualizing Digital Workplace Surveillance

Given the prevalence of workplace monitoring within highly industrialized societies, it comes as no surprise to learn that a wide range of scholars—including Martha Crowley, Daniel Tope, Lindsey Joyce Chamberlain, Randy Hodson, Patricia Wallace, and Kirstie Ball, among others—have produced research on workplace surveillance.[12] Early tools such as punch card machines, performance sheets, scheduling programs, and workplace collaborative tools were all intended to facilitate the ease of measurement and control over workers' performance and behavior. These management measures only intensified with the neo-Taylorist turn, as the various metrics of performativity and productivity became increasingly reliant on computational and technological systems in providing quantifiable measures of work.[13] Neo-Taylorism, also known as "digital Taylorism," refers to the organizational method that combines scientific management, surveillance, and digital technologies to maximize worker productivity.[14] This in turn reorients management-employee relations whereby highly skilled knowledge work becomes standardized using digital technologies. Such platforms and software also reflect how workplace oppression is increasingly imbricated with digital technologies and surveillance tools.

Shoshana Zuboff regards this as a form of "instrumentarianism," where power is enforced and expressed not through violence but through the instrumentation of behaviors via surveillance technologies such as apps and platforms.[15] In doing so, management transforms what was supposed to be qualitative spaces into quantitative spaces by which labor and precarity are disguised as promoting productivity. This reconfiguration of power relations also resonates with the organizational context of neoliberalism, characterized by increasing privatization, individualization, and deregulation of labor markets that further contribute to the precaritization and alienation of workers.[16] Here the transformation of workplace routines conforms to this neoliberal ideology of making work a personal responsibility that is supposed to be a liberating experience, as opposed to an oppressive one. Phoebe Moore and Andrew Robinson for instance, articulate the increasing adoption of wearable technologies at workplaces using various sensors and protocols. The consequence of such digital intrusions is the internalization of policing and control by the individual, hence promoting the concept of the "quantified self," by which metrics and measurements are presented as a form of self-betterment, as opposed to control.[17] Such contentions are all the more apparent in the always-on app economy, by which employee metrics and data are constantly being monitored by digital platforms connected via cloud networks.

Another major strand in surveillance studies is the metaphor of the "panopticon," where the nexus of control is largely rendered invisible, and workers are constantly being spied on without their knowledge or consent.[18] Monitoring software and digital platforms seems to fit neatly into this asymmetry of power as the processes of knowledge production, distribution, and reception are mediated via the softwarization processes that are often hidden behind opaque interfaces.[19] From wearable badges with cameras and accelerometers that can track one's arousal and performance, to infrared sensors that can monitor location and space within the office, to RFID tags and biometrics recognition, surveillance technologies have increasingly colonized the workplace in ways that allow for persistent surveillance over working life.[20] This digitally mediated workplace conforms to what Mark Andrejevic calls the "digital enclosure," where all interactions with software become incorporated as forms of labor that can be monitored and commodified.[21] José Van Dijck and Roderic Crooks further expanded on this point with the notions of "dataveillance," by which large data sources can be pooled together to form vast, networked surveillance apparatuses that can track and even predict possible patterns in user engagement.[22] Surveying this literature, Wendy Hui Kyong Chun addresses the implicit relations between software and governmentality, where interfaces provide a facade of individual choice but also confine users within the organizational powers of software.[23] Yet, the panoptical model in the Foucauldian sense often does not fully conform to the case of digital workplace surveillance. Digital platforms such as DingTalk encompass multiple layers of control that are highly visible through their metrics of self-quantification, but are also opaque through their persistent data collection. This conforms to what Selena Nemorin considers as increasingly Deleuzian or rhizomatic means of surveillance, where the loci of control are both decentralized via software interfaces and dispersed across multitudes of power structures and institutional interests.[24] In the case of DingTalk, control lies not just within the hands of the self-quantifying individual and company supervisors, but also the data centers at Alibaba.

However, such scholarly debates remain largely grounded in the Western context of the neoliberal workplace, with relatively little attention paid to how work surveillance is experienced and enacted in other regions of the world. More troubling, however, is the increasing labor exploitation in non-Western contexts, especially given the prevailing outsourcing of tech work, including both hardware and software production, to Asia. Here, the deployment of workplace surveillance compounded the existing oppression of workers in an already extractive environment. Carol Updahya's work on Indian IT knowledge workers, for instance, argues the client-driven outsourcing model has encouraged local companies to adopt harsh means of boosting productivity.[25] In applying such tensions to China, Julie Chen, in looking at DiDi's ride-hailing drivers in China, situates surveillance in the context of the on-demand economy, where workers are subjected to persistent algorithmic control.[26] Such contentions raise important questions about how new digital technologies impact workplace precarity and labor oppression, which were both made more acute during COVID-19. The pandemic-related lockdowns thus produced new intersecting layers of oppression and alienation for tech workers in China.

DingTalk and the Softwarization of Work

DingTalk in its early iterations drew close inspiration from other online collaborative software (OCS) such as Slack with a focus on office messaging and collaboration. The main interface also resembles a typical messaging app organized across different contacts and work teams, which employees must use to interact with each other on a daily basis. While Slack, as its name might suggest, can be seen as a way to foster more fun, informal, and social workplace interactions,[27] the discursive messaging behind DingTalk reflects the opposite. According to the company FAQs, DingTalk takes its name from the Chinese idiom *banshang dingding*, which literally means "nails on a board" (or pins on a bulletin board), signifying the nailing down of decisions as part of the work collaboration process.[28] But the nail metaphor in DingTalk can also be interpreted as the increasing machinization of work itself, as workers become part of the proverbial cogs in the wheel driving capitalist production.

A fellow cubicle mate in the company Ms. Tsai confided to me "I don't really trust DingTalk because it's made by Alibaba, a company that caters to businesses as opposed to the individual." While this categorization may seem overly simplistic, it implies the perception of DingTalk as not just a social-messaging tool but an instrument of control. More pertinently, however, the Chinese name DingTalk is also a homonym for the "ding" sound that alerts workers of the notifications from the app, a signifier for work to be done. In fact, Chinese workers often use "ding" as a verb (for example, "Go *ding* this person") as a way to solicit replies from co-workers or an attempt to get someone's attention. This decidedly Pavlovian response reflects how workers are conditioned to constantly anticipate and respond to messages where persistent notifications (which buzz even while the app is muted) become an integral part of the aurality of the modern workplace.

Herein lies one of the most notorious features of DingTalk—"read receipts," a feature that marks if a worker has read the message or not, which is similar to functions in WhatsApp or iMessages. However, unlike WhatsApp, which functions as a social app, the use of read receipts in workplace software carries more stake, especially when it is tied to evaluating worker engagement in the office. On the practical level, whenever a message is sent or received, a notification shows up under the message, marking it "unread" unless the user interacts with the chat box, and only then will it be marked as "read." An audible notification also accompanies the sent message, and if the user's device is muted, the taskbar will flash to notify the user of an incoming message. This results in the persistent expectations from team leaders and managers for having workers respond promptly to any work-related inquiries.

The workplace obligations imposed by read receipts also exacerbates anxieties associated with interpersonal work communication in ways that create an always-on mentality by which workers must be constantly on standby for work. This dovetails with Chun's assertion of how new media requires users to "constantly respond in order to remain close to the same," which habituates users as wholly dependent on *new* media technologies and the façade of innovation.[29] Additionally, the read receipt function is also reciprocal for both the sender and receiver whereby both can see whether the messages are read. This is especially apparent during group chats when group members can easily see which person did not read a message. As a result, the affordances of DingTalk enforce a form of "imagined surveillance" by which workers collectively surveil and supervise each other in groups.[30] Thus, the enforcement of attentiveness becomes a collective act whereby everyone must participate through constant interfacing with DingTalk. Those workers who are unresponsive were deemed inattentive at work and were often called out for it by their superiors. Read receipts are thus highly visible modes of control intended to regulate the timeliness and performance of workers' daily interactions in ways that often produce additional stress and anxiety.

The second main feature workers must interface with daily is the geolocation clock-in/clock-out attendance system in the DingTalk app, which tracks workers via their smartphones. This feature is known as *daka*, or "punch card" in Chinese, and it's a literal reference to the punch card machines used by companies in the past to record worker attendance, only in this case, the system is remediated as a digital app where employee data is collected and monitored. Each day the first thing workers must do upon arriving at the office is open DingTalk and clock in their attendance based on the time they arrived at the office. The app will also notify workers before the required attendance time in case they forgot. Since the geolocation attendance system is directly tied to company timesheets logging daily hours worked, failing to clock in or clock out regularly will negatively impact how workers are evaluated and ultimately paid. Through DingTalk, companies can set the specific time for clocking in or out of work as well as the physical proximity to the office, where attendance is geofenced within a specific area as determined by the company. Using location data from the built-in GPS on smartphones, the attendance interface features a circular radius of the area where users can clock in. Registering a location outside this perimeter or failing to clock in will prompt the message: "Please select your real current location, we will forward your current location data to your company to confirm your hours of attendance." This creates added problems for workers each morning, as many already endure long and stressful commutes to work downtown. Despite this, DingTalk in its promotional materials touts this form of digital attendance as a "simple way to clock-in, never wait in line again, and your phone is your attendance machine."[31] So while app-mediated attendance may seem convenient compared to past systems that require physical presence (i.e., the use of RFID cards and fingerprints), it also belies the offset of responsibility to the self-disciplinary individual tethered to their personal devices.

The move toward a digitalized attendance system is also not without its faults. The decentralization of the clock-in process onto individual personal mobile devices also paradoxically made it harder to keep track of who is actually doing the checking in. In theory, technically anyone can lend their phone to someone else to do the work of clocking in to work each morning, a practice known as *daiqian* or *dai daka*, that farms out the labor of clocking in to other people for a fee. As a result, DingTalk would also go on to introduce the smile-attendance feature, where workers must submit a smiling selfie that is verified through facial recognition, which will then be posted to a digital "wall" with other smiling coworkers and ranked by the best smile of the day. Many workers responded to this feature on social media saying "We don't know whether to laugh or cry" to voice their incredulity to such an absurd system.[32] While the smile-attendance system was not widely rolled out to every company (including mine), this seemingly dystopian means of fostering worker happiness and engagement belies a more ominous means of dataveillance by which users' personal information and biometrics are increasingly being harvested for the purpose of tracking their movements and behavior. In fact, the DingTalk FAQs specifically state the smile clock-in system is intended to promote "security" and to dissuade users from engaging in *dai daka* behaviors.[33] Here the use of facial recognition goes beyond simply identification to be a measurement of one's mood, feelings, and sentiments in the form of an emergent, emotional AI that works to police the affective dimensions of work itself.[34]

Pandemic and the Challenges of Control

My discursive interface analysis of DingTalk encompasses several key features that were created well before the onset of COVID-19. Yet, the increasing use of app-mediated surveillance, geolocative tracking, and facial recognition also provided some of the fundamental building blocks for the widespread adoption of the health-code contact-tracing system in China. Indeed, the DingTalk team was part of combined efforts across several product divisions within its parent company Alibaba that contributed to the first implementation of the health code on February 9, 2020—the Hangzhou Health Code that later evolved into the Alipay Health Code deployed nationwide.[35] Here, Alibaba leveraged existing expertise in QR (quick response) code payments from Alipay, its cloud computing service Aliyun, and DingTalk's portfolio of workplace monitoring tools to build a digital surveillance infrastructure that can process, collect, and monitor large amount of personal, biometric, and geolocative data for the purpose of mass surveillance.

The health code required multiple verifications and regular updates of one's health information to be active and functionally displayed. It then generates a unique QR code that is scanned to display a color-coded status of potential risk of exposure to COVID based on geolocation.[36] Because of the ubiquity of QR code systems, which are used in everything from mobile payments, to unlocking gates, to ordering off a menu, it has become an everyday routine for many Chinese, which in turn normalizes QR codes as means of self-identification that is integrated with different apps and platforms. In other words, the health-code system was not merely an ad hoc reaction to the pandemic but rather the outcome of existing forms of social controls inoculated in Chinese social life through the ongoing integration with state and corporate platforms. Similar to Elaine J. Yuan's articulation of how mobile tracing apps work to standardize and normalize the public perceptions of the pandemic, the national health code was built upon existing infrastructures quickly adapted and scaled in response to contingencies. This in turn shows how the mechanisms and infrastructures of workplace surveillance are closely aligned with the various means of biopolitical control that has already been developed in China's high-tech surveillance society.

The pandemic-imposed lockdown also opened new opportunities for more invasive technologies to penetrate people's everyday lives, particularly through the reliance on platforms such as DingTalk to keep track of workers at home. Yet, the onset of COVID-19 also brought along many new sets of challenges for tech companies to keep a watchful eye on its workers relative to their performance and productivity. While features such as read receipts can have a powerful disciplinary effect in the office, it loses much of its influence once workers are at home and outside the view of their bosses and coworkers. In the second week of teleworking, the CEO, Mr. Li, sent this urgent email to the company: "While the transition to working from home has gone smoothly, certain teams during this critical time had a noticeable decline in productivity. Many employees are hard to get a hold of and some even refuse to respond to messages [on DingTalk] from their superiors... do not think just because no one can see you, you can lower your own expectations for work!" Such reactions serve as a counter to the totalizing discourses of digital control given the ubiquity of software in tracking and collecting user data, particularly the ways workers are made legible or seen through the panoptical gaze of digital surveillance. Yet the shift to remote work during the pandemic points to how the all-seeing powers of platforms can lose their luster and effectiveness. One of my coworkers, Ms. Xiao, admitted to me how she binged TV shows while working from home and only paid scant attention to DingTalk, saying, "If everyone didn't respond to messages in a timely manner then there is no stigma for slacking off, I'm sure even the managers are not paying too much attention." Such reaction shows how quickly workers break free from the oppressive expectations of the workplace once they are at home. These avoidance strategies also highlight how the use of software and digital platforms remain very much spatially contingent despite the omnipresent

FIGURE 1. Workers waiting in long lines to get to work due to face mask requirements that rendered facial-recognition entry inefficient. COURTESY OF THE AUTHOR.

access and persistent tracking of digital software. Or in other words, once people are outside the office, the disciplinary effects of software-mediated surveillance are tempered by the various recalcitrant and subversive tactics employed by workers in their private lives. The informal nature of workplace communication tools like DingTalk, when used in the privacy of one's homes, just becomes another social messaging tool people can choose to interact with or ignore.

In addition, the restrictions that the lockdown imposed during the pandemic can also work against the affordances and intended usage of apps such as DingTalk. The most glaring example of this is the geolocative attendance feature. Even though workers were required to work from home, my company still required daily clock ins and clock outs during specific times at home. But because the attendance system is only effective within close vicinity to the company, the clock ins became largely a formality to record working hours for payroll purposes as opposed to enforcing productivity. The inability to use geolocative tracking thus defeats the very intended design of DingTalk's invasive attendance system and opens opportunities for workers to reclaim spaces for themselves. This disruption of software-mediated surveillance remained even after returning to work post-lockdown. For instance, entry to my office building required facial-recognition scans that were set up using the app, but the mandatory mask requirements made going to work particularly troublesome. This resulted in long queues in the morning to get into the office, as workers had to remove their masks to scan their faces, which defeated the purpose of the seamless, contact-free design of facial-recognition entry systems in the first place (see figure 1). The hour-long lines also forced workers to arrive much earlier to work to clock in on time, which only added to the existing long commute many had to make to the office and exacerbated the precarity in an already overworked industry through the notorious 996 work schedule.[37] Instead of facilitating getting to work, the various control measures resulting from COVID-19 only created additional red tape that prolonged workplace pressures.

DingTalk as an app that resides on personal devices works to render the mechanisms of message alerts, geolocation tracking, and daily attendance as something that is normalized as habitual, or according to Chun, dulls us from the perpetual cycles of crisis under capitalistic control only to paradoxically sustain it.[38] The plight of the COVID-19 crisis both intensified the softwarization process in the workplace and points to its deficiency in the reliance in digital platforms that must be constantly updated to keep up with shifting contingencies. On February 25, 2020, about a month after the initial lockdown, DingTalk issued a major release of version 5.0 that notably added a health-check feature intended for companies to better track employee health. This system collects data from the Alipay Health Code, where if workers are exposed to COVID-19 (code red), they will be denied entrance to the office. However, because personal information reported to the health-code system is private and stored on Alibaba's cloud service, companies in need of employee health information had to resort to other means of collecting data. For example, each morning my company will manually measure worker's temperatures and record them in a binder notebook so it can track whether an employee is potentially sick. This decidedly analogue method of data collection offers a stark contrast to the seemingly sophisticated forms of digital surveillance such as DingTalk. More tellingly, this highlights the contentions between the need to centralize dataveillance and the desire of companies to maintain control over their own data. Thus, despite DingTalk's attempt to meet the challenges of the pandemic through constant updates, the impact of the pandemic in reshaping its environs of intended use demonstrates the inflexibility and inadequacy of digital platforms when facing major disruptions that threaten its mechanisms of control.

Everyday Workplace Resistance and Counterveillance

The challenges presented by the pandemic for workplace surveillance is also applicable to surveillance in China writ large. The health-code system so touted by Chinese state media was marked by early problems, particularly in regard to its fragmented rollout, when each region used its own health codes, a process of cross-compatibility that is not always seamless. Moreover, the health code was implemented by both Alibaba and Tencent, which created rival health codes that required users to register for multiple accounts, creating a bifurcated regime of health surveillance that added to the complexity of an already tedious workplace monitoring process. For instance, the city of Guangzhou, where I was located, used the Suikang Health Code, which resides in Tencent's WeChat app as a mini program that does not have synergies with Alibaba's health code and DingTalk. This in turn required opening multiple apps each morning to register the health code and to clock in to work. Moreover, during the first weeks of the implementation of the health code, foreign employees including myself were unable to register the app because only Chinese citizens with national ID cards could sign up for the system. One of my American co-workers, Matt, expressed his frustration, saying, "I mean I can't confirm my identity in that app because it only accepts Chinese national ID cards in the form. Because despite China wanting to attract foreigners to work here, they never think to account for them in the registration software." This dilemma not only created a blind spot in the contact-tracing system, as certain people are denied access to the system, but it also indirectly points to the pre-existing notions of who ought to be included in the health-code surveillance regime to begin with. Indeed, apart from contending systems of Tencent and Alibaba, the initial rollout of the health-code system was fraught with issues regarding accessibility. Despite China's large mobile phone adoption rate, there remain significant populations without smartphone access, particularly the elderly and rural denizens in the country. Likewise, the reliance on the health-code system on geolocation as a form of contact tracing also meant that hardware failures such as the smartphone's GPS can lead to major issues in terms of identifying potential COVID-19 contacts. There have been numerous documented cases of individuals' health code "accidentally" turned red due to myriads of issues related to geolocation, lack of connection, and access to networks. These deficiencies in the system therefore point to how software-mediated forms of control can be prone to failure, which open up opportunities to exploit its inadequacies.

Having already documented everyday forms of resistance in the forms of outsourced clock ins (*dai daka*) and the refusal to respond to DingTalk messages, there are also specific strategies used by workers to directly subvert with the technical affordances of DingTalk outside the scope of its intended usage. While the pandemic highlighted the limits of digital surveillance at home, workers continue to come up with innovative means of challenging the system after returning to work post-lockdown. Such contentions echo what James C. Scott considers "hidden transcripts," or tacit forms of resistance that lie outside the view of the powers of authority.[39] The often informal and unsanctioned means of interfacing with software is a key element of workplace subversion in the digital age. Such application of offstage resistance to digital platforms brings to question the notions of "counterveillance" as a way workers can potentially break off the shackles imposed by surveillance technologies.[40] Here counterveillance does not imply a direct toppling of the structures of power but rather the various means of delaying, disrupting, and perhaps ameliorating the most harmful effects of workplace oppression. Such strategies help to reframe the totalizing dominance of the state-corporate hegemony where workers may not actually be so powerless in the face of digital control. Working at a mobile tech company has the distinct advantage of exposing me to workers with the tech know-how and proficiency to engage in recalcitrant tactics on a daily basis that can thwart many of DingTalk's most intrusive features. While these tactics range from deliberate attempts to cheat the system and exploit minor loopholes, they demonstrate different degrees of sophistication by which workers circumvent the intended design of DingTalk in their everyday working lives.

During my fieldwork, DingTalk's attendance system, with its persistent geo-locative tracking, was cited as the most frequent source of worker angst and the primary target of subversion. One co-worker, Mr. Hu, who worked as 3D designer at the company, confided to me, "I tried using an emulator in my office computer to clock into DingTalk remotely just to see what can happen but HR discovered it so they can probably see it in the backend." This ruse failed because DingTalk is inevitably tied to one's device ID, including an IP address, geolocation, and browser information, which can be easily discovered. Hu admitted that "I knew it probably would not work but since I regularly use emulators as part of my work testing new builds of apps, I figured it might go unnoticed." Another colleague, a computer programmer, Mr. Cui, said "I even contemplated using a VPN to fake [my] GPS coordinates to try to trick DingTalk into thinking I was close to the office to clock-in," but he decided against it due to fears of losing his job in the case that HR somehow found out. Cui claimed he got the idea of faking his location from playing the game Pokémon GO, where rampant cheating exists in the form of manipulating GPS coordinates. The subsequent reaction from Nintendo to permanently ban players caught cheating was also one of the deciding factors for Cui to not go through with his plan.[41] In both cases, the fear of the potential fallout of subversion was enough to deter workers from actively engaging in such activities. Likewise, the familiarity with digital software such as emulators and VPNs show how technological literacy also can ironically hinder subversive actions through the understanding of its technical limitations. As such, these tactics reveal the challenges in engaging with always-on forms of digital control where, despite the temptation of disrupting such systems, many workers are intimately aware of the risks involved in the process.

Despite these risks, workers also engage in routine, makeshift, and mundane means of everyday resistance in dealing with DingTalk. Even those who may not be technically proficient compared to IT workers and programmers can still partake in subversive acts. Ms. Zhang, one of my cubicle mates and part of the marketing team, offered her own decidedly low-tech strategy: "Before getting off [at] my metro station to work I would turn off my GPS on my smartphone then quickly turn it back on, so the GPS has to recalibrate to triangulate my location, which often tricks DingTalk into thinking I am closer to the office than where I actually was, thus allowing me to clock-in." Admitting to not being as tech-savvy as her colleagues in the development team, Zhang inadvertently discovered this loophole due to previous experiences encountering poor signals in the subway. While such tactics often only allow her to clock in ten to fifteen minutes before she's at the office, Zhang considers this worthwhile due to her hour-long commute to work each day and the time-consuming health-related checks due to COVID-19; every second saved makes the already stressful morning better. While saving time is an important part of gaming DingTalk's attendance system, workers will also attempt to prolong hours when clocking out of work. Mr. Cui explained, "Occasionally after getting off work, I would take my time getting dinner close to the office, then head back to clock-out. This way I can add a few hours to my overtime pay." Here DingTalk's invasive geolocation attendance system is ironically also the main target for workers as they manipulate their online spatial and temporal footprint to reap their own benefits.

Conclusion

The rise of DingTalk during pandemic times, of course, is not an isolated case, as numerous Western platforms such as Zoom, Microsoft Teams, Google Meet, and others have all witnessed rapid growth to meet the demands of remote work.[42] Yet, as Zihao Lin suggests, the use of Zoom during the pandemic has also raised issues of accessibility that questions the limits of digital instantiation promised by ubiquitous and seamless digital platforms.[43] In the two years since my initial ethnographic inquiries in 2020, the use of workplace software has become ubiquitous and routinized not just in China but across the globe. On one hand, work increasingly relies on digital platforms as a means of evaluating worker performance and engagement. On the other hand, the shift to remote-work software continues to blur the already hazy boundaries between labor and leisure, as workers must constantly interface with intrusive workplace software. This has also contributed to growing problems of digital fatigue and burnout associated with always-on, digitally mediated work in the global economy. But in the case of China, DingTalk being the most popular workplace-collaboration software in the country occupies a significant position as not just a digital surveillance tool but also as the building block for wider social control across China through the health-code system. Evidently, in September 2020, Alibaba announced the consolidation of Aliyun Cloud Service and DingTalk's development teams to further benefit "people's work, study, and life, along with creating more value for economic growth and social governance."[44]

It is no surprise that in the wake of the COVID-19 pandemic, DingTalk was also heavily promoted as the main learning-management software for primary and secondary schools as well as for universities across China. The sudden switch to remote teaching provided the opportunity for DingTalk to massively expand its presence in the education sector, especially with the introduction of version 5.1 in May 2020, which added educational features to the app bespoke for learning at home.[45] Thus, students, like workers, were also subjected to the same intrusive attendance, messaging, and monitoring systems that were initially developed in the workplace. This eventually led to massive organized "review bombing" of DingTalk on the app store by students across the country to express their collective disdain for the software by giving it the lowest rating (one-star).[46] While the recent application of DingTalk in education warrants additional studies in its own right, it demonstrates the broader roles of workplace-monitoring technologies in enabling surveillance across different social institutions, be it in schools or in the workplace.

The analysis of DingTalk during and after China's COVID-19 lockdown also raises several interesting questions as to the efficacy of widespread digital workplace surveillance. As this chapter has shown, the pandemic created a slew of unforeseen issues that the team behind DingTalk struggled to resolve despite its seemingly sophisticated means of data collection and control. The lockdown had the unintended consequence of allowing workers to carve their own spaces and working routines despite the outreach of companies to extend their control into private homes. While it can be argued that digitally mediated forms of resistance can play into the hands of tech companies through the persistent dependency on software, DingTalk as an always-on app also presents renewed contradictions and challenges associated with worker resistance in the age of digital surveillance. The all-seeing, ubiquitous, and totalizing aspect of the digital workplace is often contradicted by the personalization, compartmentalization, and individualization of the mobile-app experience. This tension belies the need to reimagine labor activism and worker solidarity, which are under increasing precariousness under corporate-state dominance. The various means of digital insubordination documented by this chapter during a global pandemic shows how apps like DingTalk lead to disparate, ad hoc, and makeshift tactics that are fragmented and detached from any larger movement for change. Thus, it is important to reconceptualize how workers can engage or disengage with software without simultaneously foreclosing the possibilities for collective action and advocacy against workplace oppression.

NOTES

The Chinese surnames in this article are alibis used to hide the interlocutors' identity.

1. Guobin Yang, *The Wuhan Lockdown* (New York: Columbia University Press, 2022).
2. Fan Liang. "COVID-19 and Health Code: How Digital Platforms Tackle the Pandemic in China," *Social Media + Society* 6, no. 3 (2020): 2056305120947657.
3. Huiling Ding, *Rhetoric of a Global Epidemic: Transcultural Communication about SARS* (Carbondale: Southern Illinois University Press, 2014).
4. Yusho Cho, "China's Tech Leaders Turn to Telework as Coronavirus Spreads," *Nikkei Asia*, January 29, 2020.
5. Willem Niepce and Eric Molleman, "Work Design Issues in Lean Production from a

Sociotechnical Systems Perspective: Neo-Taylorism or the Next Step in Sociotechnical Design?," *Human Relations* 51, no. 3 (1998): 259–287.

6. Yining Ding, "Tech Giants Beefing Up Digital Offerings," Shine.cn, May 18, 2020.

7. Super apps, or meta apps, are also popular in contexts such as Japan's Line, which shares similarities with China's WeChat. See: Marc Steinberg, "LINE as Super App: Platformization in East Asia," *Social Media+ Society* 6, no. 2 (2020): 2056305120933285.

8. Vidar Hepsø, "Doing Corporate Ethnography as an Insider," *Advancing Ethnography in Corporate Environments: Challenges and Emerging Opportunities*, ed. Brigitte Jordan (Walnut Creek, CA: Left Coast Press, 2013), 151–162.

9. Mel Stanfill, "The Interface as Discourse: The Production of Norms through Web Design," *New Media & Society* 17, no. 7 (2015): 1059–1074; Taina Bucher and Anne Helmond, "The Affordances of Social Media Platforms," *The SAGE Handbook of Social Media*, ed. Jean Burgess, Alice E. Marwick, and Thomas Poell (London: SAGE Publications, 2017): 233–253.

10. Ben Light, Jean Burgess, and Stefanie Duguay, "The Walkthrough Method: An Approach to the Study of Apps," *New Media & Society* 20, no. 3 (2018): 881–900.

11. Svitlana Matviyenko and Paul D. Miller, *The Imaginary App* (Cambridge: MIT Press, 2014), 4.

12. Martha Crowley et al., "Neo-Taylorism at Work: Occupational Change in the Post-Fordist Era," *Social Problems* 57, no. 3 (2010): 421–447; Patricia Wallace, *The Internet in the Workplace: How New Technology Is Transforming Work* (Cambridge: Cambridge University Press, 2004); Kirstie Ball, "Workplace Surveillance: An Overview," *Labor History* 51, no. 1 (2010): 87–106.

13. Christopher O'Neill, "Taylorism, the European Science of Work, and the Quantified Self at Work," *Science, Technology, & Human Values* 42, no. 4 (2017): 600–621.

14. Phillip Brown and Hugh Lauder, "Economic Globalisation, Skill Formation and the Consequences for Higher Education," *Routledge International Handbook of the Sociology of Education* (2009): 229–240.

15. Shoshana Zuboff, *The Age of Surveillance Capitalism: The Fight for a Human Future at the New Frontier of Power* (New York: Public Affairs, 2019).

16. Martha Crowley and Randy Hodson, "Neoliberalism at Work," *Social Currents* 1, no. 1 (2014): 91–108.

17. Phoebe Moore and Andrew Robinson, "The Quantified Self: What Counts in the Neoliberal Workplace," *New Media & Society* 18, no. 11 (2016): 2774–2792.

18. Michel Foucault, *Discipline and Punish: The Birth of the Prison* (New York: Vintage, 2012); Peter Bain and Phil Taylor, "Entrapped by the 'Electronic Panopticon'? Worker Resistance

in the Call Centre," *New Technology, Work and Employment* 15, no. 1 (2000): 2–18; Jamie Woodcock, "The Algorithmic Panopticon at Deliveroo: Measurement, Precarity, and the Illusion of Control," *Ephemera: Theory & Politics in Organization* 20, no. 3 (2020).

19. Lev Manovich, *Software Takes Command*, vol. 5 (London: A & C Black, 2013).
20. Ivan Manokha, "The Implications of Digital Employee Monitoring and People Analytics for Power Relations in the Workplace," *Surveillance & Society* 18, no. 4 (2020): 540–554.
21. Mark Andrejevic, *iSpy: Surveillance and Power in the Interactive Era* (Lawrence: University Press of Kansas, 2007).
22. José Van Dijck, "Datafication, Dataism and Dataveillance: Big Data between Scientific Paradigm and Ideology," *Surveillance & Society* 12, no. 2 (2014): 197–208; Roderic Crooks, "Cat-and-Mouse Games: Dataveillance and Performativity in Urban Schools," *Surveillance & Society* 17, no. 3/4 (2019): 484–498.
23. Wendy Hui Kyong Chun, *Programmed Visions: Software and Memory* (Cambridge: MIT Press, 2011).
24. Selena Nemorin, "Post-panoptic Pedagogies: The Changing Nature of School Surveillance in the Digital Age," *Surveillance and Society* 15, no. 2 (2017): 239–253.
25. Carol Upadhya, "Controlling Offshore Knowledge Workers: Power and Agency in India's Software Outsourcing Industry," *New Technology, Work and Employment* 24, no. 1 (2009), 2–18.
26. Julie Yujie Chen, "Thrown Under the Bus and Outrunning It! The Logic of Didi and Taxi Drivers' Labour and Activism in the On-demand Economy," *New Media & Society* 20, no. 8 (2018): 2691–2711.
27. Mel Bunce, Kate Wright, and Martin Scott, "'Our Newsroom in the Cloud': Slack, Virtual Newsrooms and Journalistic Practice," *New Media & Society* 20, no. 9 (2018): 3381–3399.
28. "DingTalk FAQ," DingTalk, https://www.dingtalk.com.
29. Wendy Hui Kyong Chun, *Updating to Remain the Same: Habitual New Media* (Cambridge: MIT Press, 2016).
30. Brooke Erin Duffy and Ngai Keung Chan, "'You Never Really Know Who's Looking': Imagined Surveillance across Social Media Platforms," *New Media & Society* 21, no. 1 (2019): 119–138.
31. "DingTalk User Manual," DingTalk, https://notes.dingtalk.com.
32. Sina, "Dingding Xiaolian Daka, Ni Zhongzhao le ma? [DingTalk's smile attendance system, did you fall for it too?]," Sina.com, May 16, 2019.
33. "DingTalk FAQ."
34. Andrew McStay, "Emotional AI, Soft Biometrics and the Surveillance of Emotional Life: An Unusual Consensus on Privacy," *Big Data & Society* 7, no. 1 (2020): 2053951720904386.

35. Paul Mozur, Raymond Zhong, and Aaron Krolik, "In Coronavirus Fight, China Gives Citizens a Color Code, with Red Flags," *New York Times*, January 28, 2020.
36. Liang, "COVID-19 and Health Code."
37. The term "996" refers a "9 AM to 9 PM, six days a week" work schedule, which is commonly employed by tech companies in China to enforce productivity. This term is also popularized by the anti-996 worker movement against overwork in the industry.
38. Chun, *Updating to Remain the Same*.
39. James C. Scott, *Domination and the Arts of Resistance: Hidden Transcripts* (New Haven, CT: Yale University Press, 1990).
40. Claudio Celis, "Critical Surveillance Art in the Age of Machine Vision and Algorithmic Governmentality: Three Case Studies," *Surveillance & Society* 18, no. 3 (2020): 295–311.
41. Julia Alexander, "Here's What Happens If You're Caught Cheating in Pokémon Go," *Polygon*, July 12, 2016.
42. Stephen Nellis, "Remote Work during Coronavirus Outbreak Puts Millions More on Microsoft Teams, Slack," *Reuters*, March 19, 2020.
43. See Zihao Lin, "Access as Method: Hopes, Friction, and Mediated Communication in a Remote Disability Reading Group," in this volume.
44. Sina, "Alibaba gongbu yunding yiti zhanlue: aliyun yu dingding quanmian ronghe [Alibaba announce merger of services: Aliyun and DingTalk officially become one]," Sina.com, September 27, 2020.
45. Jiemodui, "Dingding shangxian xuesheng ban, man xiang quanguo 1.5 yi zhongxiao xueshen [DingTalk releases education version, targeted toward 150 million primary school students]," Jiemodui.com, July 29, 2020.
46. Jane Li, "What Is DingTalk, Alibaba's Slack Equivalent That Quarantined Kids in China Hate?" *Quartz*, March 10, 2020.

Access as Method

Hopes, Friction, and Mediated Communication in a Remote Disability Reading Group

Zihao Lin

ONE EARLY MORNING IN THE SUMMER OF 2020, I WAS AWAKENED BY MY ALARM CLOCK and ran to my computer. Within a few minutes, the presence of around twenty people appeared onscreen—most simply represented by dark squares, with only the people's names shown beneath the squares. The Zoom workshop began, and some people turned on their webcams. A buzzing electronic noise accompanied by intermittent speech flew into my earphones, the sounds clashing with one another. Several people unmuted themselves and began speaking simultaneously, then all stopped, leaving several seconds of awkward silence. The woman whose video frame was pinned did not speak much, but her hands kept moving, sometimes so quickly that the video became blurry. Captions in Chinese and English appeared and quickly disappeared across the bottom of the screen—they seemingly corresponded to the live conversations yet contained typos and nonsensical words or phrases. New messages continuously popped up in the chat box along the side of the interface, demonstrating the desire of the participants, spread across several continents, to participate and be seen. In this digitally mediated space, these distant communicators established a messy but lively co-presence through crisscrossing flows of text, image, and sound.

This chapter offers a digital ethnography of a reading group committed to "barrier-free" (*wuzhang'ai*) remote communication despite continuously occurring obstacles. Taking place during the COVID-19 pandemic, the disability studies reading workshop was composed of Chinese students and scholars, as well as interested participants in Asia, Europe, and North America. My interlocutors[1] included people who identify as deaf, hearing, orthopedically disabled, multiply disabled, and non-disabled. I attended the reading group as event organizer, participant, and researcher. The reading group had neither funding nor institutional support. Consequently, there was no budget for professional video captioners. Instead, much time and energy was spent on makeshift "shortcuts": machine-generated caption applications based on voice-recognition technology, sign interpreters willing to work pro bono, and free video conferencing tools. These mediators both facilitated and complicated these remote conversations. Many moments of frustration, anxiety, and confrontation seemingly defied the reading group's initial vision of a small, amicable space where technology ensured all participants were included in the conversation. Though the complications of constructing meeting access from scratch filled the summer, the group hosted eight synchronous meetings between July and September 2020, which were regularly attended by most members.

The difficulty in establishing remote co-presence is unsurprising. Disability scholars have written on the intersection of education, technology, and disability before and during the pandemic. On the one hand, Cassandra Hartblay, Emily Lim Rogers, Ruikai Dai, and Luanjiao Hu discuss how disabled people use digital technologies to build new networks not available offline.[2] Many disabled people were involved with digital and remote communication long before lockdown; their efforts provide a rich, disability-led repertoire of innovative workarounds and built-in flexibility, as observed by Ashley Shew.[3] On the other hand, disabled people must navigate the structural constraints of virtual spaces. Linguistic and communication scholars Elizabeth Keating, Terra Edwards, and Gene Mirus have discussed technology's impact on deaf users' language practices during computer-mediated video communication at length, addressing the development and manipulation of image transmission and body relations, the creation of a radically different sign space, the impact of altered signing speed, and the dynamics of increased repetition due to low-resolution cameras and bad Internet signal.[4] Contrary to the belief that online communication facilitates smooth and easy connection, and confirming the work of the scholars cited above, our group faced myriad complications. We enthusiastically tackled many impediments, yet some workarounds left us feeling blocked off, as excluded in cyberspace as we often feel in the physical spaces of daily life.

The central puzzle this chapter explores is the commitment and desire my interlocutors exhibited in facilitating communication within the reading group despite frictions, physical distance, lack of technical support, and unreliable connectivity. Why did people keep coming back? How did they make sense of the dialogues with each other and of the technical and moral space that facilitated them? To address these questions, I have drawn mainly upon two data sources. The first is my autobiographical perspective as an event organizer involved in every step of realizing the workshop. I am a male hearing graduate student in a comparative human development program who has worked with both signing and oral deaf communities in Guangzhou, China. I have a basic level of Chinese Sign Language (CSL) that helps me understand some everyday CSL conversations, but do not claim mastery of the language. As an organizer of the reading group, I observed the WeChat conversations and Zoom workshops, treating my experience as an opportunity to analyze barrier-free social action.[5] The second source of data is interviews with participants. During the summer of 2020, I conducted nineteen interviews with fifteen reading group members.[6] Two interviews were conducted textually via Google Docs; the rest were via Zoom. The interviews were semi-structured, inviting interviewees to share their specific experiences in the reading group and general life stories about disability advocacy, access, and aspirations toward barrier-free communication.

I argue that the group's commitment to barrier-free communication was premised on a utopian desire to *think otherwise*[7] and to build an alternative space distinct from the harsh environment Chinese disability advocates currently face (discussed below). The reading group allowed an element of ethical and institutional separation from the present, a consciously hopeful resistance against ideological and institutional blockages that obstruct change in the present. In the reading group, barrier-free communication was not merely an ideal; it was enacted through practical and consequential actions. Through negotiating the settings of the Zoom discussions, group members could reflect on each other's hidden assumptions about disability's place in society and express their desire for better ways of living. As such, access was not merely a *goal*, but more importantly a *method*, an ongoing struggle that created possibilities for transcending the unsatisfactory present.

The Case of a Chinese Disability Reading Group

In May 2020, my friend Yuanjun—a Chinese anthropology graduate student with experience working in international disability advocacy in Beijing—added me to a WeChat group called Disability without Borders (DwB). Established in 2018 by a female disabled academic, this online chat group contained roughly 280 people when I joined, including scholars, students, and social workers in China and overseas. Most members are ethnically Chinese and grew up in China. Many also had experience abroad. DwB facilitated daily discussions around disability advocacy, policy, and experiences living and working in different countries as disabled Chinese people. As most members had or were completing post-graduate degrees in social work, disability studies, public health, or law, the group also served as an academic space, complete with calls for papers, webinar announcements, and grant and fellowship openings.

In China, a new generation of disability activists are increasingly internationally connected, attending conferences, traveling overseas for academic study, and applying for funding for advocacy programs.[8] Our disability studies colleagues in North America speak of the "ADA generation" to situate disability activists within an environment shaped by such landmark disability legislation as the Americans with Disabilities Act (ADA) or the United Nations Convention on the Rights of Persons with Disabilities (UNCRPD).[9] These key pieces of legislation have sought to construct an inclusive infrastructure for supporting people with disability. While the acts are imperfect, they have helped to fuel a political sea change, wherein members of the ADA generation expect certain forms of access and consider these forms a given. In contrast, China's young generation of disability activists faces ignorance and hostility toward attempts to have their agendas seen or heard. DwB members frequently invoke ideals from the UNCRPD, which stress the need for *everyone* to have suitable access to communication, and we accordingly advocate for a benchmark of information technologies to realize this goal.[10] The idea of a "benchmark" is tied to an emerging set of UNCRPD-informed criteria, standards, and best practices, by which access to technologies and design products is measured *universally*—that is, across a wide range of local settings. In this technical discourse, access is afforded by concrete, material infrastructure or assistive devices—roads, transportation, Braille signs, communication boards, screen readers, keyboards, computers, and smartphones.[11] The UNCRPD encourages states that adhere to the United Nations convention to increase the availability of these provisions for people with disabilities (article 9), and the UNCRPD committee considers such support a key indicator of the states' commitment to the convention. The Chinese state began institutionalizing disability advocacy programs in the late 1980s and adopted the legislation from UNCRPD in 2008.[12] In under twenty years, China has passed hundreds of guidelines and administrative documents touching on barrier-free information (*xinxi wu zhang'ai*). For example, after accepting the UNCRPD legislation, China passed the Regulations on the Construction of Barrier-Free Environment (2012) and the PRC Law on the Protection of Disabled Persons (latest revision in 2018),[13] which both legally recognized captions and sig- interpreting services as expected components of daily life and the building blocks for achieving barrier-free information solutions for deaf people. The PRC also adopted multiple technical standards for facilitating communication access from the Global North, including Information Accessibility Design Guidelines to Information Terminal Equipment for Persons with Physical Disabilities (YD/T 2065–2009).[14]

Though the Chinese government has embraced the idea of a barrier-free society (*wu zhang'ai shehui*) for the last two decades, disconnections between the state's claims and the lived realities of disabled people remain deep. In China, many of the UNCRPD-inspired solutions lack legal accountability and practical enforceability, as disability studies scholar Shixin Huang has observed.[15] At the spring 2020 peak of the first COVID-19 outbreak in Wuhan, people with physical disabilities living alone were trapped at home without access to healthcare.[16] Access to information was also challenging: given the lack of qualified sign interpreters, Wuhan's deaf residents experienced hindrances in obtaining personal protective equipment, filling out the requisite questionnaires, communicating with hearing volunteers who did not know sign language, and complicated delivery systems.[17] Many disability activists in the DwB WeChat group voiced these concerns, usually with deep anger and frustration.

Trapped in my Chicago apartment during the United States' international travel ban, I contacted Yuanjun and people from the DwB network to co-organize a remote group for reading and discussing social sciences literature on disability. After regular announcements in the DwB group, the reading group grew to thirty-one people. Participants' demographic information, including geographical locations, gender, disability categories, and educational backgrounds, was self-disclosed. Participants mainly fell into four categories: (1) students, (2) academics, (3) activists and social workers, and (4) sign interpreters. Seven participants identified as deaf or hearing-impaired, forming the group's largest disabled constituency.

Students

Students in the reading group, usually in their early twenties, majored in anthropology, law, cinema, special education, deaf studies, and psychology. In my student interviews, many non-disabled interlocutors told stories about how their experiences in college changed their views regarding disability and their career plans. Weizhe, for example, took an American Sign Language course at a U.S. public university and—defying his parents' wishes—decided to change his major from chemistry to clinical psychology. Since then, he has aspired to become a special education teacher or clinical psychologist for deaf people, in either the U.S. or China. Initially, he did not know many of the reading group members, telling me "It is great that the group has included talents from different sides. Many people who would have otherwise fought alone in their fields have been brought together to support each other."

Many deaf people in the group were graduates of or current students at Gallaudet University, an American private research university for deaf and hard-of-hearing students. Gui studied human resources management at a college in an inland Chinese province but was unhappy with his job after graduation and "took a gamble" by enrolling in a master's program in deaf studies at Gallaudet after studying basic American Sign Language and preparing for the English standardized test for one year. He plans to apply for doctoral programs after graduation and hopes eventually to secure an academic position in China so that he can "change the passive situation of Chinese deaf people, as now there are so few deaf scholars in Chinese universities, and deaf people are not substantially included in policy- and decision-making processes."

Academics

Like students, academics in the reading group came from various disciplines—communication, law, linguistics, and education—with a shared interest in disability studies. Except for one senior university lecturer, most academics were young scholars who had obtained their doctoral degrees in the last one to three years and were new in their professional academic tracks in China. Tingfeng, once a social worker and now a post-doctoral researcher in disability law, shared that, despite his interest, he had not had time to systematically read sociological and anthropological literature on disability during his doctorate, which the reading group could help rectify. The young academics also hoped to figure out how to bring disability studies—its training resources currently concentrated in North America—into conversations in a Chinese context. Most young scholars were also concerned about their relationships with local activist organizations and disabled communities in China.

Activists and social workers

Participants also included disability activists and social workers in Chinese cities such as Changsha, Wuhan, Chongqing, and Tianjin who were well connected through digital networks. Most deaf or disabled activists in the group have advanced degrees and are engaged in full-time or part-time disability rights advocacy projects—shooting films, participating in sign language reform, founding consulting firms, or running social media accounts. They are aware of international resources and capital for projects, and have a shared interest in the UNCRPD legislation, though they are working in different fields and advocating for different disability categories.

Disabled activists outside academia raised expectations not merely in terms of reading material, but also the forms, structures, and organization of the discussion. Xiurong, a multiple-disabled activist running a digital advocacy network, stated that her aim was "to learn more about organizing along with the reading group activities, to accumulate experiences, and to provide training for the volunteers" in her organization.

Sign interpreters

During summer 2020, six sign interpreters joined the WeChat group and subsequently the Zoom meetings. Meili, our first interpreter, learned about the group through a California-based student who had conducted an internship at Company X, one of the few start-ups providing remote sign-interpreting services to deaf people in China. Two of the reading group's deaf members recommended Company X's services. Meili invited Xiaodan, her junior colleague at Company X, to join when Meili was unavailable. Yuanjun invited the third interpreter, a child of deaf parents. All other interpreters joined after personal invitations by reading group members.

The six interpreters had little experience interpreting academic discussions before joining the group. All in their early or mid-twenties, the interpreters fell into two general categories: hearing graduates trained in special education with a basic-curriculum background in sign language, and children of deaf adults who had no formal training in interpreting but were experienced interpreters from growing up in the deaf community. None had a post-graduate degree in disability studies or sign interpreting (which are not yet offered as independent university degree programs in China).[18]

Remote Interpreting: Negotiating the Roles of Sign Interpreters

Providing sign language interpreting to deaf participants was the first and most obvious barrier-free feature decided by the reading group's initial members, two of whom were deaf. The same priority is not true for most Chinese digital academic meetings, even those with "disability" in their title. Mingxia, a female deaf graduate student in clinical psychology, angrily recounted the barrier-free arrangement of a previous Zoom workshop on inclusive therapy. Despite being organized by a physically disabled therapist who claimed to have "UNCRPD-trainings," the Zoom workshop offered neither sign language interpreting nor closed-captioning (CC). Most infuriating to Mingxia was that when she asked why no captions were provided, the speaker replied, "I can try to slow down my Mandarin," then added that "Since the workshop is unable to provide you the accommodation, you have the right to exit now." Mingxia also learned that she was criticized for her "interruption," suggesting her request for access was not taken seriously. In our hope to not reproduce such inequities, the reading group members agreed that sign interpreters were necessary for each meeting, even though the group lacked funding to pay for this inclusive support.

My interlocutors brainstormed various solutions. In late July, a deaf social entrepreneur who advocated for deaf education and family support told me her organization might be able to help:

> We are currently collaborating with different "barrier-free" workshops and disability support programs. The reading group has been a great channel for learning and

discussing things. I wish you could continue this initiative. This is not about finding a one-time solution, but about exposing the complexity of the involved ethical issues—letting different people, including sign interpreters, deaf and hearing participants, and the event organizers, get together and talk about things about and beyond money. I once had a meeting with company G and they were reluctant to pay the sign interpreter for that online workshop—I suppose they simply didn't set aside a budget for that. It was our social enterprise that paid the interpreter in the end.... I remember an interpreter's word that left a deep impression on me. She said, the lack of money had been a perennial issue in this enterprise; without devotion, it is impossible to hang in there.

In this conversation, the deaf entrepreneur emphasized how the reading group allowed dialogues between multiple stakeholders—sign interpreters, deaf and hearing participants, and event organizers. She considered these dialogues not only instrumental—that is, "about money"—but also moral, in that she thought it was worth discussing what counts as good sign interpreting, what forms (financial or otherwise) that recognition should take, and who should undertake that recognition. Anthropologists working on interpreting ethics have explored how sign language interpreters' ideological understanding of their task, in addition to their interpreting skills, influence their work.[19] There is also the problem of interpreting skills in emerging contexts like China.[20] The deaf entrepreneur's reference to her interpreter friend's word "devotion" (*chicheng*) resonated with the words of several interpreter informants I interviewed. It suggested that interpreters in the group treated sign interpreting as a morally desirable enterprise regardless of its financial prospects. Though in the early planning stage, Yuanjun and I spoke with other members about compensating the interpreters who were willing to spend their weekend interpreting for us; in the end all interpreters worked pro bono. As Meili framed it, interpreting for us was "a learning opportunity," a chance she could use and challenge she could face to improve her skills and reflect on her career. She also took the fact that we asked her to return for subsequent meetings as recognition of her skill. In this way, the roles of the interpreters evolved into a form of community gift-giving, acts of social justice and loving support.[21]

The event organizers, interpreters, and deaf participants cooperated to address the technical challenges of signal delay and breakdown. All six volunteer interpreters were based in China. When the signal delay became severe, they could not hear the presenters' words, and deaf participants could not see their signing. At first, interpreters Meili and Xiaodan thought the signal delay was caused by their offices' poor Internet and offered to switch to 4G mobile data on their personal devices for the remainder of the conference. Subsequently, we discovered that the signal delay for participants from China was occurring because data servers were overseas in the U.S.A.—something beyond our control. Yuanjun and I thus decided to stop nudging participants to turn on their cameras. In subsequent conferences, we instead emphasized that everyone except the deaf participants, sign interpreters, and presenters should keep their cameras off. Originally, we were reluctant about this, as it might single deaf people out, but after trying both arrangements, the reading group reached the consensus that signal delay was a more pressing concern.

An interpreter's presence, it should be noted, did not automatically create access, as not all interpreters possessed the same level of skill. Our discussion's academic content posed the main challenge to the interpreters—lacking formal training in academic interpreting, they were not ideal interpreters for our group.[22] The majority of our group's reading material came from disability activists and scholars in the Global North. Abstract English concepts such as "cyborg," "crip theory," or "techno-ableism" were hard to interpret.[23] As Xiaodan commented to me:

> The content [discussed in the reading group and over Zoom meetings] is such a hard nut to crack. We know every word, but it stops making sense as a sentence. There are so many theories we have never heard of. What's more, Meili shared with me after her first interpretation session that you [the participants] would mix Chinese with English expressions. For us two who have not even passed the College English Test band 4, it is such a pain!

To the young interpreters, then, the academic challenges in the reading group felt like "a hard nut to crack" and caused many pains, but also presented "learning opportunities" and a sense of achievement and creativity. Stressing the need to attend to multiple languages and new terms and ideas in our international reading group, Meili explained how she created the sign for "Bethel House"—the community site of anthropologist Karen Nakamura's ethnography of people with mental disability in northern Japan.[24]

> In that piece of literature, "bethel house" was repeatedly mentioned. I had no idea what "bethel" meant, and it was in English. Finger-spelling every letter in signs was also not helpful, because it would take too much time to do that every time and people still wouldn't understand what it means. Then, I decided to sign its initials

"B" and then followed by the sign of "House" in CSL. At the beginning of the Zoom meeting, I signed to the deaf participants that this was the name of a community in Japan and that I would be signing in this way throughout the discussion.

Meili told me that after her first interpretation, the deaf participants added her to a new WeChat group to reflect on signs they use. Meili highlighted that she did not repeat written words or speeches into mechanically corresponding signs but underwent a back-and-forth process of presenting decisions to her audiences and acting on their feedback. This ongoing process helped Meili find her presence in the study group and made her interpreting work acceptable to the deaf participants.

Though the hearing sign interpreters improved their skills with feedback from deaf participants, their insufficient interpretations created a communicatively asymmetrical situation for deaf participants in the hearing-dominated conference. It also disadvantaged hearing participants—without qualified interpreters, they could not access thoughts and analyses signed by the deaf participants. Yun, a twenty-seven-year-old deaf woman of deaf parents, was skeptical of Company X's remote interpreters. Though many of Yun's deaf friends used Company X's remote interpreting application, she was not an avid user. The primary reason: the interpreters didn't understand her signing, thereby making communication "barrier-full": "I know Company X's interpreters [Meili and Xiaodan]. But when I was signing to them, sometimes they stopped me. I would think to myself: OK, was my signing not clear to them? Thus, communicating with Company X's interpreters didn't feel comfortable and smooth. I wonder whether they have decided to focus on signed exact Chinese [*shoushi hanyu*] or Chinese sign language. I don't need signed exact Chinese."

"Signed exact Chinese" is an artificial, manual communication method based on an exact representation of Mandarin Chinese grammar and vocabulary.[25] Yun's comment revealed the politics around sign language. In the Chinese context, signing is not just about skill. The very question of what CSL should and should not incorporate is also debated.[26] To Yun, hearing interpreters' "signed exact Chinese" created barriers rather than removing them. Instead of relying on hearing interpreters as "barrier-removers" in the reading group's meetings, Yun told me her preferred and primary source of information was the closed-captions. This was not meant to devalue the interpreters' labor. In fact, Yun and other deaf participants had reminded the event organizers that interpreters should be paid decently if funding was available. Yet, Yun's critique of Company X's interpreters pointed to their overreliance on "signed exact Chinese," a common problem for hearing students taught to sign in special education programs and without enough exposure to the deaf community. Yun warned us about potential dangers of overlooking deaf people's concerns if we put interpreters with mediocre skill levels at the center of the information flow, problematizing the often taken-for-granted idea that sign interpreters make communication for deaf people in cross-disability spaces barrier-free. She also noted discrepancies between the real needs of deaf people and what state policies or programs provide ("signed exact Chinese"). The reading group was meaningful to her because of the possibility to reflect on the ideological, institutional assumptions that connect Chinese Sign Language with barrier-free communication.

Chat Box and Parallel Conversations: Negotiating Access through Ongoing Dialogues

In this section, I analyze a debate around the use of the chat box and how it triggered a reflective moment in which access was used to think about the place of disability in the reading group. The debate took place in the WeChat message group after one Zoom meeting. Luli, a deaf participant, used her cellphone to make a short recording of the Zoom conference on her iPad and posted it in the WeChat group. She wanted to show us how new messages sent through the chat box were interfering with live captions on her screen. She suggested that the event organizers should think about disabling the chat box during the Zoom meeting and using the Q/A function instead, where only the hosts see the incoming questions and can organize them into live discussions.

My immediate response was that "In my Zoom desktop, the chat box was separated from the meeting interface." I wrote this to indicate that I had been unaware of the interference between the chat box and live captions. Ai, the founder of a deaf culture organization, then joined the conversation: "Even if the two interfaces were separated, it is difficult to keep up with both the video box and the chat box at the same time under the limits of attention and senses. The chat box can be easily switched on and off by the host. I feel it can be better managed in subsequent meetings."

Yuanjun, the event co-organizer, confirmed both suggestions by reflecting on the limitations of the original plan to keep the chat box open: "We originally thought it was good to have more information pipelines to increase choice, but we ignored the fact that the content and quality of information on different pipelines are different, and we practically forced everyone to pay attention to all pipelines at the same time to get a complete picture of the information. To be honest I felt overwhelmed by the information in the chat box as well, but I didn't understand the core of the issue."

When Yuanjun spoke of "a complete picture of the information" (*quanbu xinxi*), she referenced how the conversations in the video conference and textual messages in the chat boxes had been intermingled. The chat box, which was originally intended as a "choice," an additional channel people that could opt into or out of, ended up producing parallel dialogues of its own and impacting the video conference. As such, people who paid attention to the video conference but not the chat-box conversations did not have all of the information.

However, just as the group was about to reach a consensus about the disadvantages of the chat box, a hearing participant, Jinhai, joined the dialogue and argued for usage of the chat box: "I think the question is not whether the chat box should be disabled altogether, but rather how it is functionally possible to have an active chat box that does not interfere with the viewing of captions and video screens. The provision of two pipelines going on at the same time doesn't mean everyone has to pay attention to both of them. After all, for those who prefer not to speak and show their faces, the chat box is the only way to participate in the workshop."

Jinhai's argument validated the original vision Yuanjun and I had, which positioned the chat box as a separate pipeline people could choose to engage in. Stressing how the chat box removes barriers for people "who prefer not to speak and show their faces," Jinhai argued for choice, expansiveness, inclusivity, and multiple channels, relating these with barrier-free communication. Ai, however, refuted the idea that extensive use of the chat box is a "choice," considering it instead a privilege reserved for hearing people: "When two pipelines are going on at the same time, what about those people who want to follow both but have a hard time doing so? No wonder, those who can hear and watch while typing win big."

Ai's response challenged Jinhai's evaluative stance by pointing out that the kind of access he requested was not inclusive, being only available from a position of privilege. Jinhai then nuanced his position by stressing that his support for the chat box was not about deaf or hearing people, but rather about his wish to participate in our group solely via text, a more private and comfortable mode of communication for him:

I have used the chat box a lot. When Luli mentioned that the chat box interfered with the live captions, I felt very sorry. But that wasn't my fault. I want to speak up for the chat box and show it doesn't have to be an "interference" in the reading group. The fact that we use different electronic devices and Zoom versions may also be a reason for the different experiences. I don't know if anyone in the group agrees with me on this. But I will certainly respect and obey the decision of event organizers or the majority's opinion.

The subsequent conversation considered how reading group members reconciled the concerns of deaf people who could be disadvantaged by others' use of the chat box with those people who relied on textual communication—in other words, how to address the barriers faced by two concerned groups with clashing communicative preferences. Dai, a hearing participant, commented:

Now several deaf participants have opined that the chat box messages have interfered with the reception of the video presentation, and it was impossible to keep up with the parallel conversations. I, as a hearing person, could not keep up as well. I had to give up following the parallel conversations in the chat box for several previous meetings, because the messages simply kept popping up. Yesterday, as I happened to volunteer to be the host, I paid so close attention to the chat box that I could manage to note down all the points.... The chat box was designed to be an auxiliary function of Zoom. Why not [switch] to another chat software, such as our current WeChat group. Those who can divide their attention can post things here, and others can concentrate on the presenter and check the WeChat messages later.

Dai contrasted her experience as an overwhelmed hearing participant who gave up following the parallel conversations with her experience as host who had to force herself to pay attention to the otherwise distracting flow of information in the chat box. Both experiences positioned the chat box as a source of perplexity, confusion, and interruption. Dai understood the conflict over the chat box not as between hearing and deaf people, but rather as between people "who can divide their attention" and people who preferred to "concentrate." Responding to the juxtaposition of these communicative preferences, I posted the following:

I understand Jinhai's need for chat box. [Yuanjun and] I originally also wanted to encourage the participants to communicate not only with the presenters and the host, but also with each other, and that was what we had hoped [for] the chat box as a "barrier-free" feature. But this idea was premised on the assumption that everybody was ready to process multiple tasks simultaneously, and thus those who were not used to [doing] so would feel excluded. For some, the workshop must follow one thread or otherwise it will be off track; yet for others, one more pipeline provides one more possibility for communication, and each can take what they need.

During this negotiation, the event organizer and the participants had different interpretations of the barrier-free effects of the chat box—for deaf people, for hearing people, for people who did not want to speak or show their face, and for people who could not concentrate on both mediums at once. Jinhai articulated his wish to use the chat box because of privacy concerns: since he was not willing to show his face or use his voice, the chat box was his only access to the workshop; yet he was also attentive to other participants' complaints about the chat box and adjusted his position accordingly. By considering the varying perceptions of the chat-box messages, the reading group reflected on our activities and how different concerns and communicative modes could co-exist. Friction was thus made productive, offering a pause in our habitual communicative practices and a space to consider what being barrier-free looks like. Because the participants knew and recognized each other's efforts in facilitating access, friction gave us space to negotiate.

Biased Subtitles: The Troubled Interference in Live Captioning

I will now explore how reading group participants used access as an evaluative lens through which to interrogate captioning practices inside and outside of the reading group. Closed-captions are not provided in most remote academic meetings in China hosted by hearing Chinese academics. In a few cases where captions were provided, common practice was for meeting participants to simply forego improvisation, broadcasting prepared scripts as subtitles. The subtitles' accuracy was then guaranteed, and the subtitles effectively became a teleprompter. This happened frequently in online Chinese meetings advertised as barrier-free to deaf people. While preparation of a script might be encouraged in certain visions of access,[27] Yun, one of the reading group's most active deaf members, recalled negative experiences of "being controlled by the script" in other conference spaces, especially as a deaf signer whose presentation could hardly be contained in prepared scripts:

I've seen some conferences where deaf presenters use sign language to make their statements. You wouldn't even notice if you don't know sign language, but the thing is that signers do not sign in the order of written Chinese, so it is not possible to stay 100% the same as the prepared script. In this case, if the captioner just copies and pastes the script as subtitles, while the signer conveys the information in a different grammatical order, the mismatch between the subtitles and the signs would make me confused.

To Yun, instead of facilitating the conference, Chinese captions became a new barrier to deaf people. She felt that in many instances, event organizers focused only on "getting the event done" (*wanchenghuiyi*), seeing barrier-free captioning as merely window dressing. In other words, the key problem was not specific technical settings, but that access was treated neither as a shared goal nor as a method.

Recognizing these negative experiences, the desire to facilitate access motivated our reading group to experiment with different captioning technologies. Yuanjun and I were aware from the beginning that, with no budget for professional captioners, the practical alternative was the more affordable machine-generated caption technology based on speech recognition. Zoom has a closed-caption function that allows both manually typed and third-party software entries. Meeting hosts click on the CC toolbar and authorize one participant to be a caption controller or "typer," after which that participant can open an interface wherein they can type and broadcast texts to all participants. The typing can be done manually or with help from other software. The study group experimented with iFlytek, Sogou's audio-input method, and Voibook, all built with machine-generated caption capacities in simplified Chinese. Adding live captions to Zoom required many adjustments. Like the audiovisual inputs in Zoom, the making of AI-based subtitles required stable Internet connections. It also required presenters to speak slowly and clearly, so sound input could be broken down into machine-intelligible syllables and coded back into Chinese characters.

Learning and discussing the technical aspects of captioning in the reading group gave volunteer captioners a sense of participation and achievement. Yuanjun and I would post an announcement one week in advance to let people sign up as a captioner. Novice caption volunteers encountered many technical questions in their effort to make closed captions, such as how to capture different presenters and sign interpreters' voices through their end devices (a laptop, an iPad, a cell phone, or multiple devices at once) and where to install the machine-generated caption application. Similarly, they had to consider how to put transcribed voice signals into Zoom's CC interface and broadcast them, and how to break down machine-translated text corpora into separate sentences and present them to the meeting participants, ensuring that they were neither too long nor too short. Because everybody used different devices—including computers, iPads, and cell phones—each volunteer created a specific way of captioning. These technical questions added more material for discussion and negotiation in the WeChat group, turning the ideal of access into concrete practices and decisions.

The desire to enact access also motivated participants to examine and critique each other's practices when miscommunication occurred. During one Zoom discussion, Yun decided to comment on a piece of reading. Instead of signing as she normally would during video conferences, she began speaking. Growing up, signing was her first language; Yun later told me that her decision to speak in the meeting was intended to "speed up the process and to make her points clear to the hearing participants in the group." While respectful to the volunteer sign interpreters, Yun did not fully trust their ability to fluently interpret her signs, not to mention the shaky Internet signals that prolonged the interpreting. In later interviews, Yun told me that speaking was something she would otherwise prefer not to do; it was not an ideal situation for her.

When Yun spoke, I worried that despite her well-controlled, slow speed of talking, her pronunciation—with a bit of Wuhan dialect—might create challenges in the machine transcription of her words for other deaf participants. To my surprise, the subtitles appeared to match what Yun was saying—lagging slightly, but quite accurate. What was shocking was that some "synonyms" even appeared in place of Yun's original word choices. For example, when Yun discussed her experiences as a deaf woman (*longren nvxing*), the subtitle registered "hearing-impaired women" (*tingzhang nvxing*).

Yun also noticed this change. After the Zoom discussion, she read our meeting transcript from the live captioning and posted in the WeChat group: "I saw the expression 'hearing-impaired' in the subtitles for my speech, yet I did not use that word once. I only used 'deaf.' I wonder why this descriptor appeared." My immediate hypothesis after seeing this conundrum was that the words "deaf" and "hearing-impaired" were marked as synonyms by the speech-recognition machine, with "hearing-impaired" somehow being selected as preferable by the algorithm.

This was not what had happened. A few minutes later, the volunteer captioner for that meeting posted a message explaining that it was her intervention: when Yun spoke, the machine–speech recognition accuracy was inaccurate, with too many typos, so the captioner had been manually adjusting and correcting the typos alongside the machine transcription. To keep up with the information flow, the volunteer stated, "I might have added the words and phrases that I am used to typing." She also added to Yun: "The subtitles for your speech were completely by my manual typing. The other participants spoke a lot faster and almost without any break, so I couldn't have done adjustments to the machine transcriptions simultaneously. I couldn't help feeling obsessed and bad about the machine typos and inaccuracies."

This moment reveals much frustration and miscommunication between the deaf speaker and the hearing captioner because of their different assumptions of access. The captioner thought she was helping by "correcting words" and "making subtitles more accurate." Her attention during the Zoom discussion was tuned to the machine, as it was constantly making mistakes. She decided the machine transcription of a deaf person's speech was inaccurate and must be manually modified. After hearing the deaf speaker's word choices, she rephrased sentences in a way she felt more convenient.

To the volunteer, "hearing-impaired" was a synonym, if not a better description of "deaf." To Yun, who expressed understanding to the volunteer's initiative to intervene but later shared with me her anger and antipathy toward that action, "hearing-impaired" and "deaf" were in no way interchangeable: "I identify myself as deaf, not hearing-impaired. This is because I don't see any impairment in myself. I was specific in my choice of words and made it as clear as possible. Yet the captioner simply replaced my identity with a word she preferred. She apologized in retrospect, but I couldn't forgive her for that. It felt like she imposed her subjective evaluation on me and decided on my behalf."

Yun felt especially angry because the captioner is also a sign interpreter. Yun problematized how the volunteer's training facilitated a bias: "A sign interpreter, just as a captioner, needs to stick to what they see and hear and faithfully represent them. No subjective evaluations. Her changing my words arbitrarily reminds me of all the negative experiences with unprofessional interpreters I or my other deaf friends have had. Therefore, I have chosen to point out the issue in the WeChat group. I wish everybody else could realize this is not acceptable and should be taken seriously."

The reading group's commitment to access allowed Yun to comfortably express her opinion in the WeChat group and invited the captioner to respond. To Yun, the machine-made typos and inaccurate subtitles were tolerable because they happened to deaf and hearing speakers. What annoyed her was the problematic human bias shown by the volunteer's intervention, which, to Yun, implied that deaf people need special treatment, and their speech needs more mediation than that of hearing individuals. The very fact that the caption volunteer jumped to intervene in her speech but not those of the hearing speakers exposed a discriminatory logic.

This incident did not deter Yun or the volunteer captioner from communicating with each other. Both remained active participants in subsequent meetings. The shared commitment to barrier-free communication motivated them to negotiate their different understandings of access and captioning. By reflecting on how the captions created miscommunication and friction, the reading group recognized the labor vested in calculating and making quick decisions alongside the machine: adjusting typos and inaccurate words, dividing sentences, and correctly timing the broadcasting of content. Though decisions could backfire, the shared utopian desire for barrier-free communication motivated the group's participants to stick together and adjust their practices in pursuit of better access.

Conclusion

Above, I have analyzed a group of people's insistence on communicating with each other remotely despite multiple frictions, frustrations, and unreliable access. Aspiring to barrier-free communication, the reading group allowed different visions and interpretations of access to emerge and become operative. These processes of negotiating, questioning, and reflecting upon barrier-free communication played a constitutive role in maintaining people's remote co-presence.

Chinese state media outlets often celebrate the increasing provision of accessible bathrooms, tactile pavements, and voice-recognition communication applications for people with physical, visual, or hearing disabilities to utilize in Chinese cities, linking them to the government discourses of the "China dream," the "smart city," and "serving the people" (*wei renmin fuwu*).[28] However, because no current Chinese law specifies any "right of access" for people with disabilities, disabled people are unlikely to directly bring civil suits regarding the absence of accessible public facilities against any responsible parties.[29] By foregrounding the barrier-free question, the reading group members engaged in utopian thinking that both made the existing spaces' limits explicit and constructed alternatives. Foregrounding barrier-free communication also urged people to consider and enact, at different scales, the institutional design of a better society and the ethical subjects and agents of such a society. In this light, the budgetary constraints, conflicts, frictions, frustration, and even anger became necessary reminders that the reading group was far from barrier-free, having only the partial concrete instantiation of a much broader ambition toward social reconstitution. They also showed that access is never achieved merely by installing a product or technical fix, but unfolds through negotiations, reflections, recalibration, and questioning. Using access as a method rather than a goal sustained the reading group, serving as a moral glue that held participants together.

Adopting an understanding of access as an ongoing, interpretive process can help us move beyond policy tropes about access. As anthropologist Michele Friedner notes, the cross-disability movement needs to be critically reflected upon, as it tends to obscure differences in the name of foregrounding disabled people's shared position against discrimination.[30] Although activists and scholars in the study group had a relatively high awareness of inclusion and disability rights as a generally desired good or abstract value, many people only started to examine their practices and sensibilities of access when miscommunication, perplexity, and friction arose. By observing the interactions between disabled and non-disabled students, young academics, activists, social workers, and sign interpreters, my findings show that access is more than an individual situation—that is, something that one either has or does not have. Access is also more than a tangible entity that can be quantified and facilitated by technical standards, as the UNCRPD model might imply. Conversely, I argue, these communicative frictions can trigger subsequent reflections, allowing for a reflexive form of inquiry that resists establishment of a status quo.

In the spring of 2021, while I was working on an earlier draft of this chapter, Yuanjun and I organized a collective reflection on the study group. Learning of our focus on the frictions and failures, Luli commented: "Our deaf people have spent our lives trying to communicate. For getting even a bit of information, we would have a sense of achievement, rather than frustration. Do hearing people find it frustrating when they fail to communicate with the deaf? Alas, you need to experience more communication failures."

The above remark illuminates the aspiration toward cross-difference solidarity and continued desire for communication and conversation. In pursing this goal, each of us paid greater attention to the politics we make use of to respond to the place of disability in a technically mediated space. My ethnographic observations are specific to a Chinese reading group and its online spaces during the summer of the COVID-19 pandemic, yet the desire I have highlighted—to create a cross-disability accessible digital space and make and maintain access for all—is relevant to disability communities, policymakers, technicians, Internet companies, and activists. We must also nuance our definitions of access to allow for interactive work and access as a practice, rather than a goal.

NOTES

1. In this paper, I assign pseudonyms to all participants, using thirteen machine-generated Mandarin Chinese-character first names: Yuanjun, Meili, Yun, Dai, Xiaodan, Jinhai, Ai, Luli, Weizhe, Gui, Tingfeng, Xiurong, Mingxia. I want to express my gratitude to the interlocutors who generously read earlier drafts of this paper and offered new insights, although the reading group ended nearly a year ago.
2. Cassandra Hartblay, "After Marginalization: Pixelization, Disability, and Social Difference in Digital Russia," *South Atlantic Quarterly* 118, no. 3 (2019): 543–572; Emily Lim Rogers, "Staying (at Home) with Brain Fog: 'Un-Witting' Patient Activism," *Somatosphere*, October 5, 2020; Ruikai Dai and Luanjiao Hu, "Inclusive Communications in COVID-19: A Virtual Ethnographic Study of Disability Support Network in China," *Disability & Society* (2021): 1–19.
3. Ashley Shew, "Let COVID-19 Expand Awareness of Disability Tech," *Nature* 581, no. 7806 (May 5, 2020): 9.
4. Elizabeth Keating and Gene Mirus, "American Sign Language in Virtual Space: Interactions between Deaf Users of Computer-Mediated Video Communication and the Impact of Technology on Language Practices," *Language in Society*, 2003, 693–714; Elizabeth Keating, Terra Edwards, and Gene Mirus, "Cybersign and New Proximities: Impacts of New Communication Technologies on Space and Language," *Journal of Pragmatics* 40, no. 6 (2008): 1067–1081.
5. Tanya Titchkosky, *The Question of Access: Disability, Space, Meaning* (Toronto: University of Toronto Press, 2011).
6. The research followed the protocols of the University of Chicago Social & Behavioral Sciences Institutional Review Board (IRB20–0782), and best practices were observed in conducting the interviews.
7. Ruth Levitas, *Utopia as Method: The Imaginary Reconstitution of Society* (New York:

Palgrave Macmillan, 2013).

8. Chao Zhang, "'Nothing about Us without Us': The Emerging Disability Movement and Advocacy in China," *Disability & Society* 32, no. 7 (August 9, 2017): 1096–1101; Dai and Hu, "Inclusive Communications in COVID-19."

9. Cassandra Hartblay, "Disability Expertise: Claiming Disability Anthropology," *Current Anthropology* 61, no. 21 (2020): 26–36; Americans with Disabilities Act of 1990, Public Law 101–336, 108th Congress, 2nd session (July 26, 1990); UN General Assembly, *Convention on the Rights of Persons with Disabilities: Resolution/Adopted by the General Assembly*, January 24, 2007, A/RES/61/106.

10. Victor Pickard, "Neoliberal Visions and Revisions in Global Communications Policy from NWICO to WSIS," *Journal of Communication Inquiry* 31, no. 2 (2007): 118–139; Eliza Varney, *Disability and Information Technology: A Comparative Study in Media Regulation* (Cambridge: Cambridge University Press, 2013); Gerard Goggin, "Disability and Digital Inequalities: Rethinking Digital Divides with Disability Theory," in *Theorizing Digital Divides*, ed. Massimo Ragnedda and Glenn W. Mushchert (London: Routledge, 2017), 218.

11. UN General Assembly, *Convention on the Rights of Persons with Disabilities*.

12. Na Tang and Yu Cao, "From Multiple Barriers to a Co-Prosperity Society: The Development of a Legal System for Disabled People in China," *Disability & Society* 33, no. 7 (August 9, 2018): 1170–1174; Xintong Zhao and Chao Zhang, "From Isolated Fence to Inclusive Society: The Transformational Disability Policy in China," *Disability & Society* 33, no. 1 (January 2, 2018): 132–137.

13. The State Council, *The Regulations on the Construction of Barrier-Free Environment*, 2012; Standing Committee of the National People's Congress, *Law of the People's Republic of China on the Protection of Disabled Persons* (2018 amendment) [Effective].

14. Ministry of Industry and Information Technology, Information Accessibility Design Guidelines to Information Terminal Equipment for Persons with Physical Disabilities (YD/T 2065–2009).

15. Shixin Huang, "International Rights and Local Realities: Transnational Allies of the Disability Rights Movement in China," in *Disability Alliances and Allies*, ed. Allison C. Carey, Joan M. Ostrove, and Tara Fannon (Leeds, U.K.: Emerald Publishing, 2020); Shixin Huang, "Ten Years of the CRPD's Adoption in China: Challenges and Opportunities," *Disability & Society* 34, no. 6 (2019): 1004–1009.

16. For more comprehensive statistics, see "The Rights of Persons with Disabilities and Older Persons in a Pandemic: Findings from Two Studies Conducted in China" (funded by Raoul Wallenberg Institute), https://rwi.lu.se.

17. For an example of how deaf activists in China used social media to reflect on communication barriers during the pandemic, see ProSigner, "Feelings of Doudou (Deaf)

since Wuhan's Lockdown," *ProSigner*, last modified February 12, 2020. https://mp.weixin.qq.com/s/M5AnkjWbpcXwxFpSVOJ7oQ.

18. For discussion of the history and future of sign language interpreting in Chinese higher education, see Xiao Xiaoyan, Peng Yaqing, and Deng Yi, "Exploring the Chinese Model of Sign Interpreting Education [Shouyu fanyi jiaoyu de zhongguo moshi tansuo]," *Journal of Foreign Languages* [*Journal of Shanghai Foreign Studies University*] 43, no. 5 (2020): 98–106; Meng Fan-ling and Han Lu-zhan, "Status Analysis of Sign Language Translation Occupation in Higher Institutions in China [Woguo gaoxiao shouyu fanyi zhiye xianzhuang fenxi]," *Journal of Zhongzhou University* 32, no. 2 (2015): 112–116.

19. Michele Friedner, "Negotiating Legitimacy in American Sign Language Interpreting Education: Uneasy Belonging in a Community of Practice," *Disability Studies Quarterly* 38, no. 1 (February 28, 2018); Aron S. Marie, "Enacting Dependence," *Somatosphere*, February 19, 2019.

20. Xiaoyan Xiao, Xin Gao, and Xiao Zhao, "Survey on Sign Interpreting in Mainland China: Status Quo, Issues, and Prospects [Zhongguo dalu shouyu chuanyi diaocha: Xianzhuang, wenti yu qianjing]," *Chinese Translators Journal* [*Zhongguo fanyi*], no. 06 (2018): 66–72; Yu Zhang, Yuanyuan Peng, and Feiyang Peng, "Research on Adult Deaf People's Need and Attitude towards Sign Interpreters [Chengnian longren qunti dui shouyu fanyiyuan de xuqiu yu taidu yanjiu]," *Modern Special Education* [*Xiandai teshu jiaoyu*], no. 4 (2019).

21. Leah Lakshmi Piepzna-Samarasinha, *Care Work: Dreaming Disability Justice* (Vancouver, BC: Arsenal Pulp Press, 2018).

22. Ironically, though these interpreters were unqualified (as Meili readily admitted) for interpreting international academic discussions, Company X's interpreters have a benchmark reputation for professional sign interpretation in China, as noted by many deaf activists in our group. Company X is one of the few examples where students trained in special education programs with a sign language curriculum become full-time interpreters in China. Company X currently does not charge deaf users. Their income mainly comes from government purchases of services such as helping state-owned enterprises with sign language training and interpreting. Full-time video interpreters in Company X need to answer at times hundreds of calls from deaf users during their shifts. Their services are in high demand. Company X is also prominent in international spaces, well-connected to organizations in the Global North. Thus, had we secured funding, we would likely still have employed interpreters from Company X due to their relative success and reputation among Chinese deaf people in China and overseas.

23. Alison Kafer, *Feminist, Queer, Crip* (Bloomington: Indiana University Press, 2013); Aimi Hamraie and Kelly Fritsch, "Crip Technoscience Manifesto," *Catalyst: Feminism, Theory, Technoscience* 5, no. 1 (2019): 1–33.

24. Karen Nakamura, *A Disability of the Soul* (Ithaca, NY: Cornell University Press, 2013).
25. For discussions on signed exact Chinese, see Lingling, "Sign Language, Spoken Language, Hearing Aids, Cochlear Implants . . . Two or Three Things about Deaf Identity," *Minority Voice*, last modified April 13, 2020, https://mp.weixin.qq.com/s/GTFFGkjB4EcLDH7Y-D_Z9A.
26. Linguists and educators have discussed the subtle genealogical differences between Tibetan Sign Language, Shanghai Sign Language, and Northern Sign Language, and carried out extensive effort—usually state-commissioned—to incorporate them into Chinese Sign Language (CSL) that could be used nationwide. The process is not uncontroversial. Discontent about standardization circulates on WeChat, Zhihu, blogs, and other Chinese social media: Many deaf people find the national CSL cumbersome, artificial, and ineffective in comparison to their regional vernacular sign languages. They also question why standardization is largely led by hearing special education experts, though, recently, deaf scholars trained in linguistics in China have also gotten involved. Moreover, the necessity of establishing a national standard is challenged altogether, as it rejects and wipes out diverse locally situated linguistic practices. For more discussion, see Theresia Hofer, "Is Lhasa Tibetan Sign Language Emerging, Endangered, or Both?," *International Journal of the Sociology of Language* 2017, no. 245 (2017): 113–145; Shangsheng Li, "Re-Examining the Linguistic Qualifications of Sign Language [Chongshen shouyu d yuyan zige]," *Chinese Journal of Special Education* [*Zhongguo teshu jiaoyu*] 4 (2000): 4–41; Yu Xiaoting and He Huizhong, "A Review on Chinese Sign Language Study [Guonei youyu yanjiu zongshu]," *Chinese Journal of Special Education* [*Zhongguo teshu jiaoyu*] 4 (2009): 36–41. For deaf complaints on fake CSL in social media, see for example ProSigner. "Deaf culture and Rights. Why Can't Deaf People Understand 'Signed Exact Chinese'," *ProSigner*, last modified June 16, 2017. https://mp.weixin.qq.com/s/0En6G3au0OP6Bnut8pm-Hg.
27. Jennifer Iverson, "Designing for Access in the Classroom and Beyond," in *The Routledge Companion to Music Theory Pedagogy* (New York: Routledge, 2020), 397–406.
28. Zihao Lin, "Writing Down Our Happiness and Dreams: Essay Contest and the Statist Narratives of Deaf Identity in China," *Disability & Society* 36, no. 1 (2021): 38–57.
29. Fei Qi, Luanjiao Hu, and Yuqi Wu, "Rhetoric and Reality: Litigation Rights of Chinese Disabled People," *Disability & Society* 35, no. 8 (2020): 1343–1348.
30. Michele Friedner, Nandini Ghosh, and Deepa Palaniappan, "'Cross-Disability' in India?: On the Limits of Disability as a Category and the Work of Negotiating Impairments," *South Asia Multidisciplinary Academic Journal* (April 5, 2018).

PART 2

Making Sense of the Pandemic

Chinese Students and Narratives of Freedom before and during COVID-19

Yingyi Ma and Ning Zhan

CHINESE INTERNATIONAL STUDENTS HAVE BEEN CAUGHT IN THE POLITICAL CROSS-fire of rising U.S.-China tensions in recent years.[1] U.S.-China relations had already deteriorated before the COVID-19 pandemic, and after it began, they went into freefall.[2] As Minxin Pei has argued, COVID "finished off" the already strained relationship, leaving the two nations bitter about and estranged from the other.[3]

The current generation of Chinese international students has grown up in an era as beneficiaries from China's reforms and opening-up policies—launched by Deng Xiaoping in the late 1970s—but their ambitions to become mobile, transnational citizens were met with unprecedented challenges during the pandemic.[4] We argue that the long-lasting travel bans and restrictions enacted successively on both sides of the Pacific have impacted these students' mobility and perception about America and China. Chinese students studying overseas were shut out of their own country. For example, the "Five One" policy put in place by the Chinese government during the pandemic limited all domestic airlines to one international flight per week to each country, and foreign airlines were only allowed to fly into China once per week.[5] This policy literally restricted Chinese citizens abroad, including but not limited to international students, from entering their own country, and Chinese students and their families scrambled to muster their resources and grab precious tickets.[6]

Adding to their travel troubles were new visa challenges. In May 2020, the American government announced that it was cancelling the visas of about three thousand Chinese graduate students and researchers in the United States who had direct ties to China's military universities.[7] In June 2020, the Trump administration issued a proclamation suspending the new work visas (H-1B) required for foreigners to work legally in the United States. Yet many H-1B visa applicants were international students who had received job offers after completing their studies in the United States.[8]

In the midst of travel and visa restrictions resulting from the COVID-19 pandemic, Chinese international students are witnessing and experiencing how such matters as masks and vaccines became fertile ground for contesting notions of freedom and individual liberty in the cross-national contexts of their home and host societies.[9] Recent research has focused on how COVID triggered a rise in anti-Asian racism, led to the construction of new forms of stigma, and negatively impacted the mental health of students.[10] We build upon that scholarship by addressing the neglected but powerful experiences of Chinese international students traversing the contrasting spaces of their home and host countries, among which the narratives of freedom raise critical questions. We ask: How did Chinese students understand different narratives concerning freedom during the pandemic? How did their understanding of freedom during the pandemic differ from their pre-pandemic positions? And how can we make sense of these contrasts? To answer those questions, this chapter foregrounds the voices of Chinese international students, paying particular attention to their evolving narratives about the role of individual freedom during the pandemic, as compared to their narratives before the pandemic. With semi-structured, in-depth interviews with two-cohorts of Chinese students selected before and during the pandemic, totaling 95 interviews, from a diverse set of American higher education institutions, this chapter applies a comparative lens to examine Chinese international students' narratives about freedom before and during this pandemic.[11]

Our findings indicate that Chinese international students who initially had positive views about the concept of freedom in America faced difficulties comprehending the country's confusing responses to COVID, which led to their disillusionment with the notion of freedom. To provide context, we first highlight some significant distinctions between the educational systems in China and the United States. This background is crucial since, before the pandemic, many Chinese students chose to study in the United States precisely because they perceived more freedom in the American education system. Unfortunately, the pandemic exposed them to the idea that freedom is fluid in meaning, and sometimes, deadly.

Freedom, Individualism, and Collectivism in Education Systems

In *Cultures and Organizations: Software of the Mind*, Geert Hofstede et al. discuss cultural differences and how the divide between individualism and collectivism is a major cultural dimension underlying some of the differences between Chinese and Western societies.[12] Recently, scholars have focused on the rising individualism in Chinese society, which is part and parcel of a booming market economy that started in the late 1970s. The shift to a market economy has influenced every aspect of life, from consumerism to family dynamics and work life, and has brought about enhanced personal freedom to travel, work, and consume in China.[13]

However, the rising individualism in China has not really upended the long-lasting tradition of a collectivist orientation within its education sector. According to Jin Li in *Cultural Foundations of Learning: East and West*, the education orientation in China is rooted in the ancient moral philosophy of Confucianism.[14] For example, a famous Confucius saying states "Equality of education despite differences in backgrounds". Learners of Confucius sometimes interpret this saying differently, but they all converge on the role of education for standard academic goals. In such a system, Chinese students at the same grade levels take the same courses, and freedom of choice within the curriculum is quite limited, except in a few elite schools that offer some flexibility in the choice of courses.[15] These constraints parallel the absence of early tracking in the education system, which stands in sharp contrast with the American system.[16] That is, regardless of family background and individual ability, students in China do not choose a subject track until high school, where they are usually presented with two options: arts/humanities or math/science. In other words, the two tracks are based on horizontal domain differences, not on vertical academic hierarchies. The system holds all students to similar expectations, regardless of students' abilities or interests, until they reach sixteen or seventeen years old.[17]

However, this ostensibly ideal equality in curricular and educational expectations can cause some students deep pain, as they may have to study subjects they have little interest or ability in, but they are still expected to perform at the same level as their high-achieving peers. This lack of freedom in academic studies may drive some Chinese students to study in U.S. schools, which permit students to choose courses as early as middle school, or in some private schools in the United States, where curriculums are customized to individuals' needs and learning pace, which are commodities that parents and students chase after.[18] In recent years, the numbers of Chinese students in American secondary schools are increasing on an astronomical scale, and most are concentrated in private boarding schools, where the curriculum is even more flexible than in public schools, and where students are not bound by testing regimes such as those found in the Common Core curriculum used in many U.S. states.[19]

Other than the difference in individualized curriculum in U.S. and Chinese schools, the college admissions systems in the two countries also reflect a divide between individualism and collectivism. Millions of high school seniors in China take the *gaokao*—the Chinese college entrance exam,[20] wherein their scores determine their college placement. *Gaokao* puts many students—those with test anxiety, dyslexia, and other types of learning differences—at a great disadvantage. This kind of test-based college-admissions process, despite much criticism, is still regarded as embodying the meritocratic values system, particularly for students from disadvantaged backgrounds, for whom few avenues of upward social mobility are available other than test-based college admissions.[21] This centralized and highly standardized testing has its roots in *keju*, the tests that have been used to select government officials in China for thousands of years.[22] This long-standing tradition of a collectivist and centralized approach to selecting talent in China makes students who either dislike or do not excel at test taking to suffer in Chinese schools.

On the other hand, the American education system is markedly more individualistic than the Chinese system. Nowhere is this more apparent than in the college-admission processes showcased by several high-profile Supreme Court cases. Mitchell Stevens, analyzing the Supreme Court ruling *Grutter v. Bollinger*, regarding University of Michigan Law School admissions, observed that "The term 'individualized consideration' was sprinkled throughout the Grutter decision, leaving little doubt about the kind of evaluation the Supreme Court regarded as optimal."[23] The phrase "individualized consideration" reflects the fundamental belief that informs the approach to education in the United States: students have unique abilities and temperaments, and, therefore, education should be customized and individualized to accommodate their differences. The individualized considerations in American college-admissions systems create enormous appeal to Chinese international students who struggle in the standardized Chinese system and yearn for the freedom and flexibilities in the American system.[24] If Chinese students enter the American system earlier than college, they are also able to take advantage earlier of the course electives in high schools. Other than the differences in the two education systems, Chinese students are also drawn to the American society by its general openness—the sense of cosmopolitanism in American society, to which the next section turns. There we discuss how Chinese students associate their conception of freedom with their desire for cosmopolitanism and how that association is being contested by the rising nationalism in China.

Freedom, Cosmopolitanism, and Nationalism

While the American education system is prized for its openness, which generates much freedom for students, American society more broadly embodies a similar spirit of openness, which attracts migrants from around the world. Scholars call this *cosmopolitanism*, an orientation of openness to foreign others.[25] In the era of globalization, an orientation to foreign cultures and competencies can be important assets for marshaling resources and navigating multicultural environments. Scholars interpret this as *cosmopolitan capital*. According to sociologist Don Weenink, "Cosmopolitan capital is, first of all, a propensity to engage in global-sizing social arenas. . . . Cosmopolitan capital comprises bodily and mental predispositions and competencies which help to engage confidently in such arenas."[26] Research on the motivations of international students in the United States—most of whom are from the rising middle class in Asia—shows that pursuing cosmopolitan capital is an important reason why Chinese international students study in the United States, which they perceive as the epicenter of globalization.[27] China's middle-class mindset to acquire cosmopolitan capital is part of an attempt to join the league of the "new global elites."[28]

When China joined the World Trade Organization and Beijing hosted the 2008 Olympic games, the Chinese people were immersed in a culture embracing globalization. They found themselves always on the move, if not internationally, then domestically, and the fantasy of going someplace else engulfed the psyche of Chinese society.[29] Since China's reform and opening up began, the freedom to leave one's hometown to seek a better livelihood has been a hallmark of Chinese life, and millions of migrant workers have set out from their hometowns in hope of a more prosperous life in a new city. Urban Chinese families with means—often part of the rising middle class—enjoy the freedom to travel, migrate, and choose an overseas education for their children.[30] Vanessa Fong used the phrase *pilgrimages to develop* to describe the journeys of Chinese international students who study abroad. These students aspire to become global citizens and support China's aspiration to enter the developed world community. They believe study-abroad experiences will endow them with freedoms and advantages such as "access to more prestigious, enjoyable, and useful education, greater purchasing power, better jobs, greater geographic mobility, [and] a healthier and more comfortable physical environment."[31]

One can be at once cosmopolitan and nationalistic, as Ulrich Beck has argued, claiming that "cosmopolitanism and nationalism can mutually complement and correct for each other";[32] however, a question that Beck has yet to elucidate is: Under what circumstances can nationalism and cosmopolitanism complement each other, and under what circumstances does one trump or correct for the other? Since the early 1990s, there has been an emerging and increasing sense of nationalism in China.[33] Since the 2008 financial crisis engulfed the Western advanced economies and revealed the limitations of a free-wheeling market economy, China has asserted itself in presenting alternative models for market economies, featuring a strong hand of government control while selectively opening economic sectors.[34] It is not surprising that Chinese children born in the twenty-first century tend to be more nationalistic than earlier generations, including those Chinese students abroad, as they are growing up in an increasingly prosperous and self-assured China.[35]

Previous studies on the nationalistic presentations among overseas Chinese center on filial nationalism to account for the public demonstrations launched by Chinese students in the United States and Europe in response to America's mistaken bombing of the Chinese embassy in Belgrade in 1999.[36] Both Vanessa Fong and Peter Hayes Gries have argued that these protests were stimulated out of Chinese youth's natural desire to protect their nation against what they perceived as Western imperialism.[37] At that time, Chinese students' nationalism overseas was driven more out of historical grievances than their own national pride.[38] Scholars have argued this sentiment of viewing China as vulnerable to imperial aggression, and the resulting sense of urgency to protect China from outside threats, amounts to a form of "traumatized nationalism."[39] Starting in the first decade of the twenty-first century, such feelings have started to shift away from trauma over past injuries to asserting national pride and even a sense of superiority. This shift was first seen among Chinese youth overseas protesting against Western media coverage of rioting in Tibet right before the 2008 Beijing Olympics. These overseas Chinese youth, often international students studying at global cities such as New York, London, Paris, and Sydney, embodied the promises of cosmopolitism while protesting on the streets of those global cities, expressing their international outlook and emphasizing that they were not representing the Chinese government, but just trying to add their own voices.[40] They aimed to portray a "real China" different from the caricatures of China so often seen in some Western media.

Since the Trump presidency, Chinese students' conceptions of the United States as a free world and cosmopolitan ideal have been seriously challenged. For example, the U.S. government has taken a decidedly restrictive turn against immigrants and international students, especially those from China. From FBI Director Christopher Wray's Senate speech in 2018 warning American universities against a perceived "whole-of-society threat" from China to multiple arrests of Chinese scholars and scientists out of national security concerns in recent years,[41] the narrative that Chinese students and scholars are a threat could alienate Chinese students and make them more nationalistic than before. The COVID-19 crisis in 2020 is another moment that catalyzed rising nationalism and exacerbated the chasm between Chinese students and American society. In fact, as we detail below, as anti-Asian racism and Sinophobia flamed during the pandemic in the United States, Chinese students' previously positive notions of American freedom and cosmopolitanism fell into a tailspin.[42] On the other hand, the rapid squelching of the pandemic within China in 2020–2021, compared with the ongoing ravage of the pandemic in the United States, strengthened their identification with their home China. The interviews we draw upon below were all conducted before the new Omicron variant of the pandemic hit China in 2022 and China's zero-COVID policy would not be able to control the spread of the disease anymore.

Data and Methods

The study presented in this chapter draws from in-depth interviews with two cohorts of Chinese international students who were studying before and after COVID-19 hit. The first cohort was interviewed between 2013 and 2017 as part of a book project involving a comprehensive examination of Chinese international undergraduates' academic and social experiences. The second cohort was interviewed in 2020 after COVID-19 started to spread in the United States, with a focus on understanding how the pandemic was affecting their experiences as well as their attitudes toward the ways their home and host countries were handling it.

The two cohorts are cross-sectional in nature, and they share the identity of Chinese international undergraduates studying in American institutions of higher education. The reason that we used a cross-sectional rather than longitudinal design is that the central research aim of this study is to compare and contrast the different views about freedom held by Chinese international students before and during the pandemic. Since a large majority of the first cohort had already completed their studies in the United States, and a substantial number of them have already returned to China—with the exception of a few students in advanced graduate study—a longitudinal analysis would not have been able to capture how the pandemic affected their college experiences. Therefore, a cross-sectional design was better suited to the project's objective.

We recruited study participants through snowball sampling via diverse channels of English and Chinese social media sites, including Facebook, Twitter, Instagram, and WeChat, as well as from two undergraduate research assistants, who are themselves Chinese undergraduate international students. The first cohort consisted of 65 students, and the second of 30 students (with far less time and restricted access to data collection during the pandemic). Given that a disproportionate number of Chinese college students in the United States pay full tuition, our study population was an economically privileged group, but this does not mean that they were all from wealthy families. To ensure the heterogeneity of the sample, students were recruited from diverse institutions, ranging from elite private universities to non-elite state universities.

While the interviews were semi-structured, we asked the students structured questions regarding their demographic background, academic background, and their intention to enroll in undergraduate colleges or graduate schools in the United States. For unstructured questions, we asked both cohorts questions about what motivated them to study in the United States, how they compared freedom in the United States and China, and what freedom meant to them. The unstructured questions also pertained to their international education goals, their views on the approaches the United States and China have adopted to deal with the pandemic, and their views on the influence exercised by the United States and China on the world stage. Such questions are best addressed through in-depth, semi-structured interviews. We let students choose the language they wanted to use, and most chose Chinese. All the student names are pseudonyms for the sake of privacy, but we do respect students' choices of English or Chinese names. If they presented themselves with English names, we used a pseudonym in English. The same approach applied to Chinese names. For the first cohort, every interview was conducted in person; for the second cohort, face-to-face interviews could not take place due to the pandemic and social distancing protocols, so they were handled via virtual meetings.

Findings: Before the Pandemic

The following findings pertain to the first cohort, with whom the interviews were conducted and completed before the pandemic. The main thematic narratives on freedom center on the notion of choices and respecting individuality.

Freedom means choices

When asked what freedom meant to them, the first cohort talked most frequently about choices. From their perspectives, what attracted them most to American higher education was that it afforded a greater number of choices of high-quality colleges and universities than in China. For example, Diana, a Shanghai native, first studied at the University of Washington in Seattle, and after studying there for two years, transferred to Johns Hopkins University. She talks about her choice options in China and the United States for higher education: "America has so many more good schools than China does, so I have more freedom here to choose, but in China, I feel like I have to be chosen by a few good schools. The University of Washington is pretty good, but here in America, I have the freedom to transfer to even better ones." Chinese students often consider university rankings as the primary metric when looking for a "good school." For Diana, the University of Washington in Seattle did not rank as high as Johns Hopkins University, so she reaped the benefit of the freedom to transfer. Although China has vastly expanded its own post-secondary systems—it currently has roughly the same number of higher education institutions as the United States, with a larger enrollment—it still severely lacks schools that are ranked as top in the world. Among the one hundred best universities in the world, China has three, while America has close to forty.[43] For Diana, then, "freedom" meant the ability to study where she wanted.

The enhanced freedom to access a high-quality education here in the United States further liberates students from excruciating test-based stress. While Chinese students still suffer much anxiety over college applications and admissions, they feel that they have multiple opportunities to qualify for U.S. schools. Indeed, many students take the TOEFL and SAT multiple times a year, whereas, if they want to repeat the Chinese *gaokao*, they have to wait for an entire year. Phyllis, a student from Guangdong, studied at North Carolina State University. She struggled academically in China and felt that the good colleges were beyond her reach, so she took advantage of the American system, which, according to her, "has so many more choices for people like me. I can take tests several times here, and more importantly, tests are not the only things that matter." Phyllis considered herself as someone who was deemed an academic failure in China, yet she has thrived academically in America. In Phyllis's case, the sense of "freedom" amounted to her ability to write a new narrative for herself; no longer a failure, Phyllis built a sense of herself as accomplished and capable. "Freedom" thus meant more than just choosing where to go to college, but how the student thought of herself and imagined her future.

Other than in four-year colleges, Chinese students are increasingly enrolling in community colleges in the United States. For example, Max came to Oregon from a city in North China when he was in the eleventh grade. When asked what he thought about his decision to come to the United States as a high school student, Max responded: "Definitely a right decision, as I met American friends in high school who introduced me to community college here. Otherwise, I would have never attended the community college here." Max has since transferred from his community college to Oregon State University, a four-year college that has a transfer arrangement with the community college. He marveled at his choice: "This has saved me at least two thirds of the tuition. I am so happy. My parents are so happy. We never had thought we had such great freedom to transfer schools and save money." For Max, the pre-COVID narrative of freedom included celebrating the ability to choose where to study and feeling grateful for the resulting financial savings.

Because the concept of community colleges is not familiar to most Chinese students, Max attributed his choice to attend a community college to the American friends he made in high school. However, owing to the huge industry of agents and educational consulting groups who successfully market American community colleges as a bridge to four-year universities, community college has become increasingly appealing to Chinese students from modest family backgrounds.[44] The fact that Chinese students apply to community colleges with the aim of transferring to a four-year institution, and therefore consider community college mainly as a transfer mechanism, stands in sharp contrast to the situation of American domestic students enrolled in community colleges—whose drop-out rate is high and whose transfer rate to four-year colleges is low.[45]

While Chinese international students enjoy the freedom to choose and transfer schools in America, they also appreciate the freedom to choose a major and switch if they want. In China, college majors are hierarchically linked with *gaokao* test scores, and it is thus very hard to change majors once a student is enrolled. Some majors, such as computer science, economics, and finance are more competitive and thus require relatively higher *gaokao* scores than majors such as history and philosophy, even within a particular institution. The competitive majors in the most prestigious schools, such as Tsinghua and Peking—China's top two elite universities—are often the preserve of provincial champions on the *gaokao*.

In the United States, although there is also a distinction between competitive and non-competitive fields, the system for selecting majors is not as rigid and is more amenable to change. Most institutions do not require students to declare a major until they are two years into their full-time studies. The idea is that this gives students opportunities to try out different courses and to get to know their interests and strengths better before they make their decision. Therefore, it is no wonder that Chinese students find the freedom to choose and change their majors very appealing. Research on Chinese international students shows that they are still concentrated in STEM and business fields,[46] namely, fields that are in high demand in the Chinese and global job markets. Still, some students take advantage of the flexible American system to choose and switch majors.

Freedom means respecting individuality

Chinese international students often complain that their prior schooling in China was test-oriented and suppressed their individuality. Every year, millions of students take the *gaokao* at the same time. Many Chinese students are afraid of the test; in their view, the American college-admissions system provides more freedom in its individualized approach to evaluating candidates. Besides scores on standardized tests like the SAT, American admissions offices take into account high school academic performance and documents such as personal statements and recommendation letters, which are unique to the individual. Consider the case of Sunny, a native of Shenzhen, who studied at Syracuse University. She struggled with testing in China. "I am stressed out in testing, and I've always struggled with this in China. Everyone is the same before tests and scores are everything in Chinese schools. I feel American schools respect more of individual students, not just their test scores. I certainly feel freer here [in America]."

Some students we interviewed mentioned other elements besides college admissions that attracted them to U.S. schools, including that the general learning environment in America provides more freedom in learning and being. Joy, a Shanghai native, studied at Parsons School of Design. She said, "I feel that I started to find myself after I came to America." I asked her: "What do you mean by 'find yourself'?" She explained: "American teachers encourage me to speak up, and I find my voice and I can express myself more freely. In my field [design], it is so important to have individuality, and I find more freedom to pursue this [individuality] here." Another interviewee, Christine, a native from Guangzhou, studied at Georgia State University. She felt she had always lacked self-confidence. She attributed this to her previous Chinese schooling: "[The] Chinese school environment made me lose myself in a large class setting. I cared too much about how teachers thought of me. I worked so hard to please others and earn their praise. I was also afraid to lose face for my parents. But now in the United States, whatever you do, people will praise you. This helps me focus on things I really want to do, and what I care about." This renewed sense of voice and individuality is palpable among Chinese students in America.

Our interviewees also expressed how their identities face scrutiny and even repression in China, especially around gender and sexuality, so they cherish the ways that American society has granted them respect and space to live their lives. Julianne, a Shanghai native studying at Duke University, described her struggle with sexuality and accepting herself: "I find myself struggling with being bisexual, and I am lucky that I am in America. In China, I would not be willing to be open about this, and the LGBTQ community [there] is still living with great stigma. I learned to accept myself and find great community here [at Duke]." Discrimination against the LGBTQ community in China is well-documented.[47] This freedom to choose and accept one's sexuality is much appreciated by Julianne, who has compared American society with her home country and concluded that American society has made her freedom to be herself possible.

Findings: After the Pandemic

The second cohort of Chinese students in this study experienced COVID right in the middle of the spring semester of 2020. Some have returned home to China and resumed their studies remotely. Others have stayed in the United States. Regardless, their perspectives on freedom have taken a decided turn from the positive to the negative, compared to the first cohort, who we interviewed before the pandemic. The thematic narratives on freedom from the second cohort, who we interviewed during the pandemic, centered on the notion of fear, selfishness, and at the minimum, moral ambiguity.

"Freedom brought me fear."

The pandemic triggered fear for everyone. However, Chinese students studying in America now tend to connect freedom with their fear. Xiao, a native from Beijing, arrived at New York University as a freshman in the fall of 2019. He was still in New York in April 2020 at the time of our interview, after the university had shut down the residential campus and converted to remote learning. He lived in an off-campus apartment with his Chinese friends. When asked what freedom meant to him, he said, "Americans value their personal freedom over anything else, even their own lives. That, to me, is scary." Then he went on to recount a story of his American friend's family:

> Last month, [in March], when schools started to close down and the virus already had brought many deaths in New York, my friend's grandmother, who was over 80 years old, still decided to travel to Florida, just for fun. Her family tried to stop her, but to no avail. She said: "I lived to this age to enjoy my freedom, not to be afraid." She indeed got on the plane, without a mask. When I heard about this, I was really shocked and scared. I feel very insecure here in America.... I want to go home.

Indeed, he returned to China in June, after his whole family, including his parents and himself, spent numerous hours trying to snap up air tickets, which were extremely hard to get and cost ten times more than the regular price. This sentiment of fear and insecurity is shared by all the participants in the second cohort of the study.

Granted, all people living in the pandemic more or less shared the same feelings of fear, isolation, and confusion. However, for Chinese international students, this fear was magnified through a cross-cultural and cross-national lens. For example, Cathy, from the provincial city of Changsha in Hunan Province, studied at the University of Washington in Seattle. She described her observations about life in China and the United States in May 2020: "When I woke up every day, I saw from my social media feed that my friends in China [were] dining out, traveling, and having fun. China has pretty much controlled the virus, but here [in the United States], the virus is out of control. I read news about the funeral homes in NYC struggled to keep up. It makes me very scared and sad." Other students we interviewed tried to interpret this fear from different perspectives to understand death. Andy was a visiting student at Harvard, from a liberal arts college, and he said: "In China, my hometown had one case, and then the whole city and the province were mobilized to do contact tracing, and everything else . . . but here Americans seem to not be afraid of death. Is that [because of] religion? Americans are more religious than Chinese. Those religious people believe that their death is a call from God, so they are not afraid."

Some Chinese students noted the irony that some Americans did not trust in science, though they lived in a country that boasts the strongest science and technology in the world. Tim, a Nanjing native, who studied at Tulane University, described his discovery: "They [Americans] do not listen to experts. This pandemic let me for the first time realize that many Americans do not trust science, and President Trump is the best example. Science shows that masks are important, yet people still feel free not to trust science and not to wear masks, but to believe their gut instinct of not wearing masks. As a science major, I find this totally ridiculous and frightening." Tim is a biochemistry major, and he was initially attracted by the prestige of American science and medical fields. This pandemic has made him realize for the first time that some of the American public and politicians are anti-science.[48] This new discovery has understandably shocked him and let him question the American status of leaders of science in the world.

"Freedom means selfishness."

Other than feeling fearful and frightened, some Chinese students were angry because they perceived that the freedom some Americans value, in practice, is merely a reflection of their disregard for collective well-being and that they are solely interested in their personal preferences and convenience. Jane, a Shanghai native, now studying at Ohio State University, was aghast at the behavior of some Americans in the pandemic: "I used to think that Americans have better *suzhi* [quality] than the Chinese. Now, I do not think so. Some Americans just feel that they are free to do whatever they want, even in the pandemic. I saw [in the] news that a man refused to wear a mask to enter the grocery store, and when he was stopped at the entrance by the worker at the grocery store, the man even hit the worker. Is this to fight for freedom? This is a selfish thug." That Chinese students associate freedom with selfishness gets at the core of the issue of personal freedom at the expense of others' well-being. Chinese students associate this link squarely with American culture. As Emily at Syracuse University put it, "I think this has much to do with American culture. People are very individualistic. Americans are not as social as Chinese who care more about others. Chinese put others and collectivist interest in front of self." Emily gave an example of Wuhan: "Residents in Wuhan went through huge sacrifice for the first several months of the virus outbreak, and they did not leave their apartments, and [the] neighborhood organized to deliver food to their apartments. It takes individual sacrifice to control this [pandemic]."

Amy, at University of California, Irving, was very frustrated with President Trump's decision to leave the World Health Organization: "I just could not understand why Trump left the WHO, in the middle of the pandemic. Excuse me? American leaders seem to feel that they can do whatever they want, but in my eyes, that is not assuming responsibility. That is selfish." However, when asked how she felt about her home country's policy toward international students like her, and she acknowledged the difficulty of the "Five One" travel policy in her own life, she showed a nuanced understanding: "Yes, getting a ticket is hard as hell. But I have no complaints that my country [China] shut its door. I think it is right that the government wants to keep the 1.4 billion people's lives safe and secure. I understand my government's decision to protect Chinese within its borders. But I do not understand the American government's many decisions. I do not understand why Trump discourages Americans from wearing masks. I just do not understand." Her anger toward the American government is palpable, so much so that she started to question her previous decision to come to America. She attributed her study-abroad decision to her father, who according to her "has a fantasy about the U.S. being the best country in the world." Her father's fantasy was dashed by her experience in America, particularly living through the period of COVID. According to Amy, her father used to push her to stay in the United States and become an immigrant, but after this pandemic, "He is no longer insisting that."

"Freedom is good, but . . ."

When Chinese students recognized all the problems associated with individual freedom in America and attributed the failure of pandemic management to the freedom Americans do not want to give up, I gently asked them, "So what about the upside of freedom that brought you to America in the first place?"

The responses followed the line of "freedom is good, but . . ." For instance, Joey, a Nanjing native, originally landed in a second-tier public university in the Midwest, and within a year he transferred to Johns Hopkins University, a move he could not imagine the Chinese system would ever allow: "Yes, I love the freedom to transfer schools, and that is the advantage of the American education system. But the personal freedom Americans have is just too much. How can you choose not to wear mask? You are going to infect others."

Craig, a Suzhou native, was studying at South Dakota State University. During the pandemic, he was living alone and felt quite lonely. He has a self-described passive personality, which affected his social life:

> I do not have American friends here, and I live in Pacific Time, playing video games with my Chinese friends online. I enjoy the freedom here. I mean, nobody, my parents are not watching me and I can do whatever I want. But I watched the news and our [South Dakota] governor said that it is a personal choice to wear masks or not, and she will not rob people's freedom to choose. Come on . . . I disagree with that. That is just crazy to think that it is a personal freedom to wear a mask. As a governor, she is totally crazy in saying that. . . . [T]he consequence is that our state has skyrocketing cases.

During this pandemic, Chinese students broadly shared the sentiment that they enjoy the freedom here, but the way that some Americans understand personal freedom is an extreme, which causes them enormous fear and anxiety. Some students extended their discomfort with the American notions of freedom to the *suzhi* (quality) of the American people. Amy, at University of California, Irving, offered her troubling perceptions of some Americans: "The American public are not as educated as I used to believe. Their *suzhi* is worrisome. That is why when Trump asked them not to wear masks, they will NOT wear a mask; when Trump suggests [to] them to use disinfectant to treat the virus, some did believe in it, no matter how ridiculous it is." She later concluded how this new understanding of the American public during this pandemic has influenced her life: "If anything, this experience [of COVID] in America made me realize that I never want to live in the U.S. in the future." Despite Amy's deep disappointment, she still planned to complete her studies at her university and then apply to graduate school here in the United States. She even had a very specific goal: to earn a master's degree in human-computer interaction at Carnegie Mellon University. When I asked her why, she offered a rationale that was largely pragmatic: "I am determined to complete my education with bachelor's and master's degrees in the United States. No matter how much I dislike this country, I need to make good use of my education. I will not drop out. I think undergraduate education is not enough for me to get a good job in China. I will need to work in China, and a graduate degree from a good university is important." Amy's point is broadly shared by members of the second cohort. As much as they were troubled by the behaviors and choices of Americans during this pandemic, they were determined to complete their studies in the United States so that they could land a good job in China.

Discussion and Conclusion

This chapter compares narratives of freedom expressed by Chinese students before and after COVID-19 hit in 2020. It presents evidence that the 2020 COVID-19 pandemic has created a watershed moment for Chinese students in the United States in terms of narratives of freedom, which have shifted from appreciating and enjoying personal freedom to questioning and criticizing the excessive nature of freedom as practiced in America. This shift is monumental, shaping a new view of America among the generation of Chinese youth who were often born around or after the turn of the century.

Before the pandemic, they associated freedom with abundance of choice and a respect for individuality, which is what primarily draws Chinese students to America. They experience freedom in choosing a college, academic courses, diverse extracurricular activities, and a lifestyle. Ultimately, they enjoy freedom in being away from parents and the repressive test-oriented education system in China. Some students equate the notion of freedom in American education with American values. In this sense, it is not just American education that is attractive, but American liberal values that prize personal freedom.

After the pandemic hit, freedom has taken on a different set of meanings in the eyes of these Chinese students. When they tried to make sense of why Americans were resistant to mask wearing, and when they compared the different approaches the Chinese and American governments have taken in this pandemic and their outcomes, they described the American pursuit of freedom as a barrier that hindered the American government from controlling the pandemic. In sum, a narrative of America's prioritizing of individual freedom over collective well-being emerges, which Chinese students express in a range of attitudes, from confusion to straightforward disapproval. They often associated the American failure to control the pandemic with the American value of freedom. In this case, the notion of freedom was problematized, or even blamed, rather than admired and enjoyed, as it had been before the pandemic.

On the other hand, Chinese students interpret their home country's handling of the pandemic from the standpoint of a narrative of sacrifice for the sake of collective good. They describe how one city—Wuhan—went through a huge sacrifice so that the whole country would be spared from a catastrophic infection. They understand China's stringent travel policies that even place them—Chinese citizens overseas—under enormous restrictions to enter their home country. They point to the Chinese cultural value of placing collective benefit ahead of individual freedom as a factor in China's successful control of the pandemic.

Notably, the data collection ended in 2021, which captures the period of this Chinese triumphalism;[49] Chinese students overwhelmingly endorse their home country's success in managing the pandemic, while lamenting the American government's failure. This potentially provides fertile ground for rising nationalistic sentiments among Chinese youth overseas who simultaneously embody and pursue cosmopolitanism. This chapter contributes to the literature on cosmopolitanism and nationalism. In the case of these Chinese international students, freedom was construed as an integral component of cosmopolitism. Before the pandemic, this understanding of freedom was valorized and desirable. During the pandemic, Chinese international students reconstructed the narrative in a new way, one associated with fear and selfishness. Chinese international students, as a group of transnational elites, have nonetheless experienced enormous stigmatization and marginalization and face Sinophobia and anti-Asian racism. Once aspiring to acquire flexible citizenship and straddle the best of two worlds, Chinese international students have started to worry about their decision to study in the United States, far away from their parents and home country, experiencing the pandemic at the mercy of the U.S.-China geopolitical volatility. Chinese students overseas have always tried to strike the delicate balance between cosmopolitanism and nationalism, and this chapter presents new evidence that this pandemic has created circumstances that nationalism may trump cosmopolitism, as shown by Chinese students' skepticism of the American notions of freedom they previously sought and enjoyed.

Questions remain as to whether the pre-COVID themes of freedom will come back. While China managed to control the pandemic in 2020 and 2021 with its stringent zero-COVID policy, the highly infectious Omicron variant made the zero-COVID policy unsustainable in 2022, which could have once again changed the narratives on freedom. The massive lockdowns in Xi'an, Shanghai, and Chengdu, among many other cities and towns in China have restricted people at home and deprived people's opportunities to work, socialize, and even get treated for illnesses.[50] The mandatory quarantine policies inflicted much pain on ordinary citizens and even elites of Chinese society, which has led to the widespread protests in dozens of cities in November 2022. During the protests, Chinese youth took to the streets and demanded freedom. In other words, the Chinese triumphalism experienced a slap in the face in late 2022. This could have impacted the change of attitudes among Chinese international students and their narratives on freedom as well. How have their attitudes shifted, and how do they make sense of their changed narratives? Will Chinese students continue to associate freedom with insecurity and selfishness and take that shift into account when they deliberate over whether to study in the United States in the future? Answers to these questions tap into the broader question of how the responses to this pandemic in the United States and China affect the opportunity structures and the perceptions of each country. Future studies can follow up with new data from 2022 onward about Chinese student mobility, which may shed light on the above questions.

NOTES

1. Sabrina Tavernise and Richard A. Oppel Jr., "Spit On, Yelled At, Attacked: Chinese-Americans Fear for Their Safety," *New York Times*, March 23, 2020.
2. Rick Gladstone, "How the Cold War between China and U.S. Is Intensifying," *New York Times*, July 22, 2020.
3. Minxin Pei, "COVID 19 Is Finishing Off the Sino American Relationship," *Project Syndicate*, April 29, 2020.
4. Susan L. Shirk, "'Playing to the Provinces': Deng Xiaoping's Political Strategy of Economic Reform," *Studies in Comparative Communism* 23, no. 3–4 (1990): 227–258; Vanessa Fong, *Paradise Redefined: Transnational Chinese Students and the Quest for Flexible Citizenship in the Developed World* (Stanford: Stanford University Press, 2011); Yingyi Ma, *Ambitious and Anxious: How Chinese College Students Succeed and Struggle in American Higher Education* (New York: Columbia University Press, 2020).
5. Alexandra Stevenson and Tiffany May, "Coronavirus Strands China's Students, in a Dilemma for Beijing," *New York Times*, April 5, 2020.
6. Yang Hu, Cora Lingling Xu, and Mengwei Tu, "Family-mediated Migration Infrastructure: Chinese International Students and Parents Navigating (Im)mobilities during the COVID-19 Pandemic," *Chinese Sociological Review* (2020): 1–26.

7. Edward Wong and Julian E. Barnes, "U.S. to Expel Chinese Graduate Students with Ties to China's Military Schools," *New York Times*, May 28, 2020.
8. Michael D. Shear and Miriam Jordan, "Trump Suspends Visas Allowing Hundreds of Thousands of Foreigners to Work in the U.S.," *New York Times*, June 22, 2020.
9. Yingyi Ma and Ning Zhan, "To Mask or Not to Mask amid the COVID-19 Pandemic: How Chinese Students in America Experience and Cope with Stigma," *Chinese Sociological Review* (2020): 1–26; Hu, Xu, and Tu, "Family-Mediated Migration Infrastructure."
10. Cary Wu, Yue Qian, and Rima Wilkes. "Anti-Asian Discrimination and the Asian-White Mental Health Gap during COVID-19," *Ethnic and Racial Studies* 44, no. 5 (2021): 819–835; Chuang Wang, Jian Wang, and Miranda Lin, "COVID-19 and Asian Phobia: Anti-Asian Racism and Model Minority Myth." *New Waves* 24, no. 2 (2021): i–vi.
11. This research for both the pre-pandemic and during the pandemic was approved by Syracuse University Institutional Review Board.
12. Geert Hofstede, Gert Jan Hofstede, and Michael Minkov, *Cultures and Organizations: Software of the Mind: Intercultural Cooperation and Its Importance for Survival* (New York: McGraw-Hill, 2010).
13. Liza G. Steele and Scott M. Lynch, "The Pursuit of Happiness in China: Individualism, Collectivism, and Subjective Well-being during China's Economic and Social Transformation," *Social Indicators Research* 114, no. 2 (2013): 441–451; Yunxiang Yan, "The Chinese Path to Individualization," *British Journal of Sociology* 61, no. 3 (September 2010): 489–512.
14. Jin Li, *Cultural Foundations of Learning: East and West* (Cambridge: Cambridge University Press, 2012).
15. Shuning Liu, *Neoliberalism, Globalization, and "Elite" Education in China: Becoming International* (London: Routledge, 2020); Qi Long and Rui Wang, "The Current Development of the International Class Created by Chinese High Schools in Nanjing [in Chinese]," *Shanghai Research on Education* 5 (2013): 31–34.
16. Ye Liu, *Higher Education, Meritocracy and Inequality in China* (Singapore: Springer, 2016); Jeannie Oakes, *Keeping Track: How Schools Structure Inequality* (New Haven: Yale University Press, 2005).
17. Yingyi Ma, "Is the Grass Greener on the Other Side of the Pacific?," *Contexts* 14, no. 2 (2015): 34–39; Ma, *Ambitious and Anxious*.
18. Jeannie Oakes, *Keeping Track: How Schools Structure Inequality* (New Haven, CT: Yale University Press, 2005); Mitchell L. Stevens, *Creating a Class: College Admissions and the Education of Elites* (Cambridge: Harvard University Press, 2009).
19. Baoyan Cheng, Le Lin, and Aiai Fan, *The New Journey to the West: Chinese Students' International Mobility* (Singapore: Springer, 2020).

20. Liu, *Higher Education, Meritocracy and Inequality in China*.
21. Yingyi Ma and Lifang Wang, "Fairness in Admission: Voices from Rural Chinese Female Students in Selective Universities in Chinese Mainland," *Frontiers of Education in China* 11 (2016): 44–73; Shuning Liu, "Neoliberal Global Assemblages: The Emergence of 'Public' International High-School Curriculum Programs in China," *Curriculum Inquiry* 48, no. 2 (2018): 203–219.
22. Ma, "Is the Grass Greener on the Other Side of the Pacific?"; Li, *Cultural Foundations of Learning: East and West*.
23. Stevens, *Creating a Class*, 185.
24. Andrew B. Kipnis. *Governing Educational Desire: Culture, Politics, and Schooling in China* (Chicago: University of Chicago Press, 2011); Ma, *Ambitious and Anxious*.
25. Hiroki Igarashi and Hiro Saito, "Cosmopolitanism as Cultural Capital: Exploring the Intersection of Globalization, Education and Stratification," *Cultural Sociology* 8, no. 3 (2014): 222–239.
26. Don Weenink, "Cosmopolitan and Established Resources of Power in the Education Arena," *International Sociology* 22, no. 4 (2007): 492–516; Don Weenink, "Cosmopolitanism as a Form of Capital: Parents Preparing their Children for a Globalizing World," *Sociology* 42, no. 6 (2008): 1089–1106.
27. Catherine Montgomery and Liz McDowell, "Social Networks and the International Student Experience: An International Community of Practice?," *Journal of Studies in International Education* 13, no. 4 (2009): 455–466; Ma, *Ambitious and Anxious*.
28. Jonathan Friedman, "Americans Again, or the New Age of Imperial Reason?: Global Elite Formation, Its Identity and Ideological Discourses," *Theory, Culture & Society* 17, no. 1 (2000): 139–146; Leslie Sklair, *The Transnational Capitalist Class* (Oxford: Blackwell, 2001).
29. Salvatore Babones, "China's Middle Class Is Pulling Up the Ladder Behind Itself," *Foreign Policy*, February 1, 2018; Yan, "The Chinese Path to Individualization."
30. Liu, *Neoliberalism, Globalization, and "Elite" Education in China*; Ma, *Ambitious and Anxious*.
31. Vanessa Fong, *Paradise Redefined: Transnational Chinese Students and the Quest for Flexible Citizenship in the Developed World* (Stanford: Stanford University Press, 2011), 196–197.
32. Ulrich Beck, *Cosmopolitan Vision* (Cambridge: Polity Press, 2006), 62.
33. Dingxin Zhao, "Student Nationalism in China," *Problems of Post-Communism* 49, no. 6 (2002): 16–28.
34. Yasheng Huang, *Capitalism with Chinese Characteristics: Entrepreneurship and the State* (Cambridge: Cambridge University Press, 2008).

35. Siqi Tu, "Destination Diploma: How Chinese Urban Upper-Middle-Class Families 'Outsource' Secondary Education to the United States" (PhD diss., The Graduate Center, City University of New York, 2020).
36. Vanessa Fong, "Filial Nationalism among Chinese Teenagers with Global Identities," *American Ethnologist* 31, no. 4 (2004): 631–648.
37. Fong, "Filial Nationalism among Chinese Teenagers with Global Identities"; Peter Hayes Gries, "Tears of Rage: Chinese Nationalist Reactions to the Belgrade Embassy Bombing," *China Journal* 46 (July 2001): 25–43.
38. Zheng Wang, "National Humiliation, History Education, and the Politics of Historical Memory: Patriotic Education Campaign in China," *International Studies Quarterly* 52, no. 4 (December 2008): 783–806.
39. Stephen J. Hartnett, "Google and the 'Twisted Cyber Spy' Affair: U.S.-China Communication in an Age of Globalization," *Quarterly Journal of Speech* 97 (2011): 411–434.
40. Pál Nyíri, Juan Zhang, and Merriden Varrall, "China's Cosmopolitan Nationalists: 'Heroes' and 'Traitors' of the 2008 Olympics," *China Journal*, no. 63 (January 2010): 25–55.
41. Elizabeth Redden, "The Chinese Student Threat?," *Inside Higher Ed*, February 15, 2018.
42. Ma and Zhan, "To Mask or Not to Mask Amid the COVID-19 Pandemic."
43. Jenny Lee, ed., *U.S. Power in International Higher Education* (New Brunswick, NJ: Rutgers University Press, 2021).
44. Yi Zhang. "An Overlooked Population in Community College: International Students' (In)Validation Experiences with Academic Advising," *Community College Review* 44.2 (2016): 153–170.
45. Lauren Schudde and Sara Goldrick-Rab, "On Second Chances and Stratification: How Sociologists Think about Community Colleges," *Community College Review* 43, no. 1: 27–45.
46. Ma, *Ambitious and Anxious*.
47. Yuanyuan Wang et al., "Discrimination against LGBT populations in China," *Lancet Public Health* 4, no. 9 (2019): e440–e441.
48. This is true even though the majority of Americans do have some confidence in science and scientists. Brian Kennedy, Alec Tyson, and Cary Funk, "Americans' Trust in Scientists, Other Groups Declines," Pew Research Center, https://www.pewresearch.org/science/2022/02/15/americans-trust-in-scientists-other-groups-declines/.
49. Guobin Yang, *The Wuhan Lockdown* (New York: Columbia University Press, 2022).
50. ChinaFile, "Shanghai's Lockdown: A ChinaFile Conversation" (2022), https://www.chinafile.com.

Cosmopolitan Imperative or Nationalist Sentiment?

Mediated Experiences of the COVID-19 Pandemic among Chinese Overseas Students

Bingchun Meng, Zifeng Chen, and Veronica Jingyi Wang

IN FEBRUARY 2020, WHEN COVID-19 WAS YET TO BE DECLARED A GLOBAL PANDEMIC, but the Chinese city of Wuhan was already under strict lockdown, a twenty-three-year-old Singaporean student named Jonathan Mok was attacked on the busy Oxford Street in Central London. Mok described the attack as brutal and racially motivated in his Facebook post: "The guy who tried to kick me then said, 'I don't want your coronavirus in my country,' before swinging another sucker punch at me, which resulted in my face exploding with blood."[1]

In April the same year, only a few days after lockdown measures in Wuhan were lifted, international media reported on the widespread anti-African racism in the Southern Chinese metropolis of Guangzhou. The fear of imported coronavirus cases stoked anti-foreigner sentiments. African migrants living in Guangzhou had been evicted from their homes by landlords and turned away from hotels, despite many claiming to have had no recent travel history. The news media coverage of these incidents triggered a diplomatic crisis that compelled Chinese authorities to take a public stance against racism and racial discrimination.[2]

In May 2020, as Black Lives Matter protests took place around the world in the wake of the murder of George Floyd, a group of Chinese students at the London School of Economics and Political Science (LSE) and other U.K. universities wanted to show solidarity with black students by starting a Facebook group called Chinese Students for BLM. Some of the organizers of the group, however, were told rather disparagingly by their friends from African countries that they were in no position to offer solidarity given what was happening in Guangzhou.

This series of incidents captures the conflicting states of mind and the emotional struggles of overseas Chinese students during the COVID-19 pandemic. As the epicenter of the pandemic shifted from China to Europe and North America in 2020, Chinese overseas students studying in these two regions on the one hand encountered increasing racial abuse and xenophobia, while on the other hand tried to negotiate with polarizing discourses on COVID-19 across multiple media platforms. What have been the lived experiences of Chinese overseas students during the COVID-19 pandemic, especially in relation to racism, xenophobia, and nationalism? What are the main discrepancies and incongruities that Chinese overseas students have to negotiate within their mediated understanding of the crisis? Has their assessment of the political systems both in China and in their host countries been in any way affected by the pandemic? These are the questions we intended to address when conducting in-depth interviews with university students studying in the U.K. and the U.S.

By attending to their fraught experiences of navigating racially charged political tensions during the pandemic, the study we conducted pursued two aims. First, it investigated how Chinese students studying in U.K. and U.S. universities experienced the COVID-19 pandemic at both a personal level in their daily lives and a discursive level through media coverage. Second, it explored how the mediated understanding of this global crisis contributed to a critical conjuncture prompting an elite group of Chinese youth to reassess and reformulate their views of the contemporary geopolitical order.

Conceptually, we draw inspiration from the social theory of risk society, from the analysis developed by Stuart Hall, and from theories of mediated identity formation and articulation. While the COVID-19 pandemic is a quintessential example of the kind of global risk that Ulrich Beck initially theorized three decades ago, public perceptions of the current crisis are heavily splintered, leading to great ambiguity over the prospect of cosmopolitan cooperation, which Beck considered the only sensible way for humanity to move forward. Aside from emphasizing the pivotal role of the mass media in staging the visibility of global events, however, Beck falls short in analyzing the communicative process that could lead either to stronger collaboration or to deeper antagonism.[3] This is where we seek to make a contribution, by bringing in insights from media and communication research to investigate how sense is now made of global risk by an elite group that epitomizes mobility and connectivity. The questions we examine through interview data shed light on broader debates about how the diaspora population negotiates its national identity and political allegiance, and how individuals navigate incongruence and uncertainty by piecing together varied discursive resources in their efforts to articulate a coherent narrative.[4]

Global Risk at a Moment of Hegemonic Crisis

By emphasizing the constructed and contested nature of knowledge, Beck ascribes great importance to media and communication in his theory of risk society.[5] As social constructions, risks are not defined in terms of damages incurred, but of perceptions of the intermediate state between security and destruction.[6] Such perceptions are shaped not only by information but also by the discursive frames put forward through various media outlets, which themselves are socially and politically embedded. Once global risks are staged in the media, they become "cosmopolitan events" that have the potential to produce an "imagined cosmopolitan community."[7] But Beck was careful to separate the normative connotations of cosmopolitanism from the analytical usage of the concept. While the media do raise awareness that "the global other is in our midst,"[8] uncertainty about a shared future could very well lead to renationalization and re-ethnicization, rather than to empathy and cooperation. While the anticipation of global risks could result in an "everyday global awareness" among citizens of modern societies and give rise to "the cosmopolitan imperative" of cooperation, the normative cosmopolitanism of a world without borders is far from guaranteed.

Taking the cue of a "cosmopolitan turn" from Beck, media scholars have critically evaluated the prospect of cultivating "citizens of the world"—the literal meaning of the word "cosmopolitan"—through the lens of media representation and media consumption. A good deal of research has been done on journalistic coverage of global events, especially disasters, conflicts, and distant suffering.[9] By analyzing the modalities and discursive strategies deployed in news coverage, scholars have cautioned against the estrangement and division that could result from the staging of global risks by media institutions, which do not always live up to their moral and ethical responsibilities. While digital technologies and convergent media platforms contribute to new modes of witnessing, they do not necessarily alter the fundamental logic that underpins news representation.[10]

Those who focus on the lived experience of media users, on the other hand, have examined how different populations develop an understanding of the other, either distant or adjacent, through their consumption of media content and their deployment of communication technologies. Two insights that emerge from this body of literature are particularly relevant to this chapter. First, audiences located at different positions on the social-economic ladder have varied perspectives and differing capacities in relation to cosmopolitan events.[11] Since "media and communications are spaces where identities are mobilized and to a great extent shaped,"[12] media coverage of global risk is not just providing citizens with information but is inherently a discursive space open to contestation. Second, as much as global risks are now heavily mediated, banal cross-cultural encounters in non-mediated contexts still play an important role in configuring the possibility of empathy and cooperation, especially at a time of uncertainty and adversity.[13] For example, based on ethnographic research with Kurdish youth in London, Kevin Smets argues that diasporic cosmopolitanism is not so much anchored around ethnic media as it is embedded in daily interactions across ethnic groups.[14]

Although our project builds on the aforementioned debates, our core concern is more with capturing overseas Chinese students' meaning making at a moment of crisis, rather than with identifying the "cosmopolitan imperatives" among those who happened to be living abroad during the COVID-19 pandemic. *Conjuncture* is a concept initially developed by Antonio Gramsci and Louis Althusser that designates "a specific moment in the life of a social formation and refers to a period when the antagonism and contradictions which are always at work in society, begin to '*fuse*' into a '*ruptural unity*.'"[15] In their now classic work delineating the ascendence of popular authoritarianism in the U.K., Hall and his colleagues deployed "conjunctural analysis . . . based on a distinction between moments of relative stability and those of intensifying struggles and unrest, which may result in a more general social crisis."[16] For overseas Chinese students, the crisis is three-fold. First and foremost, it is a public health crisis that demands high-level cognitive efforts from individuals when making difficult decisions while having limited information. University students are no doubt in a privileged position in terms of information access and information literacy. But, just like many other crises (e.g., ecological and financial) of what Beck calls "second modernity," the COVID-19 pandemic is yet another example of non-linear knowledge production fraught with dissent and conflicts.[17] For one thing, there is hardly any *expert consensus* on either the origin of the virus or the handling of the pandemic. For another, this symbiosis of knowledge and unawareness results in unintended consequences and in uncertainty, which means that the availability of more information does not necessarily lead to better decision making in ameliorating risk. Further, the erosion of trust in scientific expertise and technical controllability has led to the politicization of even the most basic public health advice, such as on mask wearing, not to mention the even more contested issue of vaccination.

Second, the pandemic also brought a crisis of life-planning and personal identity. Unlike diaspora populations, whose media consumption has been studied extensively,[18] students studying abroad have a rather transient relationship with the host country and only sporadic interaction with its wider society. As the pandemic disrupts their study and halts the mobility they previously took for granted, these students are compelled to think long and hard about where they want to be in the near future. Explicitly or implicitly embroiled in such practical considerations is the issue of identity and belonging. As the tension between "us" and "them" escalated, and as latent discrimination became blatant at a time of fear and anxiety, many students redrew their post-study plans of whether to stay in the host country. Their limited connection with life beyond the university setting means that they relied more on mediated forms of communication in order to evaluate the situation with the pandemic and to make sense of the world around them.

In addition to being a crisis of scientific rationality and personal identity, the COVID-19 pandemic epitomizes the crisis of a global hegemonic order. In countries like the U.S. and the U.K., continuing cuts in public spending and erosion of welfare provision have driven the underprivileged even further down the social-economic ladder. The Brexit referendum in 2016 and the election of Donald Trump later that year were only two of the most spectacular revelations of the deep resentment that many in the West feel toward neoliberal globalization. The pandemic thus threw into spotlight the deep-seated social-economic inequality and political-cultural polarization at both national and international levels. The significant variation in different countries' approaches to combating the pandemic (especially that between China and the U.S. and between China and the U.K.), the divergent views in many liberal democratic societies regarding the credibility of scientists and political elites, the intensifying racial discrimination in host countries, and the escalating geopolitical tensions between China and the West, all point to the "exhaustion of consent" that is indicative of a crisis of hegemony.[19] When even basic facts about the origin and nature of the virus were heavily contested in popular discourse, any narratives of pandemic response unavoidably became politically charged. Such contention and dissonance came as a shock to most overseas Chinese students, who were confronted with cultural, political, and medical landscapes they found challenging to navigate, yet impossible to steer clear of.

Under such circumstances of disorientation, individuals forge moments of what J. D. Slack calls "arbitrary closure" by putting together a narrative with elements that have "no necessary correspondence."[20] This process of meaning making is what cultural studies scholars mean by articulation: "Articulation is the production of identity on top of differences, of unities out of fragments, of structure across practices. Articulation links this practice to that effect, this text to that meaning, this meaning to that reality, this experience to those politics. And these links are themselves articulated into larger structures."[21] In his work along these same lines, Hall emphasizes that because the combination of fragments is an assembled structure and not a set of random associations, "There will be structured relations between its parts, i.e., relations of dominance and subordination."[22] The unique structural positioning of overseas Chinese students shaped their articulation of the conjuncture in important ways, even though there was no straightforward correlation to be drawn between structural conditions and discursive formulations. In this sense, "There is no simple 'event' here to be understood apart from the social processes by which such events are produced, perceived, classified, explained and responded to."[23] Our research participants mobilize the discursive and ideological resources at their disposal to make sense of the profoundly disorienting COVID-19 pandemic. While there is no direct correspondence between the oft-disjointed events in life and their interpretation of those events, Chinese overseas students' articulation at this moment of compounded crisis is both structurally conditioned by the broader geopolitical context and dynamically formulated through daily encounter with media and interpersonal communication.

Notes on Methodology

We used purposive snowball sampling to recruit a total of forty-five Chinese students studying in U.S. and U.K. universities in the autumn of 2020, which is when we conducted most of the interviews. In order to maximize the diversity of our sample and to strive for the saturation of interview data, we made sure there was a balanced distribution across key demographic factors, including gender (twenty-four male students, twenty-one female students), current location (twenty-four students studying in the U.K. and twenty-one in the U.S.), area of study (sixteen majoring in science and engineering, seventeen majoring in social sciences or humanities, twelve majoring business or management), and length of overseas study (twenty had spent less than five years studying overseas, while twenty-five had spent five or more years studying overseas, which often included part of their secondary education). One caveat is that we initially aimed to recruit interviewees from both elite and non-elite universities, but ended up with the majority coming from top U.K. and U.S. institutions. This was likely due to the bias of our own social networks, and it potentially leads to a further elitist bent in the data.[24]

The interview-topic guide was comprised of three sections, with seven questions in each section and a closing question soliciting further comments in an open-ended way. The first section focused on pre-pandemic life-plan and political views. The second section centered around media usage, especially the consumption of news content. The last section asked more personal questions about mediated experience during the pandemic, with a couple of specific questions on national identity and racial politics. Such semi-structured interviews typically last between one and one and a half hours. All the interviews were recorded and transcribed verbatim. We then conducted a first-stage thematic analysis in order to identify clusters of expressions and common narratives. The second stage of data analysis involved teasing out discursive strategies for sustaining the coherence of key narratives and the broader ideological articulations that link the personal with the political.

The Conundrum of Becoming "Private Alternative Experts"

In a piece published in the August 2020 issue of *Foreign Policy*, historian Adam Tooze calls Ulrich Beck "the sociologist who could save us from Coronavirus" because of his prophetic insights on global risk society. Tooze highlights in particular modern individuals' radical dependence on "specialized scientific knowledge" for assessing risk: "The harmful, the threatening, the inimical lies in wait everywhere, but whether it is inimical or friendly is 'beyond one's own power of judgment.' We thus face a double shock: a threat to our health and survival and a threat to our autonomy in gauging those threats. As we react and struggle to reassert control, we have no option but to 'become small, private alternative experts in risks of modernization.'"[25] To become "private alternative experts" means to take strong initiatives in acquiring information, which is something our research participants were well equipped to do. But this does not necessarily mean they were actual experts on either the pandemic or pandemic responses in different countries. The conundrum of trying to stay informed as individuals during a global crisis is two-fold. First, it adds cognitive and psychological burden to an already stressful situation. Second and more importantly, as knowledge of the crisis becomes so intertwined with one's own positionality, "private alternative experts" end up undermining the "cosmopolitan imperative" of cooperation and collective action.

Our data reveal a generally high level of information literacy and a fairly sophisticated pattern of media consumption. Not only did the students take great care in curating their daily media diet, they were often able to compare different news outlets or media platforms when this was probed during the interviews. They were critical of institutional media from both Chinese and Western media, but even more so of the U.S. and U.K. media, probably because they take as a given that mainstream media in China is heavily censored. Many of them also showed a nuanced understanding of social media platforms in China when discussing which was a more reliable source for certain types of information. Here are some examples:

What they reported are all filtered, biased information; the same goes for Chinese media. It is as if the world only allows black and white, no gray area in between. (LXW, male, science major, U.S.)

I don't normally watch BBC news, 'coz I feel there is something fake about it. I watch Phoenix TV more for international news. And I use Weibo for getting news in China. Maybe this is a generational thing; I think my generation tends to use Weibo a lot. . . . Even British people have issues with BBC, right? I just don't like their general negative tone in reporting on everything, domestic or international news. I understand they think that news reporting needs to be critical, but that's just not how I like it. (ZJW, male, engineering major, U.K.)

I don't like watching CNN or Fox. Nothing interesting. I mainly get news from Reuters; they just do reporting without offering you an explanation or try[ing] to sway your opinion with catchy titles. . . . I read the *Washington Post* and *New York*

Times as well. Sometimes I watch RT. RT is actually quite interesting. (TZH, male, social science major, U.S.)

Some of the students majoring in bioscience or medical science tended to gather data-driven scientific evidence from experts in their field. For example, SC is a PhD student in Structural Biology at a research institute in the U.S. She started following more scientists' Twitter accounts during the pandemic, including checking on genome sequencing data and monitoring the latest release of initial research results. But even with this level of information literacy, they did not necessarily feel that easy access to multiple sources had enabled them to make better-informed decisions. On the contrary, daily curation of media consumption was often deployed as a protective mechanism to shield themselves from negative feelings such as anger, distress, or anxiety:

There was a period of time [when] I got so depressed by those anti-China comments on Tik Tok and Twitter, I had to switch off. Just didn't want to take in those anymore. (LZY, male, engineering major, U.S.)

I remember back in April, May [2020], I almost stopped using Facebook or Twitter. I just felt reading news, any type of news, is emotionally draining. At first I looked for all sorts of reports and data about the pandemic. Then I just couldn't take it anymore.... I stopped expecting too much. It's like, I just wanted to stay alive and that's it. (DSJ, female, social science major, U.K.)

In this sense, there were no such thing as global media cultivating an imagined community through the staging of a common disaster. Rather, as the global health crisis deepened, many of our interviewees started to believe that perceptions of the crisis had less to do with what information you acquired and more to do with who you are.

The mask issue is the most absurd one. Even one of my professors, he is a well-educated person and normally very sensible. At the beginning all the media in the U.S. were saying it's useless to wear a mask. So my professor actually went to check with his colleague in the medical school, and because the anti-mask view propagated by the media was so strong, these two scientists became unsure. They said, oh well, maybe [a] mask is not that useful after all. (JH, male, science major, U.S.)

The lack of a common understanding of risk is closely linked with the individualization of responsibility. At times when our interviewees felt most fragile or helpless, the exhortation to become private experts could even lead to resentment. Such resentment is not directed toward specific individuals or entities, but is more of a general frustration over uncertainty and grievance against the "inhumane system." DSJ recalled her experience at the Amsterdam airport, when she was told there was an issue with her PCR test result, which meant she could not get on the connecting flight to Shanghai.

> They said I didn't have a valid QR code to board that plane, and because I have a Chinese passport I will need the QR code. I don't know why, but as soon as I heard that I just had a meltdown. I burst into tears in front of so many people. Maybe it was just the stress accumulated over the days leading up to that trip.... I felt all these costs, the stress, the anxiety, they were all falling on the shoulders of individuals. Yes, we sometimes help each other, but ultimately it's all down to individual responsibility. We spend time, money, and we manage our emotions, all as individuals. Even then, we don't always get the outcome we wanted. And I am not just talking about overseas students. I know we already have more resources than some other groups. What about those people who don't have the resources to take individual responsibility for everything? Shouldn't there be something bigger to support them? (DSJ, female, social science major, U.K.)

Socioeconomically and intellectually, these overseas students are members of global elites who have the cognitive capacity to figure out not only explicit or implicit institutional rules, but also the means and resources to navigate challenges and restrictions brought by the pandemic. In theory, they are better positioned to develop the kind of reflexivity that produces what Beck calls "the reciprocal relation between the public sphere and globality."[26] In reality, the students experienced an acute sense of fragmentation, confusion, and contradiction while living abroad during the pandemic. As much as these feelings were psychologically discomforting and emotionally draining, they also enabled moments of introspection and reflection. In fact, many of our interviewees attributed their political awakening to the experience of studying abroad, often recalling key events that shaped their worldview. This is the theme of the next two sections.

The Personal Is Political: Class, Race and Identity Politics

In this section, we use longer excerpts from three interviews to showcase how our participants developed a more nuanced understanding of race, gender, and class through their lived experience in the host country. In order to better convey the proceeding of a narration, which in itself was an attempt to make sense of past experience, we chose parts of the conversation with minimal interjections from the interviewer.

RK did her undergraduate study at an Ivy League university on the U.S. East Coast before moving to California to pursue a PhD in biology. When asked about her views on class and race, she responded:

> That's a good question. I actually didn't realize I was surrounded by rich White kids before I moved to California. I thought those were just normal Americans, that Americans were all like that. Then I moved to this public university in the UC system, not even the best one in the UC system, right? I guess my major has a pretty good ranking, but overall it is just an ordinary university. Students are all diligent, you know, typical good students. There aren't nearly as many parties here as in my previous school. Students all work hard and they come from ordinary family backgrounds. If you ask about their career plan, they say I want to be a teacher, or a nurse, you know, just common people's career choices. Those kids in my previous school, their aspirations are all, like, I want to be a software engineer, I want to become a doctor, I want to be a lawyer, or join a consulting firm, or become an investment banker. It's only after I moved here did I realize that I used to attend such an elite university...
>
> Back when I was living on the East Coast, in my previous school, race and class are totally intertwined. Those upper-middle-class White kids, they have a dress code. You have to follow that dress code. Like, you have to accessorize your outfit with a Longchamp bag, you need to wear North Face, you wear leggings and UGG boots. You have a cup of Starbucks coffee in your hand, and you wear a scarf. All the women look the same, with their straight hair, everyone the same, no difference. If you were Asian or Black, you still need to follow their dress code in that environment. But here in California, Asian girls are dressed like girls in Asia. That wouldn't be allowed in New York. That kind of cute kawaii style, you know, mini-skirts, flowery pattern, laced dress, stockings—just like what you see in

Japanese manga. I was like, OMG, how dare you dress like that? But it's acceptable here. Because Asian culture is accepted here. You can have your own Asian dress code. (RK, female, science major, U.S.)

There is no doubt that in a state of confusion and frustration, RK resorted to simplification and convenient stereotypes as part of the effort to orient herself. It is equally noteworthy, however, that such strategy is commonly deployed when individuals sense incongruency between their prior assumptions, which often came from media, and their lived experience. The important question here is not how *accurate* or *distorted* RK's view of American society is, but how an individual's understanding of structural conditions is always negotiated through daily encounters, therefore always patchy and constantly shifting.

XR had just finished his post-graduate study in the U.K. and was about to start a new job in China when we interviewed him. Because of his parents' work, he first moved to South Korea in seventh grade, finished middle school there, then did high school and undergraduate study in the U.K. He talked to us about how his notion of "politics" changed after moving to the U.K.

> "I think in China when people talk about politics, it tends to be at the theoretical level, in an abstract way. Like, in the U.K., people may immediately discuss the NHS when they start talking about politics. But in China people argue about all kinds of 'isms,' it's about principles and ideologies. That's very different.
>
> For example, my high-school friends in the U.K. taught me about class. It was a profound learning experience—I finally understood what class structure means in the U.K.... Let me tell you what a typical state school in the U.K. is like. You can leave education at the age of 16: if you choose to, you don't have to stay until the last year of secondary school. You can just get a certificate if you pass the exams and go find a job. In my previous school, only one third stayed for A-level study, which prepares you for university. But only one third of my cohort did A-level and the rest went on to become barbers, plumbers, etc.
>
> I remember clearly something a school friend of mine said to me when I told him I wanted to join the debating club. His comments left a big impression on me. He said, "why do you want to do that? Debating or public speaking is for posh people." Hey, we were not talking about buying a car or purchasing an apartment, for god's sake! We were just talking about public speaking, and he thinks that's posh people stuff. As a working-class kid, he didn't even think he could join that

sort of discussion. I was really shaken by that. This is hard for a Chinese person to understand. In China, regardless of your background, all parents want their children to move up on the social ladder. Nobody just accepts their fate (*renming*). But here people internalize their fate to such [an] extent that it is actually scary.

And I noticed that they are constantly, constantly making all sorts of distinctions in their daily conversation. If you have a certain accent, you are posh; if you use certain products, you are posh. They use this word "posh" a lot, in a sarcastic way, not because they aspire to become posh. That really had a strong impact on me. I just thought, wow, if this is what late capitalism would look like . . . that's bad (XR, male, social science major, UK).

Similar to RK, XR only started to notice and reflect on the politics of everyday life after moving abroad, where, after getting over the initial cultural shocks, he had to navigate the more subtle dissonance between imaginary and reality. XR's observation of how class structure is reinforced through social distinction (for example, the choice of career path, the choice of extracurricular activities, and everyday use of language) echoes some of the insights offered by academic literature on social reproduction in the U.K.[27]

MJ is a humanities major in an elite U.K. university and had been going through an emotionally difficult time when we talked to her. She attributed her depression primarily to her experience with racism and racial discrimination during the pandemic. She said she used to have faith in cultural diversity: "I used to believe that everyone has something to offer and together we make a better world." But recent experiences had converted her "from an idealist to a realist."

My worldview changed a lot in the past year. Putting aside those big events, let me just tell you a few incidents that happened to me, very unpleasant experiences, probably the culprit of my ongoing depression. The first thing is this, I had a boyfriend and he broke up with me about a year ago. I calmly accepted, but didn't understand why. So ten months after we broke up, I had a talk with him. I asked him why. It turned out me being Chinese was a problem for him. It's my ethnicity. His parents often visited him in the university, but they never asked to meet me. I always thought that was a bit weird, but tried to tell myself I was just imagining things . . . I felt that was a fundamental negation of my whole being. I couldn't take it. That was such a big blow. This guy used to tell me that 'the individual comes first and background is not important.' I thought he was a world citizen. I thought I had nothing to worry about. I just believed him. I thought he wouldn't judge me like that. Now I know it was all just a lie of political correctness.

The second incident had to do with a very good friend of mine. We became instant friends shortly after I came here. We are in the same department. I heard through another common friend that this good friend of mine said something really awful. He said to this common American friend of ours that "There are too many Chinese. Everywhere. They are like cockroaches." And when the pandemic first started in China, he said to other friends, "I'm not sure if we should go out with MJ, her parents just came to visit her, I am not sure if they carry the virus." OK, I wouldn't care if people I don't know make this sort of comments. But I thought we were friends. I thought we shared common values.

I became extremely sensitive to racist comments after these experiences. I went to see a therapist, and that helps. She is a gentle White woman. I can trust her. With others, I didn't want to say too much because people might think I was overreacting. But you know there was this period of time, after I found out my ex-boyfriend was a racist, whenever I saw a White guy on the street, I would become agitated. I felt resentful, I couldn't breathe. It's like PTSD. I would even be thinking, are all Asian women just colonial lovers in the eyes of these White men? (MJ, female, humanities major, UK).

MJ's story is one of the most traumatic experiences our interviewees shared with us. The pandemic sharpened the edge of nationalism and racial hierarchy, which intersected for MJ in an intensely painful episode in her romantic relationship. MJ's subsequent shift from "an idealist to a realist" in relation to cosmopolitanism may not be a permanent change of worldview, but her account crystalizes how even the most intimate personal space could be haunted by the specter of structural conditions.

These are just three snapshots from our total of 45 interviews that offer insights into the political awakening of overseas Chinese students, who are often given a crash course on race, class, and identity politics when facing incongruity or conflicts. Building on their carefully managed media consumption and their mediated everyday experiences, our interviewees were continually searching for ways of making sense of the disorienting reality while voicing their discontent with the hegemonic political order. These efforts were by no means coherent or consistent. In fact, the very definition of articulation implies linking elements that do not necessarily belong together.

Critiquing the Hegemonic Order

There has been lots of research in recent years on the rising nationalism among Chinese youth by scholars from political science, international relations, and media studies.[28] While we can easily recognize nationalist sentiments in most of our interviews, the intensity and the expression of nationalism vary. It is understandable that, for Chinese students living overseas in the past two years, the contrast between China and the U.K. or China and the U.S. in handling the pandemic, the thorough politicization of a global health crisis, and the hostility these students have been more likely to experience during this time could all bolster nationalist views. However, what we are more interested in exploring here is how elements of nationalism are combined with various other ideological components to formulate critiques of the contemporary global political order.

As discussed in an earlier section, our interviewees were critical of institutional media in both China and the host country, but made more extensive critical comments on the latter. During our conversations, these critical comments often led to further criticism of the political system in the U.S. or the U.K. They identified individualism and economic rationality as two primary factors driving COVID-related policymaking in Western liberal, democratic countries.

> I initially had a different set of expectations about Western developed countries. I had some wonderful fantasy that is now completely shattered by reality. I didn't expect the situation to become like this, with hundreds of thousands of people getting infected every day in the U.S. Day by day, I just gradually realized, OK, such is the reality. I think their political system led them into this shitty situation. And this also includes people's mindset. . . . They are protesting all the time against lockdown, because it's undermining their individual rights. (YT, male, business major, U.S.)
>
> I was angry when Boris Johnson said in March [2020] that people should be prepared to lose their loved ones. So he doesn't care at all about life; it's so inhumane. It's obvious the only thing he cares about is the economy. It's about

the overall economic interest of the country, not human life. (YN, female, social science, U.K.)

Some interviewees also linked the failure of the U.S. and the U.K. in fighting the pandemic with growing social inequality and erosion of public trust in government.

Now, I used to think that people in the U.S. are better educated than people in China, but not anymore. I kind of feel it's because [American] society has become so polarized? Those at the bottom really didn't receive much education. They can even be very anti-intellectual. (CQ, male, science major, U.S.)

Theoretically speaking, this [U.K.'s government] is supposed to be a better political system, right? But it's missing a lot of elements for the system to function properly. For example, there is no fact-based decision-making. And people don't trust the government anymore. This started years ago, with Brexit, with austerity, with government breaking its promises over and over again. You make a U-turn on so many policy decisions; of course people don't trust you, of course they will demand their individual rights. (YY, female, social science, U.K.)

What is more noteworthy is that, while there were considerable commonalties in their discontent toward the liberal democratic system, the alternative political order our participants imagined was rather divergent. We do not have the space in this chapter to elaborate on the nuance and ambivalence of their critiques, which is often incoherent and patchy. Instead, we group their political views into four strands, and briefly explain each strand, with short quotes from interview transcripts. An important caveat is that, given the qualitative nature of our study, we cannot make claims about these different viewpoints' overall pattern of distribution among overseas Chinese students.

We only met one individual who was a vocal Trump supporter, and he was fully aware that, as a queer person living in New York City, this was an unusual stance to take.

I don't tell many of my friends about this. I know they would probably ostracize me if I do come out as a Trump supporter. But I wouldn't fake any support for Biden either. The more I actively search for information, the more I hate the hypocrisy of Democrats. I used to think they were just being politically correct. But now they disgust me. They are so fake, so hypocritical. If Biden wins, I wouldn't want to stay in the U.S. (YS, male, science major, U.S.)

On the other end of the political spectrum, there is a small handful of participants who explicitly advocated Marxism as an approach to social critique and socialism as a political system. This group is larger than those with Far Right views but, very interestingly, they tended to preface their political commentaries with statements like "I might be in the minority here" or "My view is probably different from the mainstream." CL was doing his undergraduate studies in Japanese language and culture in the U.K. when we interviewed him. He makes anime videos in his spare time and maintains a personal channel on Bilibili, one of the most popular video-sharing platforms in China. Around 2014, a song named "Marxism Kind of Sweet" (*Ma zhe youdian tian*) became a major hit on the Chinese Internet and inspired lots of derivative digital content on Bilibili. CL made a stop-motion anime video about the International Communist Movement, using this song as the soundtrack, and the short video received more than 450,000 views. He was able to provide an unequivocal rationale for his beliefs.

> I am probably an exceptional case, because my views are different from most overseas students. My political view is very clear-cut. I am very much on the Left. I am a Communist. I drew this conclusion after reading some history books, because I think Communism is the direction that human society should be moving toward.... Many socialist countries collapsed at the end, but that's not the fault of socialism per se. Those countries had their own internal problems. So many welfare policies that capitalist countries are now carrying out actually came from socialism. People are all in favor of those policies.

JH was about to finish his undergraduate study in the U.S. when we interviewed him and move back to China to start the prestigious Schwartzman Scholars Program at Tsinghua University. He shared with us his experience with racism in the U.S. and his view of racial tensions.

> Actually, lots of people may disagree with this view of mine. I think there is no such thing as racism. It's all classism, or I should say it's all about socioeconomic inequality. Race only becomes a problem when your class position and your

appearance are linked. In other words, class issues are disguised as race issues. If everyone has the chance to move up on the social ladder regardless of their race, there won't be any issue of racism. . . . Ultimately it [racism] is class conflict. But because there is no real class struggle, the conflict manifests as racial conflict.

The third strand of critical discourse was the most common among our interviewees and, to a large extent, also the most nationalist articulation. For lack of a better term, we call it statist developmentalism, due to its emphasis on economic performance and efficient governance. Discursive elements of this view are easily detectable in our interview transcripts, although they do not always formulate a coherent narrative.

CX is a Wuhan native and was extremely critical of the Western media's reporting on China during the pandemic.

When Wuhan went into lockdown, all the Western media went berserk: oh that's draconian, that's violating human rights. But what did they know? Then they said it's all China's fault for not controlling the pandemic better. We are a country of 1.4 billion people and we ended the pandemic at around 80,000 cases. Your population of 300 million now has more than 5 million cases. Who is to blame? . . . Why are we so efficient in controlling the virus? Because our thoughts and values are unified! Maybe someone would say I have been brainwashed. But I really don't think democracy is necessarily a better system. Think about Brexit. That's the outcome of democracy, right? The value of British Pounds plummeted after Brexit. How is that good for the country? (CX, male, social-science major, U.S.)

Last, there is also an articulation of social democratic values that are critical of neoliberalism in the U.S. and the U.K., as well as of statist developmentalism in China.

Both the U.S. and the U.K. got themselves into this big hole of neoliberalism! These governments are not doing anything during the pandemic. They have such blind faith in the market, in the liberal democratic system. But at this moment of crisis their system is all bullshit! People don't even have enough to eat! My volunteering experience with the NHS taught me a lot about the failure of their system. (XN, female, social science, U.K.)

You know what's the other thing that bothers me now? That Chinese people now think of economic development as the single most important issue. Like nothing else matters, as if productivity is the only useful measurement. I feel a sense of chill whenever I think about this. Shouldn't there be other indicators for a healthy, vibrant society? Economic development and stability cannot be everything. That's just absurd. (YND, female, social science, U.K.)

Conclusion

For all our research participants, leaving China to study abroad has been both enabling and empowering. The "proper distance" these overseas Chinese students are able to maintain with both China and their host country has allowed them to gain new understanding and insights through constant comparing and contrasting of their mediated experiences. As much as living in a foreign land at times of crisis can be particularly distressing, the pandemic has served as a prism through which overseas Chinese students reflect on a host of important issues, including race, class, national identity, and ideological affiliation.

Undoubtedly, our interviewees belong to an elite population that has more resources, both material and intellectual, for mitigating global risk. But even with the resources they have, they often feel powerless, vulnerable, or even resentful of the demands of becoming a "private expert in risks of modernization." Under these circumstances, it seems that the imagined global community that Beck wished global risks could bring about is still on a distant horizon. In fact, some of our interviewees are cognizant of this when contemplating their life plan. They lamented the divisions along racial, class, and national lines that they had observed during the pandemic. They were also anguished by the constant demand to "pick sides" in the increasingly frequent occurrence of contestation. The incidents cited at the beginning of this chapter were only the more extreme cases among countless mundane occurrences that reflect the divisive force of the pandemic.

Instead of witnessing the rise of "cosmopolitan imperatives," what we can identify from our rich interview data are vigorous but fragmented attempts at making sense of a compounded crisis—a crisis at personal, societal, and global levels. As individuals of high-level information literacy living in a media rich environment, overseas Chinese students are constantly negotiating the discrepancy between media narratives and lived experience. Amid the failure of neoliberal globalization and the retreat of liberal democracy, our research participants draw on a range of political vocabularies and ideological resources to articulate critiques of the hegemonic global order without being able to formulate coherent counter-hegemonic views. These articulations cannot be void of contradictions or ambivalence, but such is the nature of meaning making in a mediated pandemic.

NOTES

1. Anna Russell, "The Rise of Coronavirus Hate Crimes," *New Yorker*, March 17, 2020.
2. Jenni Marsh, Shawn Deng, and Nectar Gan, "Africans in Guangzhou Are on Edge, after Many Are Left Homeless amid Rising Xenophobia as China Fights a Second Wave of Coronavirus," CNN, April 10, 2020; "African Expats Accuse China of Xenophobia," DW, April 14, 2020.
3. Ulrich Beck, *Risk Society: Towards a New Modernity* (London: SAGE Publications, 1992); Ulrich Beck, "World Risk Society as Cosmopolitan Society?: Ecological Questions in a Framework of Manufactured Uncertainties," *Theory, Culture & Society* 13, no. 4 (November 1, 1996): 1–32; Ulrich Beck, "Cosmopolitanism as Imagined Communities of Global Risk," *American Behavioral Scientist* 55, no. 10 (October 1, 2011): 1346–1361.
4. Myria Georgiou, *Diaspora, Identity and the Media: Diasporic Transnationalism and Mediated Spatialities* (Cresskill, NJ: Hampton Press, 2006); Wanning Sun, "Motherland Calling: China's Rise and Diasporic Responses," *Cinema Journal* 49 (2010): 126–130; Wanning Sun and John Sinclair, *Media and Communication in the Chinese Diaspora: Rethinking Transnationalism* (London: Routledge, 2015); Stuart Hall, "The Problem of Ideology: Marxism without Guarantees," *Journal of Communication Inquiry* 10 (1986): 28–44; Arlie Hochschild, *Strangers in Their Own Land: Anger and Mourning on the American Right* (New York: New Press, 2016); Shani Orgad, *Heading Home: Motherhood, Work, and the Failed Promise of Equality* (New York: Columbia University Press, 2019).
5. Ulrich Beck, *World at Risk* (Cambridge: Polity, 2009), 30.
6. Ulrich Beck, *World Risk Society* (New York: Wiley, 1999), 135.
7. Beck, "Cosmopolitanism as Imagined Communities of Global Risk," 1354.
8. Beck, "Cosmopolitanism as Imagined Communities of Global Risk," 1348.
9. Pheng Cheah, "'The World Is Watching,'" *Journalism Studies* 14, no. 2 (April 1, 2013): 219–231; Lilie Chouliaraki, *The Spectatorship of Suffering* (SAGE Publications, 2006); Lilie Chouliaraki, "Re-mediation, Inter-mediation, Trans-mediation," *Journalism Studies* 14,

no. 2 (April 1, 2013): 267–283; Simon Cottle, "Taking Global Crises in the News Seriously: Notes from the Dark Side of Globalization," *Global Media and Communication* 7, no. 2 (August 1, 2011): 77–95; Simon Cottle, "Journalists Witnessing Disaster," *Journalism Studies* 14, no. 2 (April 1, 2013): 232–248; Peter Dahlgren, "Online Journalism and Civic Cosmopolitanism," *Journalism Studies* 14, no. 2 (April 1, 2013): 156–171; Natalie Fenton, "Cosmopolitanism as Conformity and Contestation," *Journalism Studies* 14, no. 2 (April 1, 2013): 172–186; Alexa Robertson, *Mediated Cosmopolitanism: The World of Television News* (New York: Polity, 2010).

10. Lilie Chouliaraki and Omar Al-Ghazzi, "Beyond Verification: Flesh Witnessing and the Significance of Embodiment in Conflict News," *Journalism*, December 14, 2021; Lilie Chouliaraki and Tijana Stolic, "Rethinking Media Responsibility in the Refugee 'Crisis': A Visual Typology of European News," *Media, Culture & Society* 39, no. 8 (2017); Cottle, "Journalists Witnessing Disaster"; Mirca Madianou, "Humanitarian Campaigns in Social Media," *Journalism Studies* 14, no. 2 (April 1, 2013): 249–266.

11. Myria Georgiou, "Diaspora in the Digital Era: Minorities and Media Representation," *Journal on Ethnopolitics and Minority Issues in Europe* 12, no. 4 (2013): 80–99; Youna Kim, "Female Cosmopolitanism? Media Talk and Identity of Transnational Asian Women," *Communication Theory* 21, no. 3 (August 1, 2011): 279–298; Maria Kyriakidou, "Imagining Ourselves beyond the Nation? Exploring Cosmopolitanism in Relation to Media Coverage of Distant Suffering," *Studies in Ethnicity and Nationalism* 9, no. 3 (2009): 481–496.

12. Georgiou, "Diaspora in the Digital Era: Minorities and Media Representation," 81.

13. Myria Georgiou, "Conviviality Is Not Enough: A Communication Perspective to the City of Difference," *Communication, Culture and Critique* 10, no. 2 (June 1, 2017): 261–279; Kevin Smets, "Ethnic Identity without Ethnic Media? Diasporic Cosmopolitanism, (Social) Media and Distant Conflict among Young Kurds in London," *International Communication Gazette* 80, no. 7 (November 1, 2018): 603–619.

14. Smets, "Ethnic Identity without Ethnic Media?"

15. Stuart Hall et al., *Policing the Crisis: Mugging, the State and Law & Order*, 2nd ed. (London: Palgrave Macmillan, 2013), xv.

16. Hall et al., *Policing the Crisis*, xv.

17. Beck, *World Risk Society*, 109–132.

18. Nelly Elias, *Coming Home: Media and Returning Diaspora in Israel and Germany* (Albany: SUNY Press, 2008); Leopoldina Fortunati, Raul Pertierra, and Jane Vincent, eds., *Migration, Diaspora and Information Technology in Global Societies* (New York: Routledge, 2011); Georgiou, *Diaspora, Identity and the Media*; Georgiou, "Diaspora in the Digital

Era," 80; Karim H. Karim and Ahmed Al-Rawi, *Diaspora and Media in Europe: Migration, Identity, and Integration* (Singapore: Springer, 2018); Yu Shi, "Identity Construction of the Chinese Diaspora, Ethnic Media Use, Community Formation, and the Possibility of Social Activism," *Continuum* 19, no. 1 (March 1, 2005): 55–72; Wanning Sun, "Media and the Chinese Diaspora: Community, Consumption, and Transnational Imagination," *Journal of Chinese Overseas* 1, no. 1 (January 1, 2005): 65–86; Sun and Sinclair, *Media and Communication in the Chinese Diaspora*.
19. Hall et al., *Policing the Crisis*, xv.
20. Jennifer Daryl Slack, "The Theory and Method of Articulation in Cultural Studies," in *Stuart Hall: Critical Dialogues in Cultural Studies*, ed. David Morley and Kuan-Hsing Chen (New York: Routledge, 1996), 115.
21. Lawrence Grossberg, *We Gotta Get Out of This Place: Popular Conservatism and Postmodern Culture* (New York: Routledge, 1992), 54.
22. Stuart Hall, "Race, Articulation and Societies Structured in Dominance," in *Ociological Theories: Race and Colonialism*, ed. UNESCO (Paris: UNESCO, 1980), 325.
23. Hall et al., *Policing the Crisis*, 2.
24. The study was approved by the LSE Research Ethics Committee on October 9, 2020.
25. Adam Tooze, "The Sociologist Who Could Save Us from Coronavirus," *Foreign Policy*, August 1, 2020.
26. Beck, "Cosmopolitanism as Imagined Communities of Global Risk," 1350.
27. See, for example, Paul E. Willis, *Learning to Labour: How Working Class Kids Get Working Class Jobs* (New York: Ashgate, 1977); Beverley Skeggs, *Class, Self, Culture* (New York: Routledge, 2013); Tony Bennett et al., *Culture, Class, Distinction* (New York: Routledge, 2009).
28. See, for example, Hailong Liu, ed., *From Cyber-Nationalism to Fandom Nationalism: The Case of Diba Expedition In China* (London: Routledge, 2020); Stanley Rosen, "Contemporary Chinese Youth and the State," *Journal of Asian Studies* 68, no. 2 (May 2009): 359–369; Jessica Chen Weiss, "How Hawkish Is the Chinese Public? Another Look at 'Rising Nationalism' and Chinese Foreign Policy," *Journal of Contemporary China* 28, no. 119 (September 3, 2019): 679–695; Xu Wu, *Chinese Cyber Nationalism: Evolution, Characteristics, and Implications* (Lanham, MD: Lexington Books, 2007); Sheng Zou, "When Nationalism Meets Hip-Hop: Aestheticized Politics of Ideotainment in China," *Communication and Critical/Cultural Studies* 16, no. 3 (July 3, 2019): 178–195.

Contesting for Consensus

Social Sentiment toward Fellow Citizens' COVID-Related Behavior in China

Yan Wang and Yuxi Zhang

COVID-19 HAS SHIFTED HUMAN SOCIALITY PROFOUNDLY. IN THE ERA OF SOCIAL distancing, the Internet has become the main sphere where people carry out day-to-day interactions, including teaching and learning, work collaboration, political and social participation, and private gatherings.[1] Meanwhile, the pandemic makes the boundaries between individuals, the society, and the state ever more contested. In particular, private life is frequently displayed and moralized in online public spaces. Individuals subject to scrutiny are not limited to politicians such as the British Prime Minister Boris Johnson, who suffered calls to resign over lockdown breaches in a series of Downing Street parties,[2] or celebrities, like tennis star Novak Djokovic, who was deported from Australia on the ground that his refusal to get vaccinated prior to the Australian Open "may foster antivaccination sentiment."[3] During the pandemic, individual's decisions and behavior, including any that might lead to the possibility of infecting others, lent legitimacy to expanded scrutiny in public spaces. Driven by such online scrutiny of private acts, social sentiment formed toward the actions, decisions, and even lifestyles of fellow citizens.

Against this backdrop, this chapter depicts the evolving dynamics among fellow citizens in China; we use an intersubjective perspective that highlights the processes and products of sharing experiences, knowledge, and understanding with others.[4]

In particular, we ask when and how individuals reacted to others' COVID-related actions and behaviors. Such actions include demonstrating compliance or non-compliance with COVID-19 policies in people's daily routines, particularly those that could spread the virus to others. Such personal details were publicized—often as leaks—following the hyperdetailed epidemiological investigation and contact-tracing system used in China. We examine if the social sentiment change in China during the pandemic followed a psychosocial-cycle model, as the literature has found with past public health crises.[5] Within this psychosocial model, scholars track how social sentiments shift from fear and refusal to anger and moralization, eventually moving on to acceptance and action.

To capture the social-sentiment shifts during the pandemic, we address the social media data from online platforms in China. Drawing on an extensive dataset of more than four million COVID-19 related posts on Sina Weibo, we depict the information flows and discussion volumes in Chinese public spaces and estimate the general sentiment of the relevant Weibo posts in 2020 via our self-defined scoring algorithms. We also use discourse analysis to decipher the implicit beliefs, common sense, and shared knowledge sets buried inside the explicit wording of the Weibo posts (for readers interested in the details of this mixed methods approach, we have created an online appendix sharing our raw data and interpretive methods).[6]

Our findings at the national level show that the general social sentiment changes in China during 2020 echoed the psychosocial-cycle model identified in international literature,[7] while demonstrating some unique timing and sequence characteristics that were linked to China's pandemic developments and policies. The nation's all-society solidarity was built at the initial stage of the pandemic as a surviving strategy to combat the existential risk from COVID-19. However, stages featuring fear, anger, and moralization emerged even when the risk of widespread virus transmission was kept at bay for the rest of 2020. Zooming in to the local level with two focusing events, we find that changes in the general social sentiment could be triggered by local flare-ups of COVID-19 cases. The related discussions usually moved away from the severity of transmission and the degree of policy change, instead centering on normative debates around "right" or "wrong" behaviors. As the pandemic evolved, the public became more aware of problems associated with unbounded public scrutiny over private life. Such awareness and reflection encouraged discussion and efforts to build consensus in highly contested topic areas, such as individual privacy and the moral principles of COVID-related behavior. Overall, this chapter contributes to the volume's theme of *pandemic crossings* by documenting how people's lived experiences of human sociality under the pandemic were expressed within and interacted with digital technologies, especially social media, wherein public health policy, political imperatives, community scrutiny, and private lives relentlessly crossed over, mixing genres of discourse.

Psychological Shifts and Social Solidarity in the Age of COVID-19

Scholars have documented how the pandemic and correlated restrictive COVID-19 policies have affected human sociality. The disruptions and changes in people's social lives brought by the unexpected crisis inevitably led to psychological shifts, for instance, toward fear, anxiety, and anger.[8] Luca Maria Aiello et al. study how people responded to the pandemic and their fellow citizens online by analyzing a large dataset of Twitter posts.[9] In studying the language used in Twitter posts among users in the United States, they used the model of three psychosocial epidemics, based on Philip Strong's 1990 work, which identifies the three stages of distinctive interpersonal dynamics among social members during public health crises.[10] During the first stage of fear and refusal, the little-known disease triggers the frequent use of language in the form of suspecting fellow citizens as virus carriers. The cleavage lies between "me" and "others." Moving to the next stage, as social members struggle to make sense of the reality, they try to moralize pandemic-surviving strategies by engaging in both cooperation (working with fellow persons who fall into the category of "me") and stigmatization (castigating the behaviors of "others").[11] Moralization does not always mean consensus and agreement. Quite the contrary; what behavior is considered sensible and morally acceptable is usually a highly contested topic in public spaces—the controversies related to wearing face coverings in many countries at the beginning of the pandemic serve as good examples. The compliance and the non-compliance camps frequently express anger at one another, resulting in a bitter divide between imagined factions of "we" and "them." At the final stage of action and acceptance, fellow citizens often engage in more constructive social processes that start to close the cleavage by showing sympathy for others' misfortune and sorrow, mourning collective losses, giving support to the authorities, and discussing life after COVID-19. Our chapter builds from this group of literature to highlight the evolving dimensions of social solidarity among fellow citizens during the pandemic.

As a multifaceted construct, solidarity entails resource transfer, risk pooling, collective action, and shared norms about fighting for a common interest, thus becoming the moral and behavioral foundation for public policymaking around the world.[12] In this sense, it resembles the "crossings" between individual-level dynamics and the broader social and political worlds. Solidarity during a pandemic therefore relates to both the perception and evaluation of health guidelines, embodying compliance with policy measures, and engaging in the moral judgment of pandemic-related behavior. Around the behavioral component, scholars have examined how the existing level of social solidarity among fellow citizens, whether they are acquaintances or strangers, and the underlying psychosocial mechanisms, such as trust, provide conditions for the implementation of COVID-19 prevention and control measures. Jackson G. Lu, Peter Jin, and Alexander S. English find that people in collectivistic cultures consider wearing masks not only as a civic responsibility but also as a symbol of solidarity that signals they are fighting the pandemic together, and thus are more likely to conform to mask mandates.[13] Guido Alessandri et al. argue that the more people perceive their acquaintances to be trustworthy, the more they try to respect the stay-at-home order.[14] Katrin Schmelz and Samuel Bowles show that while strong trust among peer citizens often entails sufficient social capital to ensure compliance, it also implies citizens' aversion to coercive enforcement and control from the government.[15]

The moral dimension of social solidarity in the pandemic entails mainly two aspects, the "should" and "should not" in people's COVID-related behavior. The "should" side stresses citizens' adherence to moral principles; their civic duties such as donating and undertaking volunteer work; and their concern, sympathy, and responsibility toward fellow citizens.[16] However, more frequently, solidarity is strengthened through the blaming of wrongdoers. Marilena Choli and Daria J. Kuss find that social media users predominantly blame national governments for COVID-19.[17] In contrast, other research finds that accusations often targeted marginalized groups and social "others" during past epidemics, including AIDS, H1N1, and Ebola.[18] In a public health crisis, narratives usually identify "viral otherness"—most frequently posited in foreigners or immigrant communities—which ferments existing xenophobic and nationalist sentiments.[19] Lisa B. Keränen, Kirsten N. Lindholm, and Jared Woolly found that during the outbreak of avian influenza A in 2013, Hong Kong media portrayed visitors from mainland China as "the threatening, disease-ridden Other."[20] Xin Zhao depicts how social media accounts belonging to Chinese state actors employ information tactics to construct the politicized solidarity narrative of "Us (Chinese) vs. U.S." during the pandemic.[21] According to Jasper Van Assche et al., even in a society where moral emotions tend to assign support rather than punishment to the ill, the distribution of blame tends to concentrate on ethnic "outsiders," whose norm-deviating behaviors are frequently cited to justify social exclusion and discrimination.[22]

Melissa Roy et al. argue that the blame-centered dynamics may evolve as the pandemic develop.[23] At the beginning, the alienation process against those who are ill is often done through stigmatization and labeling, for example, the depiction of "super spreaders."[24] Finding a culprit for a disease helps turn the mysterious and scary nature of the virus into a narrative seemingly more comprehensible and controllable.[25] Then, the fear of stigmatization could further dissuade people from taking diagnostic tests, complying with the test-and-trace systems, or even receiving necessary treatments, thus forming a vicious spiral of "stigmatization—noncompliance—blame."[26] As Andrew E. Monroe and Bertram F. Malle suggest, blame serves as a social tool to regulate others' behavior.[27] Thus, scapegoating and heroizing are virtually two sides of the same coin unified in collective attempts to make sense of the catastrophe.[28] Nevertheless, given that extended alienation of sick social members would eventually undermine the legitimacy and effectiveness of the protective mentality, reconciliation and consensus may emerge in public spaces via the continuous destruction and reconstruction of pandemic morality.

This chapter is among the first to focus on social dynamics among fellow citizens by studying their expressed sentiments in online public spaces. It provides innovative angles and firsthand empirical evidence to understand how solidarity evolved among Chinese citizens during 2020, as mapped through the psychosocial-cycle model. Our analysis shows how social sentiment changed over time during 2020 and how it interweaved with other longitudinal forces, including the evolving pandemic situation and COVID-19 policy measures.

Contextualizing Social Sentiment during a Pandemic: China's COVID-19 Story

In January 2020, dozens of pneumonia cases from an unknown cause occurred in Wuhan City of Hubei Province in China. The outbreak soon turned into a pandemic disease that has profoundly changed the world and the way in which human beings live.[29] However, apart from the first national wave of the disease that centered around Hubei Province, the country experienced only a couple of local flare-ups for the rest of the year. After Wuhan lifted its seventy-six-day lockdown on April 8, only seven of the thirty-one provincial-level jurisdictions in mainland China witnessed a daily case growth of more than twenty throughout 2020.[30] It is fair to say that the risk of widespread transmission was kept at bay.

This relatively calm epidemic situation is relevant to this chapter in at least three ways. First, the low case level made comprehensive contact tracing and epidemiological investigation feasible. According to a news report by *South Metropolitan Press*, in order to fully establish just one transmission chain, Shenzhen city deployed 530 well-trained case workers.[31] Second, experienced epidemiological investigators, repeated mass testing, and technologies such as the health-code system, have together made it easier for the authorities to acquire personal information, but tougher than ever to keep it safe. As we show later in the "Chengdu Girl" case, the story of a confirmed case went viral possibly due to an identity leak from one of the few thousand case workers.[32] Third, the rigorous epidemiological investigation became the key to China's "success" in controlling COVID-19 in the country's official narrative, which, in turn, lent legitimacy to the activities of observing, recording, and even publicizing (under some conditions) private life.

In understanding the shifts of social sentiment, we can almost certainly eliminate the simplistic hypothesis that social sentiment fluctuated purely based on local epidemiological situations. As we show later in the empirical part of this chapter, sentiment expressed on social media continued to fluctuate during local transmissions that were small and "insignificant," even by China's standard, such as that in Chengdu in December 2020—the daily case growth during that period never reached twenty. More plausible is the assumption that the fluctuation in social sentiment resonated more with policy changes and related public communications. The sudden tightening of local policy restrictions due to a few cases could mean involuntary cancellation of leisure activities and business trips, school closures, and corresponding disruptions to the routine operation of families, supply shortage in cities, and in some cases, more consequential outcomes due to, for example, the delay of medical treatment. In other words, policy shifts might have moderated social sentiment during the pandemic. Therefore, it is important to contextualize our analysis within a changing policy environment at the local level.

The "precise control" model adapted by the Chinese government in 2020 may have had dual effects on social sentiments expressed online.[33] On the one hand, people showed more understanding toward fellow citizens who contracted the virus, especially when they themselves were not personally affected by the policy escalation. On the other hand, while people under lockdown were certainly small in number, they were shouldering a very high cost, compared with people in situations where milder but broader restrictions were applied. The group of people who were directly affected by tighter restrictions felt the loss strongly and got angry about being penalized for others' faults or carelessness. According to Laëtitia Atlani-Duault et al., in previous outbreaks of infectious diseases, such as H1N1 influenza, people tended to blame "nearby" rather than "distal" figures.[34]

In short, by contextualizing our analysis of online social sentiment with China's unique pandemic situation and policy approach in 2020, we show that the relationships among these are far from linear and neat. This highlights the necessity to take a relational and discursive approach to understanding social sentiment during the pandemic.

Research Design, Data, and Methodology

To capture the social-sentiment shifts during the different stages of the pandemic, we consider social media data from online platforms. We intend to provide a general picture of the changing sentiments and evolving discourses in COVID-related discussions in Chinese online public spaces during the crisis. We use social media data from Sina Weibo, a Twitter-like platform in China, with all posts related to the pandemic available through keyword searching on active users from December 31, 2019, to December 31, 2020.[35] Merged with policy data from Thomas Hale et al. and COVID-19 case info from Ensheng Dong, Hongru Du, and Lauren Gardner,[36] we compile the synchronized new case numbers of COVID-19, policy stringency index, and social media reaction all into one dataset.

To further clean the social media data, we use the supervised learning method to eliminate posts that are not relevant to the key research interests. We hand-coded three thousand randomly selected posts into two categories: whether the post's content related to the pandemic in mainland China, and whether the post's content referred to fellow citizens regarding social interactions, such as scapegoating, blaming, and collective honor.[37] In particular, we define "societal sentiment against fellow citizens" as social media posts containing reactions to COVID-related peer behavior, including, for instance, the ones reacting to peer citizens' compliance/non-compliance of public health rules, or praise/complaint about the behavior or lifestyles of other individuals and social groups. The key standard in our identification is that the post should be about some identifiable individuals or social groups in the society and with reaction and evaluation in the text. With high

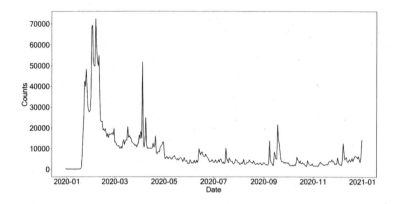

FIGURE 1. Counts of daily posts in the social media dataset.

intercoder reliability of the kappa scores over 0.86,[38] we compile a consolidated training dataset for automated classification. After testing with several classifiers,[39] we chose the Naive Bayes system to predict other remaining posts regarding the two categories, considering both the performance of the classifier and the constraints of computational power.

We then compiled the fully cleaned social media data and scored the sentiment of all posts with BosonNLP dictionary and a self-defined scoring function.[40] The essential logic of the algorithm is to use the keyword dictionaries—in our case, the BosonNLP sentiment score—that match the sentiment words, negative words, and degree words in each post, then use the function to iterate over the post and weigh the sentiment score respectively.

In addition to the machine-learning approach, we also employ discourse analysis in deciphering the implicit beliefs, common sense, and shared knowledge sets underlying the explicit wording of the posts.

Our social media dataset includes 2,739,146 unique users. The analytical dataset includes 4,517,937 unique posts, with an average length of 198 characters per post. In figure 1, we plot the counts of daily posts in the dataset. Considering the data-generation process of social media, that is, using keywords related to the pandemic and selecting the base round of posts, it is reasonable to see the heights of discussions cluster around February and March 2020, when the pandemic was at its peak in China after the Wuhan lockdown on January 23, 2020. Another peak of discussion

TABLE 1. Descriptive statistics of sentiment scores

	COUNT	MEAN	STD	MIN	25 PCTL	50 PCTL	75 PCTL	MAX
OVERALL SCORES	4,423,957	18.82	32.45	-39.46	2.77	11.56	24.52	369.51
CITIZEN SCORES	437,214	27.23	41.61	-39.46	6.14	13.89	29.01	369.47

volume came in April, when the national mourning event was held on the traditional Tomb Sweeping Day (April 4) and when the Wuhan lockdown was lifted (April 8). Then the peak in September echoed with the national commendation ceremony for heroes fighting the pandemic (September 8).

A statistical summary of the scores of overall sentiment and sentiment against fellow citizens is shown in table 1. We drop the extreme scores of the sentiment below the 1st percentile and above the 99th percentile. The distribution of scores skews to the above-zero side. Further description of the methods and the dataset is available in the online appendix.

Capturing Sentiment Changes

First, we investigate the general change of sentiment scores over the whole of 2020, with a display of synchronized policy stringency index and daily new cases. As shown by the solid line in the lower panel of figure 2, the scores are averaged daily to depict a general trend of longitudinal change in sentiment. The overall trend shows an above-zero skew, albeit the underlying sentiment scores of individual posts consist of both positive and negative values.[41]

To show the key object of our research interest, we then plot the societal sentiment expressed toward fellow citizens in figure 3.[42] After dropping the unrelated posts, we have 437,214 posts remaining for scoring and analysis. Like the overall-sentiment scores, we averaged the fellow-citizen-targeting sentiment scores on each day.

The course of sentiment change in our data demonstrates all the psychosocial stages identified in Aiello et al.[43] However, the sequence of these stages is quite unique in COVID-related social media posts in China. Moreover, as we elaborate in the following sections, these psychosocial themes reemerged over time in response to the complex pandemic situation, policy changes, and solidarity-building events.

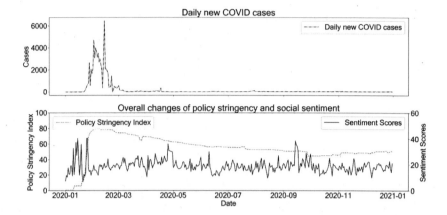

FIGURE 2. General change of social media sentiment and COVID-19 cases over 2020.

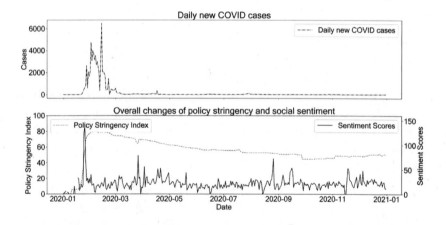

FIGURE 3. Change of social media sentiment against fellow citizens and COVID-19 cases over 2020.

Before and after the Wuhan lockdown

At the beginning of the pandemic, the sentiment expressed by social media users started to fluctuate before the significant growth of confirmed COVID-19 cases or the enactment of COVID-19 policy responses. The early "sentiment waves" reflected that public sentiment was unsettled by the fear of an unknown infectious disease, especially when users were facing the scarcity of trustworthy information. While the troughs of sentiment represented concerns and anxiety, the occasional peaks represented people's short-lived relief due to governmental assurance that the disease was "preventable and controllable."[44] The strong responses to information that downgraded the severity of COVID-19 implied the public's inclination to refuse to face the catastrophic reality of a looming crisis.

The intensity of overall sentiment dropped dramatically when the policy-stringency level rocketed for the first time around Wuhan's announcement of lockdown on January 23, 2020, which unequivocally confirmed the severity of the situation. However, public sentiment quickly bounced back to the highest level of the whole year, mainly showing support for the prevalence of donation, volunteer mobilization, and the redeployment of doctors, health workers, and other material resources from all over China to Wuhan and to Hubei Province.[45]

Respectively, while fellow-citizen-related posts were sporadic before Wuhan's lockdown, it rocketed to an all-time high soon after. It would be wrong to regard the highly positive sentiment as a sign of welcome for the high COVID-19 case level, or the strict policy measures enacted because of it. Instead, the rise in sentiment was overwhelmingly due to the acknowledgment and support directed toward doctors, nurses, volunteers, and other essential workers, meaning the psychosocial status moved quickly from the fear-and-refusal stage to the acceptance-and-action stage.

Interestingly, the process of alienation, that is, distancing the "viral others" from the "healthy us," was untypical at the very beginning of the pandemic in China, apart from occasional blame placed on fellow citizens' concrete actions that were believed to be risky, for example, consuming exotic animals.[46] This is potentially due to the fact that COVID-19 cases were first identified in China, leaving no apparent "otherness" in the conventional sense, such as foreigners, for scapegoating. Our finding echoes other research focusing on online sentiment during the first two months of 2020. Yingdan Lu, Jennifer Pan, and Yiqing Xu find that the content of criticism targeting the public included disapproval of non-compliant behavior, spreading of misinformation, and discrimination against confirmed cases or people from Wuhan or other cities in Hubei Province.[47] That is to say, instead of scapegoating the sick, early social sentiment showed strong solidarity to support them. This may be because of the sweeping transmission of the disease, which made the protective mentality of only worrying about the self an irrational choice. By late January 2020, "we" were all in this already. When the virus was widespread and the testing capacity was still low, it was too late and too difficult to identify and alienate fellow citizens who were, or who might be, infectious. Different from the experiences of other societies in the world, where COVID-19 was first known as a distant threat, the first shock from COVID-19 on the Chinese public was so close that it motivated a quick jump from the fear-and-refusal stage straight into the acceptance-and-action stage.

From the Wuhan lockdown in April to the end of 2020

Later in the year, as we discussed in the context section, the pandemic situation was relatively quiet in China, compared with most other countries in the world, with only a few local flare-ups. The local policy environment normalized through maintaining high-baseline preventative and control measures and targeted lockdowns.[48] However, social sentiment online kept fluctuating, driven by various forces. Although at the beginning of the pandemic, fear and refusal quickly turned into acceptance and solidarity-charged actions, anger became more recognizable later on, with fear being a recurring theme. The public's attempts to distinguish the "viral others" also made up for its earlier absence.

Our data show that the moralization element reflected in online social sentiment became more apparent once the initial national transmission of the virus was controlled. After February 17, 2020, many localities started the resumption of work and production, and the process sped up after February 25. As the immediate existential threat began to ebb away and people started to settle into the "new normal," the public took time to redefine the "should" and "should not" and to regulate fellow citizens' COVID-19 behaviors, mainly via denouncing those that were norm-deviating. For example, "active self-reporting of mobility trajectories" became the new code of conduct one had to adhere to.[49] The low case level and the high capacity of epidemiological investigation further contributed to exposing private life to public scrutiny.

For example, a new case (male) in Zhengzhou was confirmed on March 11, 2020. This person contracted the virus while on a business trip to Italy yet did not report his overseas travel history to local governments upon his return. His movement history, along with detailed information about his work and personal life, was leaked online. Typical social media posts commenting on this case said:

> [This case] should be filed for investigation and sentence!
> [His inaction] has consequences, the whole city's economy and schools were expected to be back to normal, now will have to delay for another half or one month—considerable economic loss. [He should be] sentenced with the highest possible punishment.[50]

Such posts are packed with outrage toward individuals' inaction in terms of self-reporting their travel history. They also revealed people's profound disappointment with the prolonged lockdown risks resulting from fellow citizens' failure to comply with policies. Apart from behavior directly related to COVID-19 transmission or policy compliance, social sentiment was also directed at people's actions, movements, and even lifestyles. For example, a post compared the mobility trajectories of confirmed cases in Chengdu to those in Beijing: "COVID-19 close contact cases in Beijing: work, meeting, eat buns, work overtime, travel by bus; COVID-19 close contact cases in Chengdu: play poker, night club, manicure treatment, hotpot, tea house."[51] Such narratives of a montage-style comparison of lifestyles encouraged the differentiation between "them" and "us." People expressed shared feelings with confirmed cases who lived a similar lifestyle, while depriving other cases of the same level of support, not on the grounds of any proven association between the activities and the pandemic, but because of their sheer differences. In this case, we see a series of stereotypes deployed to differentiate—in a facile and clichéd way—between the industrious people of Beijing and the hedonistic people of Chengdu, between the days-of-work ethic in Beijing versus the nights-of-material indulgence ethic in Chengdu. As our analysis shows, social sentiment evolved in China through, in such cases, making meaning by drawing upon pre-COVID stereotypes about alleged others.

Indeed, as we will show with the "Chengdu Girl" case in the next section, a young woman living a life outside the social norm was alienated by her fellow citizens and was categorized into the "viral otherness" group. Her existing daily routine was branded as intrinsically prone to infection, irresponsible, and dangerous. Such discussions in essence moved fellow citizens who contracted the virus from the "innocent victim" group to the "deserved villain" group.

Other easy targets of the "viral otherness" attack included Chinese students, nationals, and descendants who wanted to return to China during the COVID-19 pandemic. One Weibo post commented:

Invisible in building up the motherland, yet the vanguard to spread the virus! Miss Li, who has permanent residency in the US, paid tax to the US when things are all good, yet came back for treatment when got sick! The Guo's [another case who traveled back to China] ruined the efforts [of controlling the virus] of the 100 million people in Henan with his ONE action, yet not a single apology was heard from him! The Italian Chinese [case] questioned medical workers with "shouldn't I have better treatment considering I'm back from Italy?" The girl studying overseas was discontent with the quarantine conditions in the hotel and wanted mineral water rather than plain boiled water! And those shameless imported cases wanted free medical treatment! Those giant babies take our state as a babysitter and willfully ask for whatever they want! The state has the responsibility to protect you, but no obligations to spoil you![52]

When a rumor was spread that the family of a Chinese student who studied overseas had frictions with community workers who were enforcing the quarantine rules, comments in the retweet of the news said, "Go back to where you come from! Don't come and trouble everyone here."[53] Local anger was explicitly directed at globe-hopping international students, whose behaviors were depicted as selfish, pampered, and privileged. As this instance shows, social sentiment evolved during the early stages of the COVID pandemic along the lines of privileged and deprived, with the consciousness of relative deprivation structuring who was perceived as an "us" or a "them."[54]

As China had effectively closed its borders to most foreigners since late March 2020, there were not enough recognizable "others" to blame for the transmission of the virus. While Asian communities in Western countries were frequently discriminated against, scapegoated, and targeted by hate speech such as "Go back to your country,"[55] a considerable portion of social media users supported similar treatments to fellow citizens with expat experience. The underlying reason for this "othering" was rooted mainly in the public's fear of any new outbreak and their anger toward alleged non-compliant behavior. To justify that Chinese expats do not belong to "us," many posts leveled the ungrounded accusation that these expats thought they were superior to ordinary Chinese citizens—a narrative manifesting the long-term division between groups with high and low social-economic status. Before the pandemic, expat life was thought to be a privilege, enjoyed exclusively by the rich. Now, the social sentiment was agitated to prevent them from being "COVID free-riders" and enjoying the safety within China "unfairly." As a result, the

Chinese diasporic groups were effectively scapegoated, depicted as "viral others," and made to feel unwelcome by social sentiment in their motherland.

In short, our analysis of the overall trend in COVID-related social-sentiment change shows a psychosocial cycle existing in China in 2020. The all-society solidarity built at the beginning of the year was later challenged, and potentially eroded, by the process of moralizing fellow citizens' COVID-related behavior via blaming, discriminating, and scapegoating.

The Case of Beijing Xicheng Grandpa

To better understand the fluctuations of sentiment as the pandemic and correlated management in China entered the localized stage, we dig into two cases that raised considerable discussions in Chinese public spaces. We constructed the datasets using keyword searching through the whole collection of over sixty million posts from Yong Hu et al., which resulted in 8,699 posts related to the Beijing Xicheng Grandpa case, and 30,828 posts relate to the Chengdu Girl case.[56]

The Beijing Xicheng Grandpa case occurred in summer 2020 after nearly two months of zero local COVID cases in Beijing.[57] The new cases were first reported on June 11, 2020 (represented by the gray dotted line in figure 4), mainly connected to a wholesale market in south Beijing, the Xinfadi market. Until July 6, the outbreak led to a cluster of 400 reported cases across seven provinces, and Beijing reported 366 cases alone.[58] The first reported case was a man in his fifties, who was later referred to as "Beijing Xicheng Grandpa" on social media. He became famous after his epidemiological investigation was made public by the Beijing Municipal Health Commission, in which he reported detailed and accurate memory of all his travels. Subsequently, the Beijing government turned up the public health–emergency response level on June 13, with Xinfadi market being shut and stricter restrictions enacted over local communities. Domestic traveling into and out of the capital city as well as public transportation and schools were all affected to different degrees.[59]

We plot the social sentiment, policy stringency index, and local COVID-19 cases within the window of one week before and two weeks after the first local case identified in figure 4. The gray circles in the figure show the discussion volumes on this case. It is clear that while the ripples in social sentiment started to form as soon as a significant rise of new COVID-19 cases was identified in Beijing, the policy change was introduced around four days later. Interestingly, the pattern of social

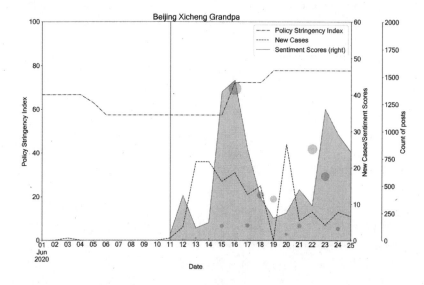

FIGURE 4. Sentiment, policy, COVID-19 cases, and social media posts for the Beijing Xicheng Grandpa case.

media reactions (sentiment scores in gray shadow under the solid line) followed neither the case number (dashed line), nor the policy stringency level (dash-dot line). Therefore, we further unpack the online discourse related to the case of Beijing Xicheng Grandpa with qualitative data.

At the very beginning, there were rumors—as frequently found at the fear-and-refusal stage of the psychosocial cycle—accused Beijing Xicheng Grandpa of traveling to another province and contributing to the case growth in Beijing (which turned out to be untrue). There were also complaints about personal life being affected by the anticipated tightening up of policies. For instance, one user grumbled in a post, "Waited and waited and waited until the date of school reopening [so the user's child could finally leave the house], and now Beijing Xicheng Grandpa got us into this [situation]."[60] At this stage, even when the government had not responded with any policy change, the common knowledge borne by normal citizens tended to think the worst of their peers due to fear, anxiety, and the unpredictability of the disease. Beijing Xicheng Grandpa was scapegoated on the ground of alleged, rather than substantiated, wrongdoing.

Yet, since the publication of the detailed epidemiological investigation, the personal life of Beijing Xicheng Grandpa entered public spaces. Starting from June 15, posts exclaiming at the impressive memory of Beijing Xicheng Grandpa dominated the discussion forum. He was commended for helping the local authority identify the source and hub of transmission, as he exhausted all close contacts quickly and potentially prevented the wider spread of the virus in Beijing. In the following three days, most of the posts in our dataset were retweets of a single post, cited below. This post received 99,921 likes and 13,732 retweets by the end of 2020.

> Beijing Xicheng Grandpa Mr. T, although he broke the great situation that there was no local COVID-19 case in Beijing for an uninterrupted 55 days, contributed to awakening the battle against the pandemic throughout the society, as well as terminating this wave of cases in time. Most importantly is that Mr. T had a clear mind and precise memory—he remembered all the places he had visited since May 30. In particular, he accurately described his visit to the Xinfadi Market for shopping on June 3 as the key joint, which immediately alerted the epidemiologists, and was reported to the decision-making center later. Meanwhile, although he was a patient, he could still calmly recall all the contacts he had in the past half month and provided the complete close-contact list of 38 names. Mr. T might be relatively weak in health, but evidently has seen the world, and is surely an educated and meticulous Beijing Xicheng Grandpa.[61]

Retweets of this post were full of praise such as "good memory is very important," "good father, good husband, and good citizen," "I could not even remember what I ate yesterday," and "respect." In addition to the moral approval of an individual, the positive reaction to "good citizen" extended to fellow community members, as shown in the quote below, which praised the collective work brought about by strong communities, responsive governments, and compliant citizens. In short, after the initial stage of fear, the moralization stage did not take the form of blame in the Beijing Xicheng Grandpa case. It, instead, centered around commending a model citizen and setting a good code of conduct for the public to follow. Moving to the action stage, the social solidarity and trust among fellow citizens built at this stage were based on the principle of reciprocity, in the sense that the government and health workers protected the public, and the public, in turn, protected the victory of pandemic control and facilitated health workers' efforts by being responsible and vigilant. As one Weibo poster wrote under the hashtag of "Beijing Xicheng Grandpa":

Following the lockdowns of middle- and high-risk communities, as well as the large-scale PCR tests, hundreds of thousands of social workers and nearly ten thousand medical workers started their work with protection suites in the high-temperature environment [in Beijing]. Many of them only finished their battles against the previous COVID-19 outbreaks very recently and had to start again with little rest. [I] sincerely consider them as great people, all the medical workers and social workers. Patients and citizens in the middle- and high-risk communities are also very compliant and understanding. . . . This demonstrates the public's confidence in the government, in the state, and in the people.[62]

The extended trust to the state reinforced the legitimacy of public measures initiated by the government and required further compliance of the society and reflections on immoral behaviors of fellow citizens. Discussions on the Beijing Xicheng Grandpa case on June 19 and 20 also reflected on the rumors and criticism at the beginning of the wave.[63] The post cited below attracted more than thirty thousand likes and was retweeted more than two thousand times.

When the first local COVID-19 case was identified this month in Beijing, the comments on the guy in Xicheng were like: "[He] traveled to Jilin and hid his itinerary," "[He] goofed around very often," "[He is] completely irresponsible to others' lives and health . . ." all kinds of rumors were flying around. He was viciously slandered and [I] have even seen many people condemning him in WeChat groups. Now what? . . . Hope everyone can fact check before spreading misinformation, and wish Beijing Xicheng Grandpa a quick recovery.[64]

In summary, the dramatic reversal of the Beijing Xicheng Grandpa's depiction from a "villain" to a "saint" suggested that scapegoating and heroizing were two sides of the same coin, which jointly contributed to moralizing and regulating fellow citizen-behavior. However, while the negative sentiment contained in the blaming posts resulted in a social division between "we" and the "viral others," the positive sentiment associated with a role model and the principle of reciprocity contributed to the construction of broad-based social solidarity, which, in turn, encouraged the public's reflection on its irrational, fearful, and angry sentiment. The trust among fellow citizens facilitated the awakening of self-awareness and the quest for consensus, both of which helped the psychosocial status evolve and adapt to and prepare for the recurring pandemic attacks.

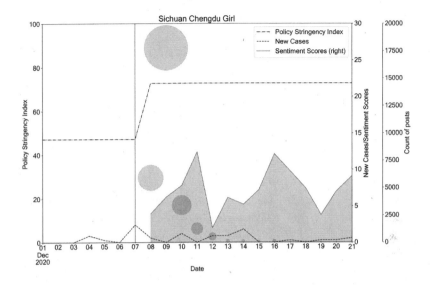

FIGURE 5. Sentiment, policy, COVID-19 cases, and social media posts for the Sichuan Chengdu Girl case.

The Case of Sichuan Chengdu Girl

In the second case, we investigate another local case that sparked enormous debates on Weibo. Chengdu City, in Sichuan Province, reported one COVID-19 case on December 7, 2020, and the following day, three more cases were reported, including a young woman whose epidemiological investigation record incurred considerable contests online.[65] Starting from December 8, the Chengdu government upgraded the risk level of one district from low to medium.[66]

We also plot the social sentiment (gray shadow under the solid line), policy stringency index (dash-dot line), and local COVID-19 cases (dashed line) within the window of one week before and two weeks after the first local case was identified in figure 5. Since the discussion volumes (shown in the gray circles in figure 5) winded down after December 14, we focus on qualitative discussions that happened during the period between December 7 and 14 to examine the public reaction to the Chengdu Girl case. Social media responses to the case of Chengdu Girl illustrated vividly the processes of scapegoating, discrimination, and stigmatization when the public faced an unexpected risk, even if the severity of such a risk was not established because the daily new case number had never exceeded five during the observation period.

Chengdu Girl's personal information was leaked online by anonymous users on December 8 soon after her epidemiological investigation was published by the local health commission. In about two days, over ten hashtags centering around this particular case hit the trending list on Weibo, with a total read amount of over one hundred million.[67] The detailed travel history in the epidemiological investigation result showed that she visited several bars and malls before being identified as a positive case. Far from being a "perfect victim," Chengdu Girl incurred much online criticism about her behavior and movements, with teases like "Young people are energetic! Her travel history is the longest and most complicated I have ever seen" and "Chengdu girls are wild."[68] Some people complained that their personal lives were affected due to the prompt policy responses from the government. A hip-hop celebrity based in Chengdu posted "Thanks to the Chengdu's COVID-19 wave, [I] can't go home" and received over one thousand likes.[69] However, many social media users supported Chengdu Girl and denounced the act of leaking personal information, showing empathy toward a fellow citizen in the vortex of blame. One post that received 3,354 likes and 12 retweets said: "If the news about the girl in Chengdu is true, please be reasonable. She did not know her family got the virus, and did not know that she already caught it. If it were you in the case of knowing nothing yet, do you not continue what you were doing? [I] saw curses and mocks and even teasing … would not you just follow your normal life?"[70]

As reflected in the discussion volumes in figure 5, the leak of Chengdu Girl's real name, home address, and even national ID number received a huge amount of contested public attention on December 8 and peaked on December 9. The hashtag "Chengdu girl may suffer potential cyberbullying" became heated, attracting enormous debates in its retweets. The discussions under the hashtag show that fellow citizens not only debated what was acceptable regarding COVID-related behavior, but also started discussing and negotiating the boundaries of public scrutiny, judgment, and interference imposed over private life during the pandemic.

The main post associated with this hashtag was a description of how Chengdu Girl's "personal information was exposed and [she was] teased as a social queen [across pubs/clubs]."[71] Some people argued that public health safety could prevail over personal privacy, for instance, in the retweet "What's wrong about the leak? This is for the sake of public safety. [If we don't] expose these people [to the public], should we just let them spread the virus everywhere?" Moreover, some posts moved from the public health risks of Chengdu Girl's mobility to her lifestyle and alleged moral imperfection: "[Being an alcohol] shill [who earns money from encouraging people to drink] in night clubs is frankly at the edge of the erotic industry, just calm [the debate] down, why encourage [her activities]."[72]

Responding to such statements, others retorted: "Being infected wasn't their fault; their lifestyles aren't in the public's judgment; [their] honestly reporting their travel history is already being responsible to the public."[73] Other posts contended for the limitation of responsibility borne by individuals based on the subjective malice regarding the externality of their behavior and actions and the bounded ex ante rationality of human beings. Such discussions suggested a broadly appealing approach to the COVID-related social contract for which ordinary citizens may be more willing to sign up because the liability it entails is not unlimited.[74]

Responding to the high volume of discussions complaining about personal information leaks, local police announced that they had started an investigation. The national TV station's official Weibo account also called for the termination of cyberbullying. The post attributed the negative sentiment around Chengdu Girl to the anxiety people experienced under the pandemic and advocated for keeping calm and fighting on. Retweets and comments were mostly supportive, especially concerning the need to draw a line between private life and public issues. For instance:

> #CCTV comments on the leakage of Chengdu Girl's information# The person who leaked her information is terrible. It is her freedom to go wherever she likes; and it is not her fault for catching the virus—she surely did not intentionally spread the virus. Doxxing others' personal information is a violation of privacy, which is illegal and should be stopped, criticized, and punished. Even if she really was responsible for spreading the virus, it is still not the excuse for exposing her personal information. Her personal life should not be a public topic; the pandemic is. Our enemy is the virus, not the person who got the virus. Fighting the pandemic should be scientific, and should be legal![75]

Interestingly, the Beijing Xicheng Grandpa also posted support and encouragement for the Chengdu Girl on Weibo, which again heated the debate under the main post: "On the 10th [of December], [Beijing] Xicheng Grandpa posted a Weibo to encourage the girl who tested positive in Chengdu: do not take [others'] words, follow the doctor's instructions and keep up with the treatment, everything will be alright."⁷⁶ The high volume of reposts, along with positive comments in the reposts, signaled the solidarity among the society supporting each other and facing the risks together.

The focus event of the Chengdu Girl case shows that as the society continued to live in the pandemic, fellow citizens started to regulate and adjust their own responses and behavior alongside those of the "viral others." Although no consensus was firmly reached, fellow citizens made continuous efforts in this regard through continuous contests in public spaces. The narratives and strategies used in these debates included not only stepping into the shoes of fellow citizens, but also following normative principles regarding the boundaries between public interest and private life, individual liberty, and legal rights. Moreover, policies started to address the issue of personal privacy being challenged in the name of public health concerns.⁷⁷

On the balance, our local-level case studies show that the psychosocial cycle did reoccur in China when the local pandemic situation changed and the real or perceived risk resurfaced, but the cycle also evolved, as the society learnt to adapt to live under the pandemic. Toward the end of 2020, negative social sentiment driven by fear and anxiety was moderated by greater self-awareness and solidarity-building efforts among fellow citizens.

Conclusion

In this chapter, we depict the COVID-related social sentiment in China's online public spaces. Drawing on an extensive dataset of Sina Weibo posts consisting of more than four million COVID-19 related posts, we present the variances of social sentiment over time in the whole year of 2020.

Overall, our findings show that the Chinese case echoed the psychosocial-cycle model identified in the international literature on social sentiment during a public health crisis, while also demonstrating uniqueness linked to China's own pandemic situation and government policies. At the initial stage of the pandemic, the sudden and widespread risk of infection motivated the all-society solidarity as a surviving strategy. Following a short period of fear and refusal, the fact that the pandemic arrived as an existential threat, rather than a distant risk, propelled social sentiment to temporarily skip the anger-and-moralization stage and enter the stages of acceptance and action. However, as the nationwide transmission ebbed away, the society entered the "new normal" for the rest of 2020, with minimal growth in the COVID-19 case number and relatively high-baseline policy measures. Subsequently, online social sentiment made up for the anger-and-moralization psychosocial stage that was missing earlier and usually marked by the construction of "viral others." Every time people found association between a recognizable figure and a local transmission event, online discussions were triggered, working toward the definition of "should" and "should not" regarding fellow citizens' COVID-19 behavior, via both denouncing norm-deviating behavior and commending good codes of conduct. The low COVID-19 case level, the high expectation for normality, and the narrative of China's success in controlling the pandemic all fueled the expansion of legitimacy for bringing private life to public scrutiny. As a result, not only COVID-related behavior but also people's daily routines and lifestyles were subject to public observation, discussion, and judgment, which in turn threatened the all-society solidarity formed at the beginning of 2020.

Our in-depth case study at the local level further shows that while the psychosocial cycle was often triggered by the change in local pandemic situations, its fluctuations were not just subject to the severity of transmission or the degree of policy change. The perceived health risk, the anticipated policy tightening, and the normative debates around "right" or "wrong" were often enough to fuel a wave of social-sentiment change. However, as the pandemic lasted for months and even years, such a cycle model also evolved. Over time, there was more awareness of and reflection upon the problems associated with unbounded public scrutiny over private life, and more empathy was shown for individuals' limited ex ante rationality. In short, the pandemic reshaped the conventional borders between private life and public spaces. While the pandemic has powered the Leviathan-style expansion of public spaces, fellow citizens have shown considerable efforts in searching for consensus on highly contested issues and reconstructing the solidarities.

NOTES

1. Minh Hao Nguyen et al., "Changes in Digital Communication During the COVID-19 Global Pandemic: Implications for Digital Inequality and Future Research," *Social Media + Society* 6, no. 3 (September 2020): 205630512094825; Yingqin Zheng and Geoff Walsham, "Inequality of What? An Intersectional Approach to Digital Inequality under Covid-19," *Information And Organization* 31, no. 1 (March 2021): 100341.

2. "Boris Johnson Faces Calls to Quit after Lockdown Party Apology," *BBC News*, January 12, 2022.
3. Daniel Hurst, "Novak Djokovic Deported for Breach of Australia's Border Rules, PM Says, at Odds with Government's Legal Case," *The Guardian*, January 17, 2022.
4. Paul T. Munroe, "Intersubjectivity," in *The Blackwell Encyclopedia of Sociology*, ed. George Ritzer (Malden, MA: Wiley, 2019), 1–3; Alex Gillespie and Flora Cornish, "Intersubjectivity: Towards a Dialogical Analysis," *Journal for the Theory of Social Behaviour* 40, no. 1 (February 2010): 19–46.
5. Philip Strong, "Epidemic Psychology: A Model," *Sociology of Health and Illness* 12, no. 3 (September 1990): 249–259.
6. The online appendix is available here https://ywangsoc.com/assets/research/covidnsolidarity/Covid_n_Solidarity_OA.pdf.
7. Strong, "Epidemic Psychology: A Model"; Luca Maria Aiello et al., "How Epidemic Psychology Works on Twitter: Evolution of Responses to the COVID-19 Pandemic in the U.S," *Humanities and Social Sciences Communications* 8, no. 1 (July 2021).
8. Samantha K. Brooks et al., "The Psychological Impact of Quarantine and How to Reduce It: Rapid Review of the Evidence," *The Lancet* 395, no. 10227 (February 2020): 912–920; Alfred Schutz and Thomas Luckmann, *The Structures of the Life-World, Volume 1* (Evanston, IL: Northwestern University Press, 1973).
9. Aiello et al., "How Epidemic Psychology Works on Twitter: Evolution of Responses to the COVID-19 Pandemic in the U.S."
10. Strong, "Epidemic Psychology: A Model."
11. Erving Goffman, *Stigma: Notes on the Management of Spoiled Identity* (New York: Simon and Schuster, 1963).
12. Peter Achterberg, Mara Yerkes, and Romke van der Veen, *The Transformation of Solidarity: Changing Risks and the Future of the Welfare State.* (Amsterdam: Amsterdam University Press, 2012); Floris Tomasini, "Solidarity in the Time Of COVID-19?" *Cambridge Quarterly of Healthcare Ethics* 30, no. 2 (December 2020): 234–247; Jeanine Grütter and Marlis Buchmann, "Developmental Antecedents of Young Adults' Solidarity During the Covid-19 Pandemic: The Role of Sympathy, Social Trust, and Peer Exclusion from Early to Late Adolescence," *Child Development* 92, no. 5 (August 2021): e832–e850.
13. Jackson G. Lu, Peter Jin, and Alexander S. English. "Collectivism Predicts Mask Use during COVID-19," *Proceedings of the National Academy of Sciences* 118, no. 23 (May 2021).
14. Guido Alessandri et al., "Moral Disengagement and Generalized Social Trust as Mediators and Moderators of Rule-Respecting Behaviors during the COVID-19 Outbreak," *Frontiers in Psychology* 11 (August 2020).

15. Katrin Schmelz and Samuel Bowles, "Overcoming COVID-19 Vaccination Resistance When Alternative Policies Affect the Dynamics of Conformism, Social Norms, and Crowding Out," *Proceedings of the National Academy of Sciences* 118, no. 25 (June 2021).
16. Niklas Ellerich-Groppe, Larissa Pfaller, and Mark Schweda, "Young for Old—Old for Young? Ethical Perspectives on Intergenerational Solidarity and Responsibility in Public Discourses on COVID-19," *European Journal of Ageing* 18, no. 2 (May 2021): 159–171.
17. Marilena Choli and Daria J. Kuss. "Perceptions of Blame on Social Media during the Coronavirus Pandemic," *Computers in Human Behavior* 124 (November 2021): 106895.
18. Melissa Roy et al., "Ebola and Localized Blame on Social Media: Analysis of Twitter and Facebook Conversations during the 2014–2015 Ebola Epidemic," *Culture, Medicine, and Psychiatry* 44, no. 1 (June 2019): 56–79.
19. Matthew Sparke and Dimitar Anguelov, "H1N1, Globalization and the Epidemiology of Inequality," *Health & Place* 18, no. 4 (July 2012): 726–736; Zheng and Walsham, "Inequality of What? An Intersectional Approach to Digital Inequality under Covid-19."
20. Lisa B. Keränen, Kirsten N. Lindholm, and Jared Woolly, "Imagining the People's Risk: Projecting National Strength in China's English-Language News about Avian Influenza," in *Imagining China: Rhetorics of Nationalism in an Age of Globalization*, ed. Stephen J. Hartnett, Lisa B. Keränen, and Donovan Conley (East Lansing: Michigan State University Press, 2017), 271–300.
21. Xin Zhao, "How China's State Actors Create a 'Us vs US' World during Covid-19 Pandemic on Social Media," *Media and Communication* 8, no. 2 (June 2020): 452–457.
22. Jasper Van Assche et al., "To Punish or To Assist? Divergent Reactions to Ingroup and Outgroup Members Disobeying Social Distancing," *British Journal of Social Psychology* 59, no. 3 (June 2020): 594–606.
23. Roy et al,. "Ebola and Localized Blame on Social Media."
24. Fahimeh Saeed et al., "A Narrative Review of Stigma Related to Infectious Disease Outbreaks: What Can Be Learned in the Face of the Covid-19 Pandemic?" *Frontiers in Psychiatry* 11 (2020).
25. Saeed et al., "A Narrative Review of Stigma Related to Infectious Disease Outbreaks: What Can Be Learned in the Face of the Covid-19 Pandemic?"
26. Saeed et al., "A Narrative Review of Stigma Related to Infectious Disease Outbreaks: What Can Be Learned in the Face of the Covid-19 Pandemic?"
27. Andrew E. Monroe and Bertram F. Malle, "People Systematically Update Moral Judgments of Blame," *Journal of Personality and Social Psychology* 116, no. 2 (February 2019): 215–236.
28. Laëtitia Atlani-Duault et al., "Tracking Online Heroisation and Blame in Epidemics,"

Lancet Public Health 5, no. 3 (February 2020): e137–e138.

29. Guobin Yang, *The Wuhan Lockdown* (New York: Columbia University Press, 2022).
30. Yuxi Zhang et al., "Chinese Provincial Government Responses to COVID-19," *BSG Working Paper Series*, 2021.
31. "What Should You Do When Receiving the Call for Epidemiological Investigation?" *South Metropolitan Press*, June, 2021.
32. "This Year on Many Covid-19 Patients' Privacy Were Leaked, How Should We Protect Patent's Privacy," *Beijing News*. December 10, 2020.
33. State Council Information Office, China's Moves in Fighting the COVID. June 7, 2020, http://www.gov.cn.
34. Atlani-Duault et al., "Tracking Online Heroisation and Blame in Epidemics."
35. Yong Hu et al., "Weibo-COV: A Large-Scale COVID-19 Social Media Dataset from Weibo," *Proceedings of the 1st Workshop on NLP for COVID-19 (Part 2) at EMNLP 2020* (Stroudsburg, PA: Association for Computational Linguistics, 2020). Our data is a subset of the dataset cited in this note (10 percent of the full dataset, resulting in 6,501,006 posts initially, then we removed duplicated posts and fandom posts using keywords selection, and end up with 4,517,937 unique posts). The cited dataset uses monthly updated COVID-19 related keywords to capture data in a pool with twenty million active Weibo users. For more information on the dataset, see https://github.com/nghuyong/weibo-cov.
36. Thomas Hale et al., "A Global Panel Database of Pandemic Policies (Oxford COVID-19 Government Response Tracker)," *Nature Human Behaviour* 5, no. 4 (March 2021): 529–538. For more information on the dataset, see Ensheng Dong, Hongru Du, and Lauren Gardner, "An Interactive Web-Based Dashboard to Track COVID-19 in Real Time," *Lancet Infectious Diseases* 20, no. 5 (February 2020): 533–534.
37. We present the hand-coding flowchart in the online appendix.
38. We present the intercoder reliability report in the online appendix.
39. We present the classification report of Naive Bayes, Support-Vector Machines, and Natural Language Process (Chinese BERT-wwm-ext, https://github.com/ymcui/Chinese-BERT-wwm) classifiers in the online appendix.
40. BosonNLP is a commercial NLP platform that aims to find business value from numerous texts, and its sentiment dictionary is built upon learnings with millions of social network–balanced corpus and hundreds of thousands of news-balanced corpus. For more information, see http://bosonnlp.com. Replication code is available upon request.
41. We are aware of the existence of censorship in Chinese online public spaces (as discussed in Yuan's chapter) but consider it tolerable in our case here. Our research focus is on the general trends of the averaged social sentiment, especially the fluctuations in

42. various time periods. Even if the censorship is not a constant variable as we assumed, our data still captured the dives of sentiment just before the Wuhan lockdown and in many other cases, as shown in figures 2 and 3.
43. Since the daily volume of posts related to sentiment against fellow citizens is different from that related to the overall sentiment, the scale in figure 3 is different from that in figure 2.
44. Aiello et al, "How Epidemic Psychology Works on Twitter: Evolution of Responses to the COVID-19 Pandemic in the U.S."
45. "Prevention and Control Are Feasible—Wuhan City Responds to Questions from Journalists on Comprehensive Prevention and Control of Novel Coronavirus Pneumonia," *News.cn*, January 9, 2020..
46. Yang, *The Wuhan Lockdown*.
47. Yingdan Lu, Jennifer Pan, and Yiqing Xu, "Public Sentiment on Chinese Social Media during the Emergence of COVID19," *Journal of Quantitative Description: Digital Media* 1 (2021).
48. Lu, Pan, and Xu, "Public Sentiment on Chinese Social Media during the Emergence of COVID19."
49. The description applies to 2020. Notably, in China's dealing with the Delta- and Omicron-waves in late 2021 and 2022, the "normalized" policy measures were found to be less effective, and the country sometimes had to implement extended lockdowns, as we have seen in Shanghai in spring 2022.
50. "Hu Shanlian: Publicizing the Patient's Activity Trace Helps Prevent and Control without Any Omissions," *Kankan News*, February 7, 2020.
51. Iy9KlpCbn, March 11, 2020. Hu et al. (2020) generates nine-digit unique character strings, like "Iy9KlpCbn," as the IDs of Weibo posts in the "Weibo-COV" dataset. The authors of this book chapter follow the same style when referencing Weibo posts to facilitate the replication of analysis. See more, including the way of accessing the dataset, from note 35 in this chapter.
52. JzEgah2Cs, December 12, 2020.
53. Iz1QYfYfM, March 17, 2020
54. IAVke340x, March 30, 2020.
55. Amelie Mummendey et al., "Strategies to Cope with Negative Social Identity: Predictions by Social Identity Theory and Relative Deprivation Theory," *Journal of Personality and Social Psychology* 76, no. 2 (1999): 229.
56. Purna Kambhampaty, "'I Will Not Stand Silent.' 10 Asian Americans Reflect on Racism during the Pandemic and the Need for Equality," *Time*, June 25, 2020.

56. Due to the fact that the whole dataset was collected afterward, many of the posts may have been deleted or made invisible at the time of collection. Also, the original collection from Hu et al., "Weibo-COV: A Large-Scale COVID-19 Social Media Dataset from Weibo" does not contain the comments following each post; therefore we don't claim to have the absolute full dataset on the two cases.
57. "Beijing Shuts Down Seafood Market after Dozens Test Positive for Coronavirus," *New York Times*, June 13, 2020.
58. "Update on the COVID-19 Situation in Beijing during June to July 2020, No. 2," *China CDC*, 2020.
59. "The Public Health Emergency Event Response Level Switched Up to Level Three," *Gov. cn*, June 17, 2020.
60. J6cuAhwKt, June 11, 2020.
61. J6M8K11Oa, June 15, 2020.
62. J76kY9DPa, June 17, 2020.
63. We provide more discussion and evidence on the social reaction after June 19, 2020, in the Beijing Xicheng Grandpa case in the online appendix.
64. J7b9H2Cjs, June 18, 2020.
65. "Xinhua Opinion: Where Is the Origin of Virus? When Will the Screen Finish? How to Stop the Transmission Chain of Virus?—at the Frontline of Pandemic Control in Chengdu," *News.cn*, December 19, 2020.
66. "Huadu Yunjintai Community, Cuijiadian, Chenghua District, Chengdu City Is Switched to Mid Risk Area," *Sc.gov.cn*, December 8, 2020.
67. "From Teasing to Privacy Protection: Public Sentiment Data Reveal the 48 Hours after 'Chengdu Girl' Tested Positive," *Sohu.com*, 2020.
68. JxtZu0tG0, December 8, 2020.
69. JxuwkrIP8, December 8, 2020.
70. JxsigF0wn, December 8, 2020.
71. JxvdXFpjI, December 8, 2020.
72. JxWbViTO5, December 11, 2020.
73. JxWc6tclG, December 11, 2020.
74. Patrick Mileham, "Unlimited Liability and the Military Covenant," *Journal of Military Ethics* 9, no. 1 (February 2010): 23–40.
75. JxDjUoYh8, December 9, 2020.
76. JxWaNfTS8, December 10, 2020.
77. "Emergency Announcement from the Pandemic-prevention Control Center," *Chengdu Municipal Health Commission*, December 13, 2020.

PART 3.

Contesting over Narratives

Narrating the Nation during the Global Pandemic

The "K-Quarantine" and Biopolitical Nationalism in the Era of COVID-19

Ji-Hyun Ahn

THE YEAR 2020 WILL BE REMEMBERED FOR THE OUTBREAK OF COVID-19 AND ITS multiple impacts on nearly every individual and society worldwide. Amid the ongoing public health crisis, the call for "big government" solutions intensified, as national governments sought to control the spread of the disease and protect their citizens. Forms of biopolitical governmentality, wherein sovereign power is exercised at the level of the population—as analyzed by Michel Foucault, Giorgio Agamben, and others—have therefore evolved in most countries, to greater or lesser effect.[1] In their COVID-19 regional safety assessment, for example, the Deep Knowledge Group (a consortium of NGOs who pool resources) tracks the success of nations in combatting COVID. East Asian countries fared well in the study, with South Korea (hereafter simply "Korea") ranked third, Japan fifth, China sixth, Singapore ninth, Taiwan thirteenth, and Hong Kong fourteenth (as of July 30, 2020).[2] As Jeroen de Kloet, Jian Lin, and Yiu Fai Chow observed, East Asian countries, as they combatted the virus, often competed for the right to claim that "we are doing better."[3] These scholars coined the term "biopolitical nationalism" to describe a situation in which "biopolitics has morphed into a field of competition, of rivalry, [and] of nationalistic power games."[4] While their analysis focused on Hong Kong,

Taiwan, and mainland China, I argue Korea exemplifies the development of biopolitical nationalism in East Asia.

Korea has been praised as a model for "successful" control of the virus, at least during the early stage of the pandemic, when it deployed such innovative digital technologies as a self-quarantine app, CCTV, and GPS to track the infected.[5] Indeed, in response to requests from numerous countries, the Korean government offered webinars to share the experiences of Koreans combating the coronavirus and strategies that had proved effective. The government offered nine webinars between May and July 2020, in which approximately 3,780 people from 118 countries participated.[6] The Korean government also took the initiative to systematize its "K-quarantine" model and to implement it as a global standard. The term "K-quarantine" (*k'ei pangyŏk*), which was introduced by the mainstream media and soon picked up by the Korean government as a policy term, makes clear the nationalist context in which this approach has been framed as *the* successful model.

In this chapter, I examine the domestic and international discourse about the K-quarantine model from a media studies perspective. Specifically, I consider how the Korean government exercised biopolitical power through the K-quarantine project, and I document the narration of biopolitical nationalism within the government's attempts to standardize the model. First, I describe the COVID-19 situation in Korea in 2020 and the context in which K-quarantine discourse emerged both within and outside Korea. Second, I demonstrate that media outlets in some Western countries, including the United States, the United Kingdom, Germany, and Spain, differently represented the Korean way of doing things under quarantine (in short, K-quarantine) over time. Within this discourse, I critique the recourse to a clichéd "West versus East" narrative. Next, I analyze the formulation of a particular type of biopolitical nationalism through the K-quarantine project and argue that the Korean government has sought to establish the K-quarantine model as a national brand by standardizing specific technologies and promoting the global distribution of domestically produced biomedical products. Lastly, I explore the implications of the intervention of sovereign power during a national emergency and the normalization of the use of surveillance technology and digital media to track and treat the infected. I argue that the success of the K-quarantine model is primarily attributable to the fact that everyday surveillance had already been normalized and rendered mundane in Korea before the advent of the pandemic. My overall aim in this chapter is to advance the understanding of the operation and transformation of biopolitical governmentality during the global pandemic by considering the K-quarantine model as a case study.

COVID-19 and the Emergence of the K-Quarantine Discourse

Following the first outbreak of the disease in Wuhan, China, in December 2019, COVID-19 quickly spread around the world. Four distinctive phases were evident in the progress of the pandemic in its first year.[7] Up to mid-January 2020, cases of the novel coronavirus infection were registered only within China, during what can thus be called the "Chinese phase."[8] The second phase, lasting the next few weeks to early February 2020, was aptly described as the "East Asian explosion," during which cases in East Asian countries (excluding China) accounted for around three-quarters of the total worldwide.[9] During the third, "European explosion" phase, cases continued to soar, with the declaration of the situation by the World Health Organization (WHO) that COVID-19 was a global pandemic on March 11, 2020, marking the transition to the fourth phase.[10] Thus, the "U.S. explosion" began in late March 2020 when the number of confirmed cases in that country exceeded the number in any other country.[11]

Korea was among the countries immediately impacted by the early mass outbreak in Wuhan. After the first Korean case was reported on January 20, the number of confirmed cases for a while remained small and largely limited to travelers from overseas. However, cases soared through February and into March during the first wave of infections, spread in large part by the adherents of a particular religious group (*Shinch'ŏnji*) in the city of Daegu. On February 29, the number of new daily reported confirmed cases reached the peak of 909 for the first wave, making Korea the country with the largest number of confirmed cases at the time outside China.[12] The number soon stabilized, in late March, but a second wave arrived in August, with multiple mid-sized outbreaks originating from multiple epicenters, particularly in churches, nightclubs, and similar mass gatherings in the heart of Seoul.[13] Then, during a third wave starting in November and peaking in late December, daily reported confirmed cases reached 1,237 on December 24, marking the highest number so far in Korea.[14]

Despite the early large-scale mass infection in February 2020, followed by multiple mid-sized outbreaks in certain populations afterward, the total number of confirmed cases in Korea remained relatively small compared with the numbers in other regions, such as North America and Europe, with fewer than thirty thousand total cases and fewer than five hundred deaths as of November 2020.[15] Hence, Korea was praised by many countries and health organizations around the world for effectively flattening the COVID-19 curve; some media outlets in Europe and North America especially reported on Korea's success in this regard.[16] According to an analysis by the Ministry of Culture, Sports, and Tourism of foreign media reports from January 20 to April 28, 2020, the one hundred–day period after the first confirmed Korean COVID-19 case, 5,589 of 8,610 articles about Korea—nearly two-thirds—concerned the country's response to the pandemic.[17] The broad range of the foreign media outlets in which these articles appeared—including CNN and Voice of America (U.S.A), BBC and *The Guardian* (U.K.), *El País* (Spain), AFP (France), and *Asia Times* (Hong Kong)—attested to the international praise for Korea's early quarantine strategies.[18]

It is no coincidence that the term "K-quarantine" became established in the everyday vernacular across sectors in Korea immediately after the first wave of infections subsided, when it began appearing in mass media publications and government statements. A key moment in the history of the term came in late March 2020, when then Prime Minister Sye-kyun Chung stated at a press conference that the Korean government was attempting to create a roadmap for systematizing the K-quarantine model in response to increasing interest from WHO and various countries. The impact of the prime minister's statement was immediate: while only 2 newspaper articles in February and 30 in March contained "K-quarantine" as a keyword, 463 additional instances were added in April, 1,620 came in May, and 1,640 more were added in June, with the total number of articles or stories using the term reaching 8,400 by October 31, 2020. Hence, by the start of November 2020, the term "K-quarantine" had become a ubiquitous trope, capturing a surging sense of Korean pride in how the nation was handling COVID-19.

Basking in the international and domestic enthusiasm for the K-quarantine model, the Korean government commenced branding the nation as a global leader in biotechnology and as an exemplary model for responding to the pandemic. Beginning in early May by offering webinars in which Koreans shared tips, experiences, and strategic responses to COVID-19 with the rest of the world, the government went on to announce an official roadmap on June 11 for making the Korean quarantine model a global standard.[19] The government officials summed up the approach in English as the "3Ts," that is, test, trace, and treat. The 3T model included a proposed eighteen programs using innovative drive-through testing and screening stations ("test"), self-monitoring and self-quarantining applications ("trace"), and infectious disease centers ("treat") submitted to the International Standard Organization (ISO) in an effort to establish it as a global standard. As discussed, the government's effort was a success, as the model was widely praised, shared, and replicated in many countries.

The primary factors in the success of the K-quarantine model seem to have been the innovative use of media and technology, openness and transparency, and civil engagement.[20] Thus, healthcare workers were able to conduct large numbers of tests quickly thanks to the development of a test kit by Korean biotech companies that delivered accurate results in only a couple of minutes. According to the government, "As of September 2020, 90,000 tests can be processed a day at full capacity, enabling the country to operate nationwide tests pre-emptively and proactively."[21] In addition, the number of confirmed cases was immediately reported and constantly updated on a central COVID-19 website, and the leading officials from the Korean Center for Disease Control (KCDC) delivered daily national debriefing conferences during which they shared the most up-to-date information about the COVID-19 situation in Korea. All of these steps helped to reassure the Korean population.

Moreover, whereas many countries, including Israel, Russia, and Australia, decided to shut their borders completely and undergo a national lockdown to prevent the virus from infecting their populations, Korea never did so during any of the three waves of infections. By avoiding national and local-level lockdowns, which negatively impact national economies, Korea weathered the pandemic better than nearly every other country. Thus, "In the latest economic projections by the OECD, South Korea is looking at a mere 1% GDP contraction for 2020, whereas the Euro area is expected to shrink by around 8%."[22]

The K-quarantine model, then, has been presented by the Korean government and hailed by international authorities and media outlets as a competent and successful response to the COVID-19 pandemic. In this regard, the K-quarantine project is by nature simultaneously domestic and international. It shapes a particular national image (that is, of Korea as confident and competent in fighting the virus) that both national and global authorities construct and legitimize by presenting Korean COVID-19-related efforts at home positively, again for both domestic and international audiences. More precisely, the K-quarantine project speaks to audiences at home by sifting through what commentators and authorities have said about it abroad; the Korean effort therefore combines external validation with local success stories to frame the government's preferred narrative for the nation. Simultaneously, the project speaks to global audiences while projecting Korea's soft power. In the following section, I consider how both domestic and international media portrayed the K-quarantine model to reveal in greater detail the role of the K-quarantine project in constructing nationalistic discourse.

Situating the K-Quarantine Discourse: Beyond the East-West Dichotomy

During the "East Asian phase" of COVID-19, the Korean response was promoted and praised by some of the media outlets in Europe and North America as the success of a democratic political system, in contrast to the supposed failure of the Chinese communist authoritarian regime.[23] The narrative swiftly and radically shifted when the virus began to spread widely in Europe, especially in Italy, the U.K., and France, and then in the U.S.A, since the democratic/authoritarian dichotomy could not explain the failure of countries in Europe and North America to respond effectively to the pandemic. With the failure of the so-called advanced societies with much longer histories of democracy to control the virus, the success of the Korean model came to be associated not with Western values but with "Asian values" or Confucianism, thereby explaining Korean success together with, rather than in opposition to, the success enjoyed by the Chinese after the East Asian phase passed.

Some Western-based intellectuals, for example the renowned French intellectual Guy Sorman, likewise explained Korea's success with reference to its Confucian tradition.[24] The Berlin-based, South Korean-born philosopher Byung-Chul Han also attributed Asian states' success in combatting the COVID-19 to "an authoritarian mentality which comes from their cultural tradition [of] Confucianism."[25] Han added, "People are less rebellious and more obedient than in Europe. They trust the state more."[26] Along the same lines, Sung-yoon Lee, an international relations professor at Tufts University, said in an interview with the *Wall Street Journal*, "Most people willingly submit themselves to authority and few complain. The Confucian emphasis on respect for authority, social stability and the good of the nation above individualism is an ameliorating factor in a time of national crisis."[27]

Such arguments are rooted in a notion of Asian exceptionalism, thus framing the Asian strategy as something neither attainable nor replicable by those who adhere to Western norms.²⁸ Put differently, the active participation of East Asian citizens, including Koreans, in quarantine efforts is due to so-called core "East Asian values," which can be summed up as authoritarianism, conformity, and collectivism. Conversely, the response to COVID-19 in Europe and North America was slow because the citizens of Western countries value individual freedom and privacy more than their personal health or national economies. However, such a binary opposition between Western democracy and individualism and Eastern Confucianism and collectivism seems inadequate and simplistic, at least without the support of empirical research, to explain the success of East Asian countries in responding to the pandemic. Moreover, this narrative, to the extent that it reinforces pre-existing notions of Orientalism, exists "only in a racist fantasy that imagines a society made up of meek, compliant Asians."²⁹

Notably, a national survey of one thousand Koreans (both male and female above the age of eighteen) conducted jointly by the Korean Broadcasting System (KBS), SisaIN, a national politics magazine, and Seoul National University in May 2020 told a different story about the success of K-quarantine. The empirical data provided by the survey presented a challenge to the untested claims endlessly repeated and re-narrated by intellectuals and media outlets. Thus, the results of the survey showed that Korea's success in combating COVID-19 had nothing to do with "East Asian values."³⁰ Rather, the most statistically significant factor in that success was "democratic citizenship." According to the survey, democratic citizenship correlates with the tendency to participate in a quarantine.³¹ The influence of democratic citizenship cannot be captured by such binary oppositions as collectivist/individualist or liberalism/authoritarianism because the virtue of democratic citizenship is that it combines these qualities,³² valuing individual freedom but holding that such freedom is only fully actualized in the context of a strong community. In other words, citizens who contributed willingly to the betterment of their communities while equally valuing individual freedom performed democratic citizenship. The survey thus suggested the possibility that the argument that Korea has been successful because its populace has been weaned on Confucian values and rendered submissive to authority is simply wrong.

As the COVID-19 situation has worsened globally, the gap between East and West in the number of new daily confirmed cases and the mortality rate has increased, and narratives that reinforce the East/West dichotomy have, if anything, become more prevalent.³³ Thus, many academic analyses, while avoiding mention of Confucianism, continue to contrast Western incompetence with Asian competence.³⁴

Indeed, even the SisaIN report on the survey just discussed was not entirely free of the dichotomy, for it situated Korea's praiseworthy democratic citizenship in the broader context of the East-versus-West narrative. The story being told this time is that Korea is doing better than the West and is presented as a model democratic society to the world in the time of global public health crisis.

The Narrativization of Biopolitical Nationalism in the K-Quarantine Project

The ways in which COVID-19 has been transforming politics and sovereign power recall Foucault's notion of "biopolitics" as well as Agamben's extended reworking of Foucault in developing his notions of "homo sacer" and the "state of exception."[35] Indeed, Agamben joined the COVID-19 discussion by arguing prominently that mere survival has now become the top priority and that, predictably, sovereign power is seeking to normalize a state of exception as the regular governing paradigm, as was the case with terrorism in the past.[36] From this perspective, COVID-19 catalyzed the emergence of biopolitical governmentality—for which national security and the lives of individuals alike are tools and objects—as a hegemonic form of control across nations, regions, and political systems. Every government was expected to implement various types of monitoring and actions to limit the casualties in a "war" against the coronavirus and to minimize its impact on its citizens. Thus Foucault, in theorizing biopower, affirmed that, in the modern era, "The ancient right to *take* life or *let* live was replaced by a power to *foster* life or *disallow* it to the point of death."[37] These notions of biopower and biopolitics are especially evident in the measurements used to quantify the current COVID-19 situation, with the real-time reporting of mortality rates, numbers of confirmed case per capita, and various indices, such as the safety index and economic projection index, that experts carefully calculate and compare. These statistics all serve as governing tools for justifying the state's decisions and actions as being intended to preserve life and to protect the economy—such, precisely, is the work of biopolitical governmentality.

The deployment of biopolitical nationalism as each nation races to improve its efficiency in managing the crisis is now especially apparent. As Kloet, Lin, and Chow described the situation, the "biopolitical efforts of nation-states are being compared, applauded and supported"[38] and "citizens pride themselves on living in a country with the 'best' and 'most efficient' containment measures."[39] Already in

2009, Herbert Gottweis, renowned for his extensive study of bioscience, bioethics, and biopolitics, wrote in the editorial introduction to the special "Biopolitics in Asia" issue of *New Genetics and Society*, "Web 2.0 tools of communication, deliberation, and mobilization have demonstrated in some countries such as South Korea their significant potential for reconfiguring biopolitics."[40] He accurately predicted the impact of the rapid development and wide deployment of information communication technology (ICT) in the nation. In the following discussion, I explore the particular type of biopolitical nationalism that the K-quarantine model has constructed.

Unpacking the K-quarantine model: A nexus of information and bio(medical) technologies

Korean biopolitical nationalism is deployed through internationalization of the K-quarantine model and propelled by the amalgamation of bio(medical) technology and information technology. As has been seen, the Korean government has made aggressive attempts to brand the nation as a world leader in terms of responding to the global pandemic through its promotion of the K-quarantine model as a global standard. Notably, Korea's advanced ICT and bio(medical) technology have directly supported all of the 3Ts—testing, trace, and treating—that form the core of the K-quarantine model.

Korea's achievement in this regard has not been fortuitous. Since the 1990s, the government has been investing heavily in bioscience as the future of national industry. This effort peaked in the 2000s, with the story of Dr. Woo-suk Hwang's rise to the status of national hero for his cloning of stem cells and subsequent fall into national disgrace for fabrication of the research, epitomizing the workings of biopolitical nationalism in the first decade of the present century.[41] The ways in which the K-quarantine model has been constructed as a national product during the current pandemic showcases the most recent iteration of biopolitical nationalism in Korea.

As discussed, the conceptualization of the K-quarantine as a model for export is apparent in the Korean government's efforts to standardize and globalize it. Specifically, the government allocated for the project 163.5 billion won (about U.S. $148 million) for research and development (R & D), of which 157.5 billion won (U.S. $142 million) went toward industrialization and 6 billion won (U.S. $5.4 million) toward globalization specifically.⁴² The expenditures on industrialization involved investment in biomedical and biotech companies for the development of COVID-19 vaccines and treatments (111.5 billion won; U.S. $101 million) and for the distribution of test kits and essential quarantine and protective equipment (46 billion won; U.S. $41 million).⁴³ I emphasize that more than 96 percent of the allocated budget was directed to industrialization of the K-quarantine model and that most of that amount went into developing and producing the vaccine and other medicines.

Five diagnostic reagent companies—KogeneBiotech, Seegene, Solgent, SD Bio-sensor, and Biosewoom—obtained emergency-use approval from the government. The first three of these had received R & D funding from the government for developing diagnostic products as of April 2020.⁴⁴ According to the Korea Customs Service, one country bought 4 million won worth of Korean test kits in January; three months later, 103 countries purchased 247 billion won worth in April, representing the development of an enormous market almost overnight.⁴⁵ Notably, the outstanding reliability and quality of Korean products such as test kits and masks have propelled their branding.

The Korean government's expenditures on the globalization and export of biomedicine and biotechnology included financing the K-Quarantine Expo 2020, which Korea International Exhibition Center (KINTEX) and Korea Trade Promotion Corporation (KOTRA) co-hosted and presided over. The exposition was the country's largest thus far and focused on infectious diseases and quarantine industries, and it offered space and opportunities for small business and venture start-ups to promote their products and technology as well as opportunities for consultations about export, including matching potential domestic sellers with international buyers.⁴⁶ This close cooperation between the government, private companies, and health experts epitomizes the concerted promotional and industrial effort that is the national K-quarantine project.

A strong nationwide ICT infrastructure has likewise played a key role in branding the K-quarantine model as a national project, as is particularly evident in the development of various mobile applications for tracking the infected and those in need of self-quarantine. The Korean government's specialized app offers step-by-step guidance through two weeks of self-quarantine, directing users to log their condition daily. Other mobile apps for self-diagnosis, telemedicine service, and coronavirus information were also introduced as part of the effort to flatten the curve of COVID-19, again taking into account all of the 3Ts.

Further, the government used the nationwide telecommunication infrastructure to alert citizens about the most up-to-date information on COVID-19 through

Cellular Broadcasting Service (CBS) and introduced KI-Pass, "which contains QR codes to keep a customer or visitor entry log digitally at high-risk facilities and to implement rapid response measures."[47] Other measures included the Drug Utilization Review (DUR) system and the International Traveler Information System (ITS), the latter of which served "to obtain travel history and quickly share information on confirmed cases."[48] This innovative marshaling of digital technology proved highly effective, though the government's widespread use of personal information without consent (which was authorized under the 2015 Infectious Disease Control and Prevention Act) increased concerns regarding biotechnological surveillance—an issue to which I return below.

In sum, the branding of the K-quarantine model as a global standard has emphasized technologies for detecting the infected rapidly and accurately and isolating and treating them effectively. The spotlight, accordingly, has been on Korea's ICT and bio(medical) technology. Korea's 3T model nicely shows the operation of biopolitical nationalism on multiple levels: first, by presenting and celebrating the K-quarantine model as a global standard; second, by commercializing and globalizing Korea's quarantine-related technology and products, the total revenues from which have been recorded and celebrated as a marker of national (economic) competitiveness; and, third, by implementing various measures and practices based on the 3T model that have been optimized in terms of keeping the numbers of confirmed cases and the mortality rate low.

The articulation of Korean democracy and biopolitical nationalism through the K-quarantine project

The Korean biopolitical nationalism driven by the K-quarantine project is not simply based on the sense that "Korea is doing a good job handling the COVID-19." Rather, the sentiment is more that "Our country is not simply doing a good job but is doing a *better* job than the other countries." The key to this aspect of the K-quarantine discourse is the collective sense that the Korean way of doing things—of testing, tracing, and treating—is *superior to* the way things are done in the "inefficient" West, especially Europe and the U.S.A. This discourse has been repeatedly reaffirmed and re-narrated by health officials to national approval.

As Herbert Gottweis and Byoungsoo Kim aptly put it, "This bionationalistic mobilization was never to be separated from the attempt of the government to push Korea into a position of world leadership in biotechnology."[49] In an interview with the *Wall Street Journal*, Jun-wook Kwon, the deputy director of the KCDC said, "In the past, we had treated the regulations from the World Health Organization and the U.S. as the Bible. But I had to apologize to our citizens because it was time for us to create our own regulations based on our own evidence."[50] Echoing Kwon, Yoonmo Sung, head of the Ministry of Trade, Industry, and Energy, who announced the roadmap, said at a press conference: "It is meaningful that Korea is leading the international standardization of the quarantine models—this is something that the international community had not been able to do in the event of a deadly infectious disease in the past. We will strengthen our global leadership through the international standardization of the K-quarantine model and use it as a stepping stone for a leap forward to lead the new international order."[51]

Thus, the Korean media and the government have continuously presented the K-quarantine model as the global standard, with some support from foreign media and authorities. In this discourse, Korea is leading the new global order through the COVID-19 crisis thanks to its superior quarantine technology. Korea's achievement in this regard stands in stark contrast with the incompetence and inefficiency of the Western response to the pandemic, as exemplified in its "three *no*'s"—no panic, no hoarding, and no lockdown—as observed by both domestic and foreign media outlets.[52]

This biopolitical nationalism has not, of course, been entirely top-down but rather has benefited from a more organic, if contested, relationship between the government and the governed. According to the same May 2020 SisaIN survey discussed earlier,[53] 67.8 percent of Koreans expressed the opinion that Korea was not "a hellish place" while 25.9 percent were of the opinion that it was. The term used to express this notion in the survey was *Hell Chosŏn*, a cynical, self-deprecating coinage popular mainly among young people distrustful of the patriotic and nationalist logic of Korean nationalism. These numbers may not seem particularly encouraging, but the promise represented by the K-quarantine project and the discussion about it has had a dramatic impact on attitudes across the political spectrum, so that even those who have mocked what they considered blind patriotism have come to feel pride in Korea through the collective experience of responding to the global pandemic. Furthermore, 63.7 percent of the respondents to the survey said they would choose to be a Korean citizen again in a future life, and, when asked to compare Korea with advanced Western countries in terms of civic capability, 58 percent said that Korea was superior, while only 25.5 percent said it was similar and 14.1 percent that it was inferior.[54] These figures reveal a qualitative transition in Korean nationalism in the sense that it is no longer based on the sense that Korea has become an advanced society but is, in fact, *superior* to many other such societies.[55] Put differently, "Koreans did not feel pride in the K-quarantine alone but also in their sophisticated sense of citizenship and in a national system that successfully navigated the difficulties of quarantining."[56]

The K-quarantine project has, then, emerged as a space in which citizens collectively experience national pride and excellence through a coordinated war against the enemy, which is the virus. In the process, they learned to trust the government's ability to manage crises, which, in turn, bolstered national competitiveness. Thus, to some extent, the global pandemic is a kind of "World War III" (metaphorically speaking), with nations confronting a mutual, global foe. In this war, Korea experienced an early victory that reinforced such virtues as comradeship, solidarity, and responsibility. Further, by encouraging Koreans to *sense* these virtues collectively as a nation, the K-quarantine project formulates a particular version of nationalism.[57] That is, this new kind of patriotism is not simply about superiority in bio/informational technology but involves citizens *feeling their country is superior* to the West more broadly, especially in terms of political systems and civility. The K-quarantine model manifests the Korean way of doing things—flattening the curve without a lockdown, successfully conducting a national election in the midst of the pandemic, and cooperating on new measures and norms without losing individual freedoms—and gives Korean people pride by demonstrating what an advanced democratic society should look like to the world.

In the Shadow of the K-Quarantine Model: Biopolitical Surveillance and Digital Technology

Amid the current global public health disaster, it seems obvious that the role of the state must expand along with its sovereign power. The function of the state during the pandemic is simultaneously to prevent the virus from spreading and the economy from stagnating. Under the current situation, it has been noticeable that countries in which digital media are under centralized control have been successful in controlling the spread of the virus. In particular, Taiwan, Singapore, China, and Korea have used digital technology proactively in testing and tracing. It is no exaggeration to describe the COVID-19 era as the point in human history when biopolitical surveillance regimes came fully into operation, at least in countries with advanced and centralized digital-media infrastructure.

To trace the infected, control their movements, and manage individuals at high-risk for infection, the governments in these states have encouraged their citizens to make use of digital technologies, in some cases demanding that they do so. The technologies have increased the effectiveness of authorities in exercising new forms of power for the express purpose of protecting citizens' health and lives. The datafication of the personal information relating to location, health, and contacts has at the same time served to optimize state governmentality.[58] By gathering increasingly large amounts of data, governments increase their effectiveness in managing the spread of the virus, calculating the associated risks, and implementing the best possible response—for example when prioritizing sectors of the population for vaccination and allocating limited resources to save the most lives possible. The citizens, considering governmental surveillance inevitable, even *desire* monitoring that, they believe, will make them safer. The government's mandates that citizens establish a digital presence (e.g., "Use this self-safety application" or "Make sure to register through this QR code wherever you go") increase their sense that they *feel safe* irrespective of the effectiveness of the actual measures taken.

I emphasize that biopolitical surveillance is not exercised unidirectionally, from the state to the individual. Rather, citizens' surveillance of each other complements the actions of governments in this regard. Thus, despite the praise for the K-quarantine system in foreign media, the early success of this system in the country that developed it was only possible because of already pervasive daily surveillance (e.g., through CCTV), cyberbullying, and peer-monitoring in Korean culture. Korean media outlets initially referred to COVID-19 as "the Wuhan virus," thereby fueling fear and hatred toward ethnic Chinese, especially members of the country's Chinese immigrant community. A little later, in February, mainstream media outlets as well as personal blogs and social media posts aggressively blamed followers of the *Shinch'ŏnji* in Daegu, as mentioned earlier as the epicenter of an early outbreak of the virus, and the city and people from the city were shunned; for instance, it was reported that a hotel in Seoul rejected customers from Daegu, and products manufactured in Daegu or parcels sent from Daegu were canceled or returned for a refund owing to the fear of infection,[59] which further aggravated Korea's already serious regional tensions. Similarly, when another mass infection occurred in May, this time in the Itaewon area in Seoul, where, it was reported, gay clubs were among the sources, Korean media and netizens alike stigmatized gays and queer communities as being reluctant to comply with the government's rules, irresponsible, and selfish for prioritizing their pleasure over the nation's safety.[60]

Such stigmatization of the infected were facilitated by the enormous amount of information about individuals that was readily accessible online in the name of transparency.[61] Specifically, the Infectious Disease Control and Prevention Act empowered Korean health officials to collect sensitive personal information about those who tested positive for the virus as well as those suspected to be infected and made it public. Health agencies at the national and local levels sent cell phone message alerts about new confirmed cases to citizens, including the age and gender of infected individuals and a detailed log of their movements prior to their testing positive.[62] Beyond the cell phone messages, the same information was also shared on national and local government websites as well as free COVID-19-related smartphone apps.[63] While the publication of this information was intended to identify individuals who may have been exposed to the virus and encourage them to undergo testing as well as to help other citizens avoid infection hotspots, there was considerable debate regarding whether this level of disclosure was necessary.

Small businesses that had been identified by name as places visited by the infected were hit especially hard, in some cases being driven into bankruptcy. Further, though the personal information was anonymized before being made public, it was often sufficiently specific to identify infected individuals, especially those living in small communities. Once the identities of the infected had been deduced based on the information revealed by the government, their personal information (names, phone numbers, Facebook accounts, and more) were quickly spread online, where they could be judged and blamed for supposedly careless or irresponsible behavior.[64] Hence, unsurprisingly, a survey conducted by researchers at Seoul National University's Graduate School of Public Health in February 2020 indicated that Koreans feared the "criticisms and further damage that they may suffer from being infected" more than the infection itself.[65] The stigmatization and even criminalization of the infected were made possible by a networked interpersonal surveillance system made up of citizens ready to look askance at and punish their fellow citizens for failure to share the responsibility to prevent harm to Korean society.

Thus, I further emphasize that Korean biopolitical nationalism is not possible without a combination of (1) state-level surveillance involving bio(medical) and ICT and (2) citizen-level networked, interpersonal surveillance. Remarkably, both levels of surveillance are perceived not as an infringement on a fundamental right to privacy, but as a shared civil responsibility to protect the society from the virus. To be more precise, under the current biopolitical nationalism regime, as each nation races to be the most efficient in combating the coronavirus, it transforms its citizens' very notion of surveillance. The agents of the regime insist that submission to this digital(ized) surveillance is a civic duty, a sacrifice made *in exchange for* public safety. Therefore, each individual is expected to use the surveillance devices *willingly*, which is the mark of a "responsible" citizen. Perhaps it is this convergence between biopolitical nationalism and (digital) surveillance that simultaneously shapes a new subjectivity and drives the establishment of biopolitical surveillance regimes that will be the norm across the globe in the post-COVID-19 era.

Conclusion

Korea's response to the early phase of the COVID-19 pandemic was deemed effective and efficient and, as a result, quickly received praise and emerged as a global model. The K-quarantine project, which can be summed up as the 3T model, demonstrates Korea's biopolitical nationalism in that this model is exportable in like manner as K-pop and K-drama, the country's highly successful cultural exports. The K-quarantine model, driven by the combination of biomedical technology and communications technology, projects Korea's desire to be a leading global player, in this case by demonstrating its capacity to handle a global public health crisis. The narrative of K-quarantine as a national project has been forged simultaneously by the government's initiatives and by civic engagement and participation. In this way, Korea has projected its soft power, branding itself as both a high-tech powerhouse and a society to be admired worldwide, especially during the pandemic.

More importantly, Korea treats the praise that it has received from international health authorities and global news media outlets as external validation for the K-quarantine project. However, this success narrative is precarious since the pandemic is ongoing globally, and the situation remains highly volatile. Paradoxically, this uncertainty gives each East Asian nation grounds to claim that its model is superior by defining success with the most favorable criteria—whether in terms of technological achievement, its political system, or even its culture.

In the meantime, the fact that Korea has never officially declared a state of emergency, despite the multiple waves of infection that the country has faced, deserves attention. The emergency measures currently in place were based on the provisions of a bill passed after the severe outbreak of MERS in 2015. Accordingly, it is not certain when or whether the digital surveillance and datafication tolerated under the ongoing pandemic will cease. From this perspective, it is in Korea during the pandemic that Agamben's state of exception[66] has appeared in its most extreme form, for a state of emergency has become normalized.

Analyzing the Korean experience of this state of emergency, Jaeho Kang insisted that "The current crisis of the COVID-19 pandemic is not a breakdown of normality but a continuation of the state of emergency" that "serves to normalize the state of emergency and perpetuate the crisis for the marginalized, vulnerable and unprotected citizens."[67] He further claimed, "We cannot go back to normal because normal is a state of emergency. A 'real' state of emergency is required to stop the 'normal' state of emergency in which South Korea exists."[68] The untangling of this dialectic of "the state of emergency" then is among the most important tasks facing governments and citizens in the post-COVID-19 era.

NOTES

1. Michel Foucault, *The Birth of Biopolitics: Lectures at the Collège De France, 1978–79*, ed. Michel Senellart, trans. Graham Burchell (New York: Palgrave Macmillan, 2008); Giorgio Agamben, *Homo Sacer: Sovereign Power and Bare Life* (Stanford, CA: Stanford University Press, 1998).
2. Deep Knowledge Group, "Covid-19 Regional Safety Assessment 30 Countries & Regions," https://www.dkv.global/covid-regional-assessment-july-30.
3. Jeroen de Kloet, Jian Lin, and Yiu Fai Chow, "'We Are Doing Better': Biopolitical Nationalism and the Covid-19 Virus in East Asia," *European Journal of Cultural Studies* 23, no. 4 (2020): 635–640.
4. Kloet, Lin, and Chow, "'We Are Doing Better,'" 635.
5. I put "successful" in quotation marks here to acknowledge the complexity (and difficulty) of defining success in efforts to handle the spread and impact of COVID-19. To be sure, Korea's response to the virus prior to the availability of vaccines—i.e., the quarantining effort in general, including "flattening the curve" that represented the numbers of the infected—was deemed successful by both domestic and international communities, as I show in this paper. Nevertheless, Korea's vaccination effort has been slow and inefficient, thereby inviting criticism and fueling both domestic and international cynicism and, thus, challenging the very notion of what counts as success in combating the

unpredictable and ongoing pandemic. Therefore, in this paper, I use the terms success or successful to describe the K-quarantine project with specific reference to Korea's early effort and response to the virus before the third wave in the country in the full knowledge that the meaning of success has become highly contested.

6. The Government of the Republic of Korea, "All about Korea's Response to Covid-19," (2020), 212.
7. Caroline Kantis, Samantha Kiernan, and Jason Socrates Bardi, "Updated: Timeline of the Coronavirus," https://www.thinkglobalhealth.org/article/updated-timeline-coronavirus.
8. Andrei Illarionov and Natalya Pivovarova, "Two Supertypes of Coronavirus: 'East Asian' and 'European,'" *CATO Institute*, May 8 2020.
9. Illarionov and Pivovarova, "Two Supertypes of Coronavirus."
10. Illarionov and Pivovarova, "Two Supertypes of Coronavirus."
11. Illarionov and Pivovarova, "Two Supertypes of Coronavirus."
12. The Government of the Republic of Korea, "All about Korea," 13.
13. The Government of the Republic of Korea, "All about Korea," 14.
14. The spread of COVID-19 worldwide has varied as much as the efforts to combat it and was still ongoing in January 2021 as I completed this chapter. Given the evolving nature of the situation, the data and argumentation here only take into account the first through the third waves of infection in Korea.
15. The Government of the Republic of Korea, "All about Korea," 14.
16. Ministry of Culture, Sports and Tourism, "100 Days of Covid-19 Quarantine in Korea," (2020).
17. Ministry of Culture, Sports and Tourism, "100 Days of Covid-19," 1.
18. Ministry of Culture, Sports and Tourism, "100 Days of Covid-19," 2–5.
19. To encourage the wide participation of health officials across the world, the webinars were offered with simultaneous translations in multiple languages, including English, French, and Russian, and were accessible through the government's official website anywhere in the world in real time.
20. The Government of the Republic of Korea, "Flattening the Curve on Covid-19: How Korea Responded to a Pandemic Using ICT," (Seoul: The Government of the Republic of Korea, 2020); The Government of the Republic of Korea, "All about Korea."
21. The Government of the Republic of Korea, "All about Korea," 36.
22. Morten Soendergaard Larsen, "Covid-19 Has Crushed Everybody's Economy—except for South Korea's," *Foreign Policy*, September 16 2020.
23. Gwan-yul Cheon, "'The World of Koreans' That the Covid19 Exposed—Unexpected Response," *SisaIN*, June 2, 2020.

24. Jérôme Béglé, "Le Con Nement Nous Fait DéCouvrir Qu'avant, Ce N'éTait Pas Si Mal," *Le Point*, April 27 2020.
25. Patrick Wintour, "Coronavirus: Who Will Be Winners and Losers in New World Order?," *The Guardian*, April 11 2020.
26. Wintour, "Coronavirus."
27. Timothy W. Martin, "East vs. West: Coronavirus Fight Tests Divergent Strategies," *Wall Street Journal*, March 13, 2020.
28. Minjung Noh, "Understanding South Korea's Religious Landscape, Patient 31, and COVID-19 Exceptionalism," in *Teaching about Asia in a Time of Pandemic* (Asia Shorts), ed. David L Kenley (Ann Arbor, MI: Association for Asian Studies, 2020), 31–40.
29. Nathan Park, "Confucianism Isn't Helping South Korea Beat the Coronavirus," *Foreign Policy*, April 2, 2020.
30. Cheon, "The World of Koreans' That the Covid19 Exposed—Unexpected Response."
31. Cheon, "The World of Koreans' That the Covid19 Exposed—Unexpected Response."
32. Cheon, "The World of Koreans' That the Covid19 Exposed—Unexpected Response."
33. Margherita Stancati and Dasl Yoon, "Covid-19's Global Divide: As West Reels, Asia Keeps Virus at Bay," *Wall Street Journal*, October 20, 2020; Byung-Chul Han, "Why Asia Is Better at Beating the Pandemic Than Europe: The Key Lies in Civility," *EL PAÍS*, October 30 2020.
34. Victor Cha, "Asia's Covid-19 Lessons for the West: Public Goods, Privacy, and Social Tagging," *Washington Quarterly* 43, no. 2 (2020): 1–18; Faculty of Social Science & Public Policy, "Preventing the Next Pandemic: Lessons from East Asia" (London: King's College London, 2020).
35. Foucault, *The Birth of Biopolitics*; Agamben, *Homo Sacer*; Giorgio Agamben, *State of Exception* (Chicago: University of Chicago Press, 2005).
36. Giorgio Agamben, "Contagio," *Quodlibet*, March 11 2020.
37. Michel Foucault, *The History of Sexuality 1*, trans. Robert Hurley (New York: Vintage Books 1990), 138 (emphasis in original).
38. Kloet, Lin, and Chow, "'We Are Doing Better,'" 636.
39. Kloet, Lin, and Chow, "'We Are Doing Better,'" 637.
40. Herbert Gottweis, "Biopolitics in Asia," *New Genetics and Society* 28, no. 3 (2009): 204.
41. Dr. Woo-suk Hwang, a research scientist specializing in stem-cell research, was hailed as a national hero for supposed breakthroughs in the laboratory but was later found to have fabricated his research. The resulting scandal in the mid-2000s dealt a severe blow to Korea's biotech research and industry; see Herbert Gottweis and Byoungsoo Kim, "Explaining Hwang-Gate: South Korean Identity Politics between Bionationalism and Globalization," *Science, Technology, & Human Values* 35, no. 4 (2010): 501–524.

42. The Government of the Republic of Korea, "Strategies for International Standardization of the K-Quarantine 3T (Test-Trace-Treat)," (June 11, 2020).
43. The Government of the Republic of Korea, "Strategies for International Standardization."
44. The Government of the Republic of Korea, "Flattening the Curve on Covid-19," 21.
45. Soon-yu Kwon, "Biotech and Webtoon Take a Leep into the Global Market," *Hankyoreh*, June 8, 2020.
46. For more information, please see K-Quarantine Expo 2020 brochure, https://kotrasiberia.ru/wp-content/uploads/2020/07/K-Quarantine-Broshyura.pdf.
47. The Government of the Republic of Korea, "All about Korea," 51.
48. The Government of the Republic of Korea, "All about Korea," 222.
49. Gottweis and Kim, "Explaining Hwang-Gate: South Korean Identity Politics between Bionationalism and Globalization," 519.
50. Timothy W. Martin and Dasl Yoon, " How South Korea Successfully Managed Coronavirus," *Wall Street Journal*, September 25, 2020.
51. Youngmee Kim, "We Have a Guide to Making the K-Quarantine Model the World's Standard," *Ministry of Health and Welfare*, June 11, 2020. Translation from Korean to English is mine.
52. Ministry of Culture, Sports and Tourism, "100 Days of Covid-19."
53. Yoo Min Lee, Ji Yeon Yoon, and Han Sol Woo, "The Changes That K-Quarantine Has Brought? Sympathy, Solidarity, and Pride," *KBS News*, May 20 2020.
54. Lee, Yoon, and Woo, "The Changes That K-Quarantine Has Brought?"
55. Eun Young Song, "Disaster Nationalism: The Quality Transformation of Korean Nationalism in the Covid-19 Era," *Culture/Science* 103 (2020): 118.
56. Song, "Disaster Nationalism," 131.
57. As the pandemic has continued, the value of these virtues for building a better society has come into question. Thus, Seoul Nation University, KBS, and SisaIN teamed up for a follow-up to the March 2020 survey in November 2020 in which the respondents expressed grim frustration that the situation seemed unlikely to improve any time soon, and many expressed the opinion that individuals should focus more on their own lives than on the broader community or society.
58. Jaeho Kang, "The Media Spectacle of a Techno-City: COVID-19 and the South Korean Experience of the State of Emergency," *Journal of Asian Studies* 79, no. 3 (2020): 589–598; Jeehyun Jenny Lee, "Vital Dataveillance: Investigating Data in Exchange for Vitality through South Korea's COVID-19 Technogovernance," *Communication, Culture and Critique* 15, no 4 (2022): 499–506.
59. Woo Young Kim, So Yeon Lee, and Yoo Jeong Kwon, "'Reservation Refused,' 'Not Buying'

... Daegu/Gyeongbuk Citizens Hurt by Corona Tag," *Choson Daily*, March 17, 2020.
60. Jake Kwon and Julia Hollingsworth, "Virus Outbreak Linked to Seoul Clubs Popular with Lgbt Community Stokes Homophobia," *CNN*, May 13, 2020.
61. Yeran Kim, "Bio or Zoe? Dilemmas of Biopolitics and Data Governmentality during COVID-19," *Cultural Studies* 35, no. 2–3 (2021): 370–381. Kim argues that Korea's controlling system under COVID-19 is characterized by totalization, exclusion, and stigmatization.
62. Jung Won Sonn, "Coronavirus: South Korea's Success in Controlling Disease Is Due to Its Acceptance of Surveillance," *The Conversation*, March 19, 2020.
63. Sonn, "Coronavirus."
64. Hyung Eun Kim, "Coronavirus Privacy: Are South Korea's Alerts Too Revealing?," *BBC*, March 5, 2020.
65. Kim, "Coronavirus Privacy."
66. Agamben, *State of Exception*.
67. Kang, "The Media Spectacle," 598.
68. Kang, "The Media Spectacle," 598.

What Motivated the Sharing of Disinformation about China and COVID-19?

A Study of Social Media Users in Kenya and South Africa

Herman Wasserman and Dani Madrid-Morales

CONCERNS THAT DISINFORMATION HAS BEEN ON THE INCREASE ON THE AFRICAN continent, like in much of the rest of the world, have been at the forefront of academic debates for some time.[1] Some scholars refer to a "crisis of disinformation," which has "ravaged electoral, social and cultural processes with devastating consequences."[2] Others have found high levels of perceived exposure to disinformation in several African nations.[3] This happens as other sociopolitical factors affect the media's ability to facilitate knowledge sharing in the interest of social progress. Globally, public perceptions about declining levels of trust in the media have been on the rise, with a range of surveys indicating public concerns about "impartiality, sensationalism, relevance and lack of depth" in the media.[4] Research by the Reuters Institute suggests that, although trust levels in news media rebounded during the COVID-19 pandemic, the spread of disinformation on social media, particularly messaging platforms in the Global South, continues apace.[5] On the African continent, for instance, there is a long history of media that have been "captured" by elites and are seen not to work in the interest of the broader citizenry. This has led to different levels of trust in public and private media.[6]

The increased presence of Chinese media outlets in Africa has made some of these matters more complex. Since the 1990s, Beijing has embarked on a "going out strategy in its international relations policy, which includes increasing its media footprint on the continent.[7] African audiences and journalists have responded to this influx in different ways: some actively resist Chinese media, others take a skeptical stance, while some use Chinese media content in their own reporting.[8] Those who were resistant or skeptical have mostly expressed concerns about the negative impact that China's state-controlled-media model might have on the fragile cultures of free expression and media independence on the continent.[9] Some of these processes have coincided with increasing tensions between China and a wider range of liberal democracies, notably the U.S.[10] Sino-American tensions have also extended to the media industry, with both U.S. and Chinese officials imposing restrictions on visas, operating licenses, and access to media products from each other.[11]

In this context, recent events have created challenges for China's "going out" strategy. Allegations of ethnic cleansing in Xinjiang, suppression of pro-democracy protests in Hong Kong, and China's handling of the COVID-19 pandemic through a series of prolonged lockdowns have made it harder for China to promote its image globally, including in Africa.[12] The global public-image crisis experienced by the Chinese government has led to a more assertive approach to the management of foreign public opinion. Beijing has taken to more aggressively countering criticism through coordinated top-down information campaigns, led by "Wolf Warrior" diplomats, and by "borrowing boats to sail overseas" (*jie chuan chu hai*), an expression that refers to inserting content in the domestic media in the target countries to promote ideas aligned with China's preferred strategic narratives.[13]

China's attempts to steer specific narratives of COVID-19 around the globe should be seen against this background of changing geopolitical and media contexts. Some of the resistance and skepticism about China's influence and its media presence in Africa has emerged in some of the disinformation campaigns, rumors, and "fake news" circulating online.[14] Given that China has often been perceived in global media discourses as the origin of the virus outbreak on the one hand and as a global provider of aid and assistance on the other, the 2020 COVID-19 outbreak provides a case study to understand how the discourses about the pandemic tie into wider geopolitical narratives. Within this broader goal, this chapter looks at the link between social media users' perceptions of and attitudes toward China and their motivations to share disinformation related to COVID-19 and China. The focus will be on Kenya and South Africa, as examples of African countries with vibrant media environments and active online communities where Chinese media's "going out" strategy has been felt most prominently.

Kenya and South Africa have democratic political systems and robust citizen engagement in the mediated public sphere. The wide availability of and access to social media, mostly accessed through mobile phones, has facilitated public participation in political debates, but has also played a big role in the spread of disinformation. We find one such example in the 2007–2008 elections in Kenya, where rumors about election rigging spread via SMS technology.[15] Rumors and falsehoods circulating on these circuits of informal exchanges of information may result from the lack of trust in the mainstream news media but could also be read as a result of political disillusionment with local politicians and elites, as well as global superpowers. When people feel disempowered, they might be more likely to share and believe rumors rather than trust the mainstream news. This could be because rumors have a stronger emotional appeal, or offer a better explanation for their own lived experience, than mainstream news does. The appeal of rumors can be increased further by pre-existing views about an individual, a group, or a country, in this case China, which elicits polarized views in the sub-Saharan-Africa context.

Global Chinese Media, Public Opinion, and COVID-19

The increased economic presence of China on the African continent, which is part of its larger "going out" policy, has been a core component of Beijing foreign policy since the early 2000s.[16] An important part of this strategy has been the growth of Chinese media outlets on the continent. This expansion of China's footprint in African media spheres included establishing regional headquarters of the Xinhua news service in Kenya, opening a regional hub of China Radio International (CRI) in Nairobi, developing Africa-focused programming by China Global Television Network (CGTN), producing localized journalistic content (e.g., *Chinafrica* magazine), distributing content (e.g. the StarTimes satellite television platform), developing infrastructure (e.g. cell phone networks), channeling direct investment into African media (e.g. the Independent Media group in South Africa), and launching various training and exchange sponsorships for African journalists and students.[17] In addition, Dani Madrid-Morales has suggested that, since 2018, Chinese media and other actors working in engaging foreign audiences have also been active in "managing" foreign public opinion by other means, including running multilingual coordinated campaigns on social media or paying news media outlets to distribute content created by Chinese media.[18]

The diversification of China's media presence should be seen as part of the nation's broader initiatives to harness "soft power."[19] By promising better and more sympathetic coverage of both Africa and China, Chinese media outlets aim not only to build better relationships with governments in the region and increase their market share internationally, but also bolster China's discursive power (*huayu quan*) in the global arena.[20] Some NGOs and civil-society organizations, like Washington-based Freedom House, have seen these mediated activities in Africa as part of a larger global campaign that is "leveraging propaganda disinformation, censorship, and influence over key nodes in the information flow," which undermines "democratic norms, erodes national sovereignty, weakens the financial sustainability of independent media, and violates local laws."[21] Despite these concerns, little evidence exists of the actual impact of China's media on audiences. Only a few studies have begun to explore the influence of Chinese media on public opinion.[22] These studies find a much less direct, causal, and homogenous impact on African audiences than is often assumed.

Globally, attitudes toward China seem to have grown more negative in recent years, with the COVID-19 pandemic marking a significant inflection point. While an Afrobarometer survey of sixteen African countries in 2014–2015 found respondents to have largely positive views of China's economic involvement on the continent (65 percent of respondents said China had a "somewhat" or "very" positive influence on their country), a subsequent survey (2018–2019, prior to the COVID-19 pandemic) found a decline in that number: only 60 percent of respondents across sixteen countries thought that China had a positive influence.[23] Pointing in the same direction, a Pew Research Center survey in late-2020 found that across fourteen advanced economies, a majority had a negative opinion of China, the most unfavorable findings in a decade. These views appear to be closely linked to the COVID-19 outbreak: a median of 61 percent across these countries said they thought China did a poor job in handling the outbreak.[24]

What these data suggest is that despite the efforts the Chinese government has made in recent years to extend its soft power in Africa, the outbreak of the COVID-19 pandemic could potentially have damaged its image on the continent. The spread of disinformation relating to China's presence in Africa as well as the country's association with the origins of the pandemic might have amplified existing attitudes, perceptions, and biases toward China. Issues such as the accusations of genocide in Xinjiang, the suppression of dissent in Hong Kong, threats against Taiwan, and China's handling of the COVID-19 pandemic may have further eroded China's attractiveness and reversed some of its soft power gains, but no evidence exists to date on such possible causal links. Considering all this, in this chapter we first ask, *What were the prevailing views toward China and toward COVID-19 among South Africans and Kenyans during the first wave of the pandemic*? (We refer to this question later as research question 1, or RQ1.)

There are multiple reasons why the COVID-19 pandemic provides an appropriate entry point into an analysis of African attitudes toward China. China has been blamed for not only being the most likely origin of the pandemic, but also for covering up information about the virus, mishandling the initial outbreak, and punishing whistleblowers who raised concerns about its coming impact.[25] The pandemic has also given cause to some political leaders to engage in anti-Chinese rhetoric and xenophobic discourse, for instance by labeling COVID-19 the "China virus" or referring to COVID-19 as "kung flu."[26] In response to these accusations, China has relied on its global media network, diplomatic missions, and social media users to counter anti-Chinese rhetoric by using a range of communicative strategies that range from disseminating self-congratulatory news and reports, to more conventional forms of propaganda. In addition, Chinese media have also engaged in disinformation campaigns to criticize the failures of democratic governments in dealing with the pandemic. For example, to attack the response of the U.S. government to China's failures in handling the virus, Chinese media and diplomats have peddled unfounded conspiracy narratives about the origin of the COVID-19 outbreak being at Fort Detrick, in the U.S. State of Maryland.[27]

The COVID-19 pandemic also offers a unique opportunity to explore how African publics engage with disinformation about China, given how prominent it was on social media.[28] As we noted earlier, in this chapter we understand "disinformation" as an umbrella term to refer to all types of false information that have the potential to cause harm. This would include false news stories, coordinated disinformation campaigns aimed against China, and viral hoaxes. In Africa, for instance, disinformation campaigns promoting anti-vaccination messages have drawn on existing anti-China sentiment. One such example would include media posts blaming China (and India) for providing ineffective vaccines to Africans.[29] The virality of many of these messages might have contributed to eroding audiences' perceptions of China. For this to happen, it might be important that those exposed to disinformation about China and COVID-19 would need to believe these messages were true. All of this leads us to ask our second research question: *To what extent did South Africans and Kenyans believe in disinformation related to China and COVID-19 on social media?* (We refer to this question later as research question 2, or RQ2.)

For false information to spread and have an impact, it must also be shared and amplified. Understanding what motivates the sharing is, therefore, important. When studying sharing motivations, it is imperative to examine how media users reflect on their sharing practices, how they display agency in choosing what information, true or false, to share, and how these practices relate to their trust in the news media. While there is abundant work on users' motivations to engage with disinformation,[30] the COVID-19 pandemic might have brought to the fore new motivations. Given the blame placed on China for the origins of the pandemic and its initial cover-up of the outbreak,[31] social media users may find in China a scapegoat upon which to project their frustrations. The pandemic may also give cause to social media users to amplify existing stereotypes and biases toward China by sharing disinformation relating to the country and its influence in Africa. These considerations lead us to ask our final research question: *What were the prevailing motivations expressed by South Africans and Kenyans to share disinformation about COVID-19 and China on social media?* (We refer to this question later as research question 3, or RQ3.)

We address each of the research questions separately in the next three sections. To do so, we refer to data collected in April 2020 through online surveys in Kenya ($n = 970$) and South Africa ($n = 991$) distributed among adults over the age of eighteen. Because online surveys tend to overrepresent urban and young residents, during the collection of responses we enforced quotas around age, gender, and region/province to better reflect each country's demographic breakdown. Our sample includes 51.1 percent women (50.9 percent in Kenya and 51.4 percent in South Africa), has a median age of thirty-four (thirty-one in Kenya, thirty-six in South Africa), and comprises social media users from all South African provinces, as well as in all Kenyan counties, with the exception of Mandera and West Pokot. In addition, post-stratification weights (by gender and age group) were used during the data-analysis process. All the results presented below are done with weighted data. Despite our efforts to draw a diverse, representative, and inclusive sample, our data can only speak about those Kenyans and South Africans with regular access to the Internet, not the entire population. That said, and given that this study focuses on social media content, our methodological approach—while not ideal—can still provide a meaningful description of how social media users in the two countries engaged with disinformation about China during the early stages of the COVID-19 pandemic.

Attitudes toward China and COVID-19

At the peak of the first wave of the COVID-19 pandemic, attitudes toward China in both Kenya and South Africa were far from positive (RQ1). To measure these attitudes, we used a modified version of the scale developed by Simon Anholt in his study of nation branding and soft power to measure how attractive nations are abroad.[32] Survey respondents were asked about their level of agreement with five statements included in the original scale, plus one additional statement that referred to China's influence on Africa. The scale ranges from 0 (strongly disagree) to 4 (strongly agree). We present a summary of the results in table 1, which also includes, for comparative purposes, a summary of responses to the same prompts about the United States. In all questions, both Kenyans and South Africans had a more negative view of China than they did of the U.S.; differences between the two nations were more pronounced among Kenyans. For example, to the item "China/U.S. is competently and honestly governed," both Kenyan and South African respondents gave a higher score to the United States than China (Kenya: M_{China} = 1.79, $M_{U.S.}$ = 2.35; South Africa M_{China} = 1.44, $M_{U.S.}$ = 1.67). The differences between responses about China and the U.S. were statistically significant in both the Kenyan—$t(1928.6) = -9.28, p < .001$—and South African samples—$t(1974.9) = -3.10, p < .005$. Differences were most pronounced for the item "China/U.S. is a country where I would like to live and work," while scores were most similar, with differences not statistically significant in the South African sample—$(1963,1) = -1.43, p = .153$—for the item "China/U.S. has a positive economic and political influence on Africa."

As we noted earlier, public sentiment toward China in several African countries appears to have been in decline in recent years. This trend might have been accentuated because of COVID-19. An alternative explanation is that despite all of China's efforts to boost its soft power, Kenyans, and South Africans—with all their nuanced views—still gravitate more toward U.S. cultural products and social/political values, and therefore exhibit more positive attitudes toward the United States. This might be occurring even though, to many Kenyans and South Africans,

TABLE 1. Attitudes toward China and the United States in Kenya and South Africa (0 to 4 scale)

	KENYA N = 970		SOUTH AFRICA N = 991	
	CHINA	U.S.	CHINA	U.S.
X is competently and honestly governed.	1.79	2.35	1.44	1.67
X respects the rights of its citizens and treats them with fairness.	1.65	2.83	1.44	2.07
X behaves responsibly to protect the environment.	1.59	2.66	1.33	1.88
The media in X are free and objective.	1.42	3.00	1.26	2.20
X has a positive economic and political influence on Africa.	2.53	2.88	2.14	2.23
X is a country where I would like to live and work.	1.10	2.97	1.03	2.26

TABLE 2. Kenyans' and South Africans' assessment of government responses to COVID-19 (0 to 4 scale)

	KENYA N = 970	SOUTH AFRICA N = 991
Chinese government response	2.38	2.07
U.S. government response	1.89	1.51
WHO response	2.87	2.61
Own country's government response	2.22	2.77

Washington did not handle the pandemic well. When asked about government responses to the COVID-19 pandemic, survey respondents appeared to be particularly critical about the way the Trump administration responded to the crisis (see table 2). South Africans gave the highest score to their own government's response (M = 2.77, SD = 1.30), followed by the World Health Organization, or WHO (M = 2.61, SD = 1.24) and China (M = 2.07, SD = 1.89), leaving the U.S. last (M = 1.51, SD = 1.46). In the case of Kenya, the rank from highest to lowest was WHO (M = 2.87, SD = 1.06), China (M = 2.38, SD = 1.82), Kenya (M = 2.22, SD = 1.42) and, finally, the U.S. (M = 1.89, SD = 1.58). Without longitudinal data to compare views before and after the pandemic, it is difficult to pinpoint what explains differences in attitudes toward the U.S. and China. However, and given respondents' relatively positive views about how the Chinese government responded to the crisis, a possible hypothesis would be that the differences (more positive views of the U.S. than China) existed before the pandemic. This gap in perceptions might have been made more evident given that many, even while acknowledging the effective response taken by the Chinese government, might associate the outbreak of the virus to China.

During the early days of the outbreak, a significant amount of the information circulating online about COVID-19 and China could have been labeled as disinformation. Two of the most prevalent topics on social media included discussions around the origins of the virus and (often xenophobic) comments that contributed to the stigmatizations of East Asians.[33] In table 3, we present a summary of Kenyans' and South Africans' views on these two issues. We asked respondents to indicate how much they agreed or disagreed with a list of statements that either referred to conspiracy theories about the origins of the virus or xenophobic attitudes toward Asian communities. We adapted the statements from those developed by J. Hunter Priniski and Keith Holyoak.[34] There were no significant differences in the average support for conspiracy theories about the origins of the virus between South Africans (M = 2.05; SD = 0.91) and Kenyans (M = 2.11; SD = 0.89), nor in their level of agreement with xenophobic responses to the pandemic (Kenya: M = 2.03, SD = 0.84; South Africa: M = 2.02; SD = 0.78).[35] While, overall, the average scores in both countries fell right at the middle of the scale (from 0 to 4), there were some differences between participants' support for different items. When it comes to xenophobic responses, the predominant view was that referring to the virus as the "Chinese coronavirus" or to COVID-19 as the "Wuhan disease" was racist (38 percent of Kenyans strongly agreed with the statement, and 33 percent of South Africans did). At the same time, however, many supported the closing of borders to foreigners

TABLE 3. COVID-19 related attitudes in Kenya and South Africa (0 to 4 scale)

	KENYA N = 970	SOUTH AFRICA N = 991
Xenophobic beliefs		
I am extra cautious around Asian people to protect against COVID-19.	1.74	1.52
One of the best ways to reduce the spread of COVID-19 is to stop immigration into our country.	2.94	2.82
Because of COVID-19, my country should reduce its interactions with China.	2.01	2.19
I find it racist when people refer to the coronavirus as "Chinese coronavirus" or "Wuhan disease."	2.58	2.44
Conspiracy beliefs		
The global spread of COVID-19 was planned and orchestrated.	2.23	2.10
COVID-19 emerged from natural conditions.	1.61	1.84
COVID-19 was engineered in a laboratory.	2.48	2.26
The scientific community is spreading fake news about COVID-19.	1.33	1.68

(39 percent of South Africans strongly agreed with the statement "One of the best ways to reduce the spread of COVID-19 is to stop immigration into our country," compared to 49 percent of Kenyans), even though there is limited evidence that this measure could have helped stop the spread of the virus once it was already circulating domestically.

There is also some discrepancy in the views of Kenyans and South Africans regarding conspiracy theories about the origins of the virus. For instance, most Kenyans (52.2 percent) and many South Africans (42.4 percent) agreed or strongly agreed with the statement "COVID-19 was engineered in a laboratory," as was often posited on social media posts. The Wuhan "lab leak theory" has since been refuted by scientific evidence.[36] At the same time, in an apparent contradiction, a large number of respondents in both countries (Kenya: 55.4 percent; South Africa: 40.6 percent) disagreed or strongly disagreed with the statement "The scientific community is spreading fake news about COVID-19."[37] The fact that COVID led to a dizzying array of theories, hoaxes, and conspiracies comes as no surprise, given the wide range of studies that show how scientific discourse is misunderstood by publics.[38] What our data suggest, in turn reinforcing the findings of prior studies, is that even the scientific misunderstandings can bear the markings of prior assumptions about nations and cultures. Those social media users who held conflicting views about the scientific and medical questions pertaining to COVID-19 also expressed views about China, or the U.S., or their home countries, that reproduced many pre-COVID-19 attitudes. This underlines the importance of understanding scientific disinformation within social and geopolitical contexts, rather than in isolation.

Hoaxes about China and COVID-19

Between January and August 2020, the eighty-eight organizations that belong to the International Fact-Checking Network (IFCN) investigated the veracity of more than eight thousand claims about COVID-19. Two fact-checking organizations based in Africa, PesaCheck and Africa Check, verified the accuracy of at least 180 claims, that is, approximately one per day during the first six months of the pandemic. Out of the eight thousand claims collected by the IFCN, around 10 percent referred to information about China. For example, claims included "Chinese influencer caused the new coronavirus outbreak after eating bat soup" and "Chinese scientists expelled from a Canadian microbiology lab took the novel coronavirus strain

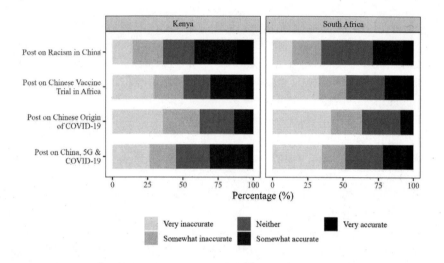

FIGURE 1. Perceived accuracy of hoaxes on social media about China and COVID-19 among Kenyans and South Africans.

with them to China."[39] Using a list of hoaxes, fake social medias posts, digitally manipulated screenshots, and similar materials collected by AFP Fact Check, an international fact-checking organization, we identified four recurring themes in inaccurate information about COVID-19 and China during the early days of the pandemic: theories about the origin of the virus; unproven claims that there is a link between 5G networks and the outbreak of COVID-19; conspiracies related to Chinese vaccines and therapeutics; and, instances of racism against Africans in China, beyond the proven cases of discrimination against some groups of African residents that occurred in the southern Chinese city of Guangzhou.[40]

We tested the believability of these hoaxes (RQ2) by asking survey respondents to indicate how accurate they thought a series of social media posts were. We showed participants four posts, each of which refers to one of the four disinformation narratives listed above. These were posts shared on social media that we retrieved from the collection of fact-checks available on the website of AFP Fact Check.[41] To avoid survey fatigue, each participant only saw two posts selected randomly. After seeing each post, respondents were asked to rate its accuracy (on a scale from 0, for very inaccurate, to 4, for very accurate).[42] We summarize the frequency of responses (in percentages) in figure 1. On average, Kenyans were significantly more likely to believe that the posts they saw were accurate ($M = 1.55$; $SD = 1.04$) than South Africans ($M = 1.39$; $SD = 0.91$). The differences between the two countries were statistically significant—$t(1949.7) = 3.035$; $p < .005$. These scores (below the mid-point of 2 in our scale) indicate that, overall, most survey respondents did not believe the posts to be accurate. However, some differences emerge when we compare the perceived accuracy of different posts.

Two of the hoaxes referred directly to Africa, Africans, or both. One, a video tweeted by a Kenyan social media user, appeared to depict a street fight between Kenyan and Chinese couples in Wuhan. While the video claimed to be from April 2020, it was in fact a much older recording unrelated to COVID-19. Nonetheless, and maybe because other instances of racist responses had occurred against Africans in China in the weeks before we fielded the survey, approximately one-quarter of respondents believed the post to be accurate. The other post related to Africa was a screenshot of a Facebook message shared on WhatsApp that claimed to show the arrival of Chinese vaccines in Burundi. The post asked why the vaccinations would be first distributed in Africa, instead of Europe or America. The images, however, were not from Burundi and did not depict the delivery of vaccines, which were yet to be developed in April 2020. As with the case of the previous post, Kenyans appeared to be marginally more likely to believe the message was accurate than South Africans, but the difference between the two groups was not statistically significant—$t(938.6) = -1.409$; $p = .159$. Furthermore, the percentage of respondents who believed the vaccine post to be somewhat or very accurate was much smaller (Kenya: 30.6 percent; South Africa: 20.8 percent) than for the post about alleged racial abuse in Wuhan (Kenya: 42.1 percent; South Africa: 29.2 percent). This finding suggests that some respondents might have a strongly held belief about racist attitudes in China toward Africans, a possible deterrent for China's attempts to increase its soft power on the continent.

The social media post that was perceived as the least accurate was the screenshot of a video posted on Facebook by an obscure TV network by the name of MOB TV. The post claimed to show a press conference by the U.S. Department of Justice to discuss the arrest of "a Chinese scientist that created coronavirus." Only a very small fraction (Kenya: 13.7 percent; South Africa: 9.3 percent) labeled this post as accurate. Kenyans were overall more inclined to believe the Facebook post was true than South Africans. This also held true for the final post, which depicted a tweet by an American songwriter who linked 5G towers and the outbreak of COVID-19 in China and used a statement by philanthropist Bill Gates as proof of the veracity of the claim. Around 30.9 percent of Kenyans and 21.7 percent of South Africans gave some credence to the tweet. While these two hoaxes referred to China, they were part of wider global narratives and might reveal less about Kenyans' and South Africans' imagery of China and Africa-China relations than the first two posts. Although to some extent contradictory (respondents were unlikely to believe that the U.S. arrested a Chinese scientist but more likely to believe that Bill Gates endorsed disinformation about COVID-19 and 5G), these responses might say more about Kenyans' and South Africans' views of the U.S. and its cultural exponents than it reveals about their attitudes toward China.

Sharing Disinformation to Discuss, Connect, and Take a Stand

Based on the data we collected, it is safe to say that a large majority of Kenyans and South Africans did not believe in hoaxes and rumors on social media about COVID-19 and China. Still, somewhere between a third and a quarter of survey respondents did attribute some level of accuracy to the posts. These values went up significantly when we asked participants about their sharing intentions, that is, how likely they would be to share the social media posts with family, friends, co-workers, and community or church members. Over 45 percent of Kenyans and slightly over 32 percent of South Africans in our survey said they would be "likely" or "very likely" to share the posts they saw, even though many perceived them as inaccurate. Sharing intention was highest with friends (Kenya: 54 percent; South Africa: 38 percent), and lowest with community or church members (Kenya: 35 percent; South Africa: 24 percent). Sharing intention with family (Kenya: 49 percent; South Africa: 38 percent) was higher than with co-workers (Kenya: 46 percent; South Africa: 29 percent).

In this final section of the chapter, we focus on understanding what motivated some survey participants to say they would share the hoaxes they were presented with (RQ3). We also explore the connection between some of the variables described earlier (*attitudes toward China, views on conspiracy theories,* and *xenophobic responses*) and the different motivations to share disinformation. To identify users' sharing motivations, we make use of responses to the question: "You said that you'd be likely/very likely to share the post above with [family; friends; co-workers; community or church members]. Could you briefly tell us why?" This question was posed to survey participants after they saw two of the hoaxes. Each open-ended

TABLE 4. Kenyan and South African media users' motivations for sharing hoaxes related to China and COVID-19 by topic of social media post and country (in percentages)

	ARREST OF SCIENTIST		5G AND COVID		RACISM IN CHINA		VACCINE TRIALS	
	KE	SA	KE	SA	KE	SA	KE	SA
Duty to warn	16.6	15.2	4.6	4.7	13.8	11.8	22.9	18.1
Connecting & caring	9	3.8	7.3	3.7	8.4	4	9.5	6.6
Social currency	0.7	0	0.5	0.2	0.1	0.9	0.2	0.3
Just for fun	0.7	1.6	0.7	2.6	3.3	5.4	0.4	1.2
Just in case	4.4	4.9	2.8	3.3	1.2	1.3	3	3.1
Sharing everything	0.8	1.6	1.4	0.9	0.2	3.8	0.6	1.4
To make a statement	13	13.7	12.4	13.6	31.4	25.9	13.3	15.9
Information is to be shared	22.8	29.9	31.1	34.3	19.2	23.4	25.2	27.2
To warn the post is fake	1.5	2	5.3	4.2	0.4	0.4	4	1.9
It's the truth	2.2	2.4	2	1.2	2.1	2	1.2	1.4
It's interesting/relevant	1.9	5.7	2.5	7.2	1.5	8.3	0.4	4
To spark discussion	20.6	13.4	21.3	15.9	13.2	10.3	14	12.7
To verify	5.4	5.5	7.8	7.5	4.4	0.9	4.4	4.5
Other	0.4	0.2	0.2	0.7	1	1.6	0.9	1.6

response was classified by one of two coders using a taxonomy of motivations that was derived from that introduced in our previous work. We identified fourteen motivations. In table 4, we offer a breakdown, divided by social media post, of frequencies of motivations invoked by those users who said they would "likely" or "very likely" share one of the posts they were exposed to (N = 4,917 statements). Because some of the responses were rather detailed, more than one motivation was identified for several of the posts.

The prevailing motivations were the desire to inform others about current events, to keep them in the know, and to help them make more informed decisions related to COVID-19 (e.g., "I like to share important information with people I know" and "so they can share it with their families to make them aware"). Overall, around 24 percent of responses belong to this category, followed by responses that we labeled as "to make a statement" (18 percent). As shown on table 4, this motivation was most prevalent among those who saw the hoax about a racist incident in Wuhan (over 31 percent for Kenyans and close to 26 percent in South Africa). Many participants made it clear that they would share the post—even in instances where they were not sure about its accuracy—to make a broader political statement (e.g., "That [statement] is racism, and therefore there is need to spread the news maybe for justice"), or to express their discontent with the way other countries, including China, treated Africans (e.g., "to show them how fellow Africans are being mistreated in China while [C]hinese people barely get mistreated in Africa"). Discrimination also featured in responses to other posts. For example, a South African respondent who saw the hoax about vaccine trials in East Africa wrote: "I would share this with family so they know the happenings around the globe and be aware of the things Americans are going to bring into Africa." Around 5 percent of all the statements mentioned China explicitly. Of those, 87 percent were labeled by the coders as "to make a statement," with views ranging from "China must be exposed" to "Kenyans do not like or trust Chinese" and "Chinese have really help[ed] Africa."

The third most common motivation was "to spark discussion" (16.8 percent), followed by "duty to warn" (15.3 percent). Respondents tended to refer to their civic/moral duty to warn others more often when they described reasons to share a post with family members, and they appeared most likely to refer to their desire to spark debate when explaining why they would share it with friends. In line with what Madrid-Morales and his co-authors found through focus group discussions, we observed differences between the motivations for sharing posts related to health and those that might be of a more political nature.[43] For instance, those who saw the post about the conspiracy theory around the links between 5G and COVID-19 were the most likely to share it "just in case" it turned out to be true (e.g., "It is better they know, than if [t]hey don't. We share info, even rumours," and "Better to be safe than sorry and if it turns out true, we would be on the safe side").

We identified two additional motivations that had not been included in previous literature on the topic. The first one, which we labeled as "connecting and caring" accounted for around 9 percent of all responses. This response may be indicative of the strong cultural value of *ubuntu*, a relational ethic found in some African societies, according to which "human beings have a dignity in virtue of their capacity for community, understood as the combination of identifying with others and exhibiting solidarity with them."[44] In some cases, respondents referred directly to how important family, friends, and others were to them (e.g., "because I care for them" or "to create positive hope"). In other cases, there was a religious component to care and connectedness (e.g., "so that we can pray for Africa and Africans in diaspora" or "for spiritual connection comfort in this needy period"). Finally, in some other instances, responses elicited a desire to build or strengthen ties with others (e.g., "mostly to spread friendships around the neighbourhood by learning from other people" or "community is supposed to be there for each other"). We also identified a number of users (5.3 percent overall) who said they would share the hoax to seek the help of others in verifying its veracity. This type of engagement with disinformation was a lot more prevalent than the desire for correcting/confronting (2.6 percent). Some researchers have indicated that in more group-oriented and collectivistic societies, social media users tend to avoid correcting others or confronting those who post content, as this might break important social ties.[45]

To further understand how each of the motivations to share inaccurate information connects to attitudes toward China in general, we fitted a series of regression models.[46] A summary of these analyses is presented in table 5. We did not observe any consistent relationship between attitudes toward China and any specific motivation to share inaccurate information on social media. Negative attitudes toward China did not consistently explain why some users decided to engage with and share the hoaxes. As could be expected, the strongest predictor of sharing was respondents' perceived accuracy of a social media post. Those who believed the post to be true were consistently more likely to say that they were sharing it as a "duty to warn," "to make a statement" or, simply, to pass information along. On the other hand, lower levels of perceived accuracy of the posts were

TABLE 5. OLS regression results for selected motivations to share disinformation related to COVID-19 and China

PREDICTOR	DUTY TO WARN	SHARE INFORMATION	SPARK DISCUSSION	MAKE A STATEMENT	CONNECTING AND CARING	WARN IT IS FAKE
	b	b	b	b	b	b
(Intercept)	-0.35*	0.05	1.12**	-0.09	-0.11	0.25**
Gender (0 = female)	0.04	-0.10	-0.24**	0.21**	-0.01	0.04
Age	0.00	0.00	-0.01*	0.00	0.00	0.00
Country (0 = Kenya)	-0.15*	0.03	-0.22**	-0.17*	-0.19**	-0.03
Attitudes toward China	0.04	0.19**	-0.04	-0.04	0.06*	0.00
Chinese government's response	0.01	0.01	0.07**	-0.05*	0.01	0.00
Xenophobic attitudes	0.05	0.09*	-0.06	0.04	0.06**	-0.02
Views on origins of virus	0.03	-0.01	0.02	0.06	0.01	0.01
Perceived accuracy of posts	0.31**	0.24**	-0.07*	0.33**	0.09**	-0.08**
R^2	.090**	.049**	.042**	.090**	.050**	.039**
			n = 1,278			

* = $p < .05$; ** = $p < .01$

associated with users sharing a post to "warn it was fake" or "to spark discussion." After controlling for multiple other explanations, South African respondents appeared to be significantly less likely than Kenyans to share content as a "duty to warn" others, "to spark discussion," "to make a statement," or "to connect and care." Age did not play any role in explaining users' engagements with the posts, but gender identity did. Female-identifying participants were more likely to share a post to spark discussion, while male-identifying respondents were more likely to share a post to make a statement.

Conclusion

This chapter examined the rise of disinformation in Africa within the context of the COVID-19 pandemic. We argued that the intersection between 1) an increased presence of China in Africa in recent years as part of its geopolitical strategy; 2) the intensification of tensions between China and liberal democracies like the U.S.; and 3) the wide circulation of disinformation around China's role in the COVID-19 pandemic provided a useful lens for viewing the motivations for social media users to share false information. We posited that disinformation about COVID-19 and China provided an entry point into a more broad-ranging analysis of media users' attitudes toward China, its handling of the COVID-19 pandemic, and its cultural attractiveness in general.

Data presented in this chapter show that a significant number of Kenyans and South Africans had a negative view of China, which may have been amplified by the outbreak of the COVID-19 pandemic. Although respondents also displayed strongly critical views about how the U.S. handled the pandemic, they still viewed China in a more negative light overall than the U.S.. This finding may suggest that similar to the limited impact that China's soft power attempts have had on journalism on the continent,[47] the country's appeal among other sectors of the population might also be relatively low.

Despite the robust criticism offered by South African news coverage, South African participants gave the highest score to their own government's response to the pandemic, with the U.S. in last place, after WHO and China.[48] The U.S. was also in last place of the ranking offered by Kenyan respondents. The positive views of China's handling of the crisis, despite respondents' overall negative attitudes toward the country, may have influenced the resistance to xenophobic messaging and implied attribution of blame toward China for the COVID-19 pandemic. The predominant response in South Africa and Kenya was that references to the virus as originating in China or linked to Wuhan were racist. Somewhat contradictorily, respondents from both these countries demonstrated a more xenophobic attitude to foreign travelers, despite limited evidence that halting international travel would mitigate the spread of the virus.

With some exceptions, a large majority of Kenyans and South Africans in our sample did not believe in hoaxes and rumors on social media about COVID-19 and China, but they did show interest in sharing these posts. It is also instructive to understand the reasons why those who indicated that they would share one of the posts they were exposed to would do so. We found that the most prevalent motivations were a sense of "moral/civic duty" to share information and make others aware, and a desire to spark discussion, debates and gather other people's views. We also saw differences between the types of posts, with those about racial injustices making people more likely to want to share to make a statement about their political views. We also identified two motivations that had not been included in previous literature on the topic. Media users indicated that they would share disinformation because it made them "connect and care."

Overall, our study provides new evidence about Kenyans' and South Africans' engagement with disinformation. In line with our previous work,[49] we show that a significant number of social media users do share content that they might consider inaccurate. Our findings are also in line with previous research about what motivates social users to share content.[50] We provide quantitative evidence to support the findings of previous qualitative studies suggesting that a sense of "moral/civic duty" to share information and to create awareness is what drives most sharing on social media. This study further contributes to studies of disinformation by applying existing taxonomies to one case study and by showing that, when it comes to disinformation about China and COVID-19, existing attitudes toward China might not be the main drivers in information sharing, but that contextual factors such as social and cultural motivations play an influential role in sharing practices.

NOTES

This work is based on research supported by the South African National Institute for Humanities and Social Sciences.

1. There has been much debate in the academic literature around terminology such as "fake news" as well as "dis-," "mis-," and "mal-information." These terms refer to varying degrees of harm and falseness and refer to the fact that messengers have different intentions in sharing inaccurate information. See Claire Wardle and Hossein Derakshan, *Information Disorder: Toward an Interdisciplinary Framework for Research and Policymaking* (Strasbourg: Council of Europe, 2017). To avoid confusion, we use disinformation as an umbrella term to refer to all types of false information that have the potential to cause harm.
2. Dumisani Moyo, Admire Mare, and Hayes Mabweazara, "Editorial: Social Media, the Press, and the Crisis of Disinformation in Africa," *Communicatio* 46, no. 4 (2020): 1–6.
3. Herman Wasserman and Dani Madrid-Morales, "An Exploratory Study of 'Fake News' and Media Trust in Kenya, Nigeria and South Africa," *African Journalism Studies* 40, no. 1 (2019): 107–123.
4. Caroline Fisher et al., "Improving Trust in News: Audience Solutions," *Journalism Practice* (2020).
5. "Digital News Report 2021," Reuters Institute, https://reutersinstitute.politics.ox.ac.uk.
6. Devra C. Moehler and Naunihal Singh, "Whose News Do You Trust? Explaining Trust in Private versus Public Media in Africa," *Political Research Quarterly* 64, no. 2 (2011): 276–292.
7. Xiaoling Zhang, Herman Wasserman, and Winston Mano, *China's Media and Soft Power in Africa: Projection and Perceptions* (New York: Palgrave Macmillan, 2016).
8. Dani Madrid-Morales and Herman Wasserman, "Chinese Media Engagement in South Africa: What Is Its Impact on Local Journalism?," *Journalism Studies* 19, no. 8 (2017): 1218–1235.
9. Madrid-Morales and Wasserman, "Chinese Media Engagement in South Africa."
10. Daya Kishan Thussu, Hugo de Burgh, and Anbin Shi, eds., *China's Media Go Global* (London: Routledge, 2018).
11. Bates Gill, "China's Global Influence: Post-COVID Prospects for Soft Power," *The Washington Quarterly* 43 (2020): 97–115.
12. Helen Davidson, "China Police Move to Deter Zero-COVID Demonstrations and Trace Protesters," *The Guardian*, November 29, 2022. See also Guobin Yang, *The Wuhan Lockdown* (New York: Columbia University Press, 2022); Dani Madrid-Morales and Herman Wasserman, "How Effective Are Chinese Media in Shaping Audiences' Attitudes towards China? A Survey Analysis in Kenya, Nigeria and South Africa," *Online Global Media and Communication* (2022). For discussion on resistance in Hong Kong, see,

Hsin-I Cheng and Hsin-I Sydney Yueh, *Resistance in the Era of Nationalisms: Performing Identities in Taiwan and Hong Kong* (Ann Arbor: Michigan State University Press, 2023), which features the chapter "Public Transportation as a Vehicle of Resistance against the Mainlandization of Hong Kong" by Andrew Gilmore.

13. Frédérick Douzet et al., "Mapping the Spread of Russian and Chinese Contents on the French-speaking African Web," *Journal of Cyber Policy* 6, no. 1 (2021): 50–67; Nadège Rolland, "A New Great Game? Situating Africa in China's Strategic Thinking," *NBR Special Report. Washington: The National Bureau of Asian Research*, 2021.

14. Yan Hairong and Barry Sautman, "Chasing Ghosts: Rumours and Representations of the Export of Chinese Convict Labour to Developing Countries," *China Quarterly 210*, (2012): 398–418.

15. Maarit Makinen and Mary Wangu Kuira, "Social Media and Postelection Crisis in Kenya," *International Journal of Press/Politics* 13, no. 3 (2008): 328–335.

16. Jean-Pierre Cabestan, "Beijing's 'Going Out' Strategy and Belt and Road Initiative in the Sahel: The Case of China's Growing Presence in Niger," *Journal of Contemporary China* 118, no. 28 (2018): 592–613.

17. Dani Madrid-Morales et al., "Motivations for Sharing Disinformation: A Comparative Study in Six Sub-Saharan African Countries," *International Journal of Communication* 15, (2021): 1200–1219.

18. Dani Madrid-Morales, "Sino-African Media Cooperation? An Overview of a Longstanding Asymmetric Relationship," in *It's about Their Story: How China, Turkey and Russia Try to Influence Media in Africa* (Johannesburg: Konrad-Adenauer-Stiftung, 2021). See also Eric Olander, "China Paid for a Second Article in South African Media to Promote Vaccine Agenda," *China-Africa Project* 15 June 15, 2021.

19. Catie Snow Bailard, "China in Africa: An Analysis of the Effect of Chinese Media Expansion on African Public Opinion," *International Journal of Press/Politics* 21, no. 4 (2016): 446–471.

20. Keijin Zhao, "China's Rise and Its Discursive Power Strategy," *Chinese Political Science Review* (2016): 1–25.

21. Sarah Cook, *China's Global Media Footprint: Democratic Responses to Expanding Authoritarian Influence* (Washington, DC: National Endowment for Democracy, 2021).

22. For example, see C. S. Bailard, "China in Africa: An Analysis of the Effect of Chinese Media Expansion on African Public Opinion." *International Journal of Press/Politics* 21, no. 4 (2016): 446–471; Madrid-Morales and Wasserman, "Chinese Media Engagement in South Africa: What Is Its Impact on Local Journalism?"; Dani Madrid-Morales and Herman Wasserman, "How Effective Are Chinese Media in Shaping Audiences' Attitudes

towards China? A Survey Analysis in Kenya, Nigeria and South Africa," *Online Global Media and Communication*.

23. Edem Selormey, "Africans' Perceptions about China: A Sneak Peack from 18 Countries" (presented at the Afrobarometer, online, September 3, 2020, https://afrobarometer.org/sites/default/files/africa-china_relations-3sept20.pdf).
24. Pew Research Center, "Unfavorable Views of China Reach Historic Highs in Many Countries," October 2020.
25. Shadi Hamid, "China Is Avoiding Blame by Trolling the World," *The Atlantic*, March 19, 2020.
26. Jérôme Viala-Gaudefroy and Dana Lindaman, "Donald Trump's 'Chinese Virus': the Politics of Naming," *The Conversation*, April 21, 2020.
27. Joshua Kurlantzick, "How China Ramped Up Disinformation Efforts during the Pandemic," *Council on Foreign Relations In Brief*, September 10, 2020; Dani Madrid-Morales, "Sino-African Media Cooperation? An Overview of a Longstanding Asymmetric Relationship," in *It's about Their Story: How China, Turkey and Russia Try to Influence Media in Africa* (Johannesburg: Konrad-Adenauer-Stiftung, 2021), 9–70.
28. Austin Horng-En Wang et al., "Influencing Overseas Chinese by Tweets: Text-Images as the Key Tactic of Chinese Propaganda," *Journal of Computational Social Science* 3, no. 2 (2020): 469–486; Chen Yang, Xinyi Zhou, and Reza Zafarani, "CHECKED: Chinese COVID-19 Fake News Dataset," *Social Network Analysis and Mining* 11, no. 1 (2021): 58.
29. Tendai Dube, "Misleading Claims about Pharmaceutical Company's Covid Vaccine Circulate in South Africa," *AFP Fact Check*, February 11, 2021.
30. Madrid-Morales et al., "Motivations for Sharing Disinformation."
31. Hamid, "China Is Avoiding Blame by Trolling the World."
32. Simon Anholt, "Branding Places and Nations," in *Brands & Branding* (London: Profile Books, 2009), 206–216.
33. Jonathan Corpus Ong, "The Contagion of Stigmatization: Racism and Discrimination in the 'Infodemic' Moment," *MediaWell*, Social Science Research Council, February 4, 2021.
34. J. Hunter Priniski and Keith Holyoak, "Preregistration for Misconceptions Surrounding COVID-19 and a Route to Change Them," http://osf.io/z4ds3.
35. The first measure is the average mean score of the last four statements (*conspiracy beliefs*) in table 3; the second measure is the average mean score of the first four statements (*xenophobic beliefs*) in table 3.
36. Edward C Holmes, "The COVID Lab Leak Theory Is Dead. Here's How We Know the Virus Came from a Wuhan Market," *The Conversation*, August 14, 2022.
37. Dominic Dwyer, "I Was the Australian Doctor on the WHO's COVID-19 Mission to China.

Here's What We Found about the Origins of the Coronavirus," *The Conversation*, February 22, 2021.
38. Ala Irwin and Brian Wynne, eds. *Misunderstanding Science? The Public Reconstruction of Science and Technology* (Cambridge: Cambridge University Press, 1996).
39. The authors were granted access to this unpublished dataset of fact-checks through the Poynter Institute in late 2020. Since then, another version of the database has been made available to the general public at https://www.poynter.org.
40. Hangwei Li, "Mistreatment of Africans in Guangzhou Threatens China's Coronavirus Diplomacy," *The Conversation*, April 17, 2020.
41. The list is available at https://factcheck.afp.com/Covid-19-debunked-rumors-and-hoaxes.
42. At the end of the survey, all participants were debriefed about the nature of the posts and made aware that they were hoaxes.
43. Madrid-Morales et al., "Motivations for Sharing Disinformation."
44. Thaddeus Metz, "Ubuntu as a Moral Theory and Human Rights in South Africa," *African Human Rights Law Journal* 11, no. 2 (2011): 532–559.
45. Andrew Duffy, Edson Tandoc, and Rich Ling, "Too Good to Be True, Too Good Not to Share: The Social Utility of Fake News," *Information, Communication & Society* 23, no. 13 (2020): 1965–1979.
46. We fitted one model for each motivation, which was measured as the total number of times a survey respondent referred to that motivation.
47. Madrid-Morales and Wasserman, "Chinese Media Engagement in South Africa: What Is Its Impact on Local Journalism?"
48. Herman Wasserman et al., "South African Newspaper Coverage of COVID-19: A Content Analysis," *Journal of African Media Studies* 13, no. 3 (2021): 333–350.
49. Herman Wasserman and Dani Madrid-Morales, "Audience Motivations for Sharing Disinformation: A Comparative Study in Four Sub-Saharan African Countries," (paper presented at the International Communication Association, online, May 2020).
50. Madrid-Morales et al., "Motivations for Sharing Disinformation."

China's Twitter Diplomacy

Crafting Narratives of COVID-19

Wendy Leutert and Nicholas Atkinson

"I'M PLEASED TO JOIN TWITTER AND LOOK FORWARD TO ENGAGING WITH MORE Batswana. Feel free to follow me and stay looped in."[1] This was the first tweet by then Chinese Ambassador to Botswana, Zhao Yanbo, after he opened a Twitter account in February 2020. From June 2019 through July 2020, more than twenty Chinese ambassadors created Twitter accounts, a sharp increase from the seven such accounts among Chinese ambassadors from 2015 up until that time.[2] Although several Chinese diplomats, such as former Ministry of Foreign Affairs Information Department Deputy Director and spokesperson Zhao Lijian and then Chinese Ambassador to Brazil Yang Wangming, were already active users, the global COVID-19 pandemic coincided with a surge in ambassador Twitter debuts. As the virus surfaced in China and spread globally, messaging related to COVID-19 became a core theme of Chinese diplomats' Twitter activity during the first half of 2020.

Many government officials worldwide use Twitter as a communication tool. As of June 2020, 163 heads of state and 132 foreign ministers had Twitter accounts.[3] During the COVID-19 pandemic, world leaders actively employed social media like Twitter to soothe, rally, update and inform the public. Take for example Canadian Prime Minister Justin Trudeau, who tweeted in March 2020: "To deal with COVID-19, we need everyone to do their part—this needs to be a Team Canada effort. That's why we're helping businesses right across the country produce supplies that will keep you safe. Watch this video and click this link for more info."[4] Former United States President Donald Trump also routinely used Twitter to disseminate competing narratives characterizing COVID-19 as simply "the flu" and downplay its risks.[5] Twitter's unique ability to instantaneously convey messages to a mass audience in a direct, accessible, and personalized way make it especially well-suited for official use during crises. The rapid evolution of the global pandemic in particular, which amplified uncertainty and the value of time-sensitive information, also enhanced the platform's appeal.

Government officials also used Twitter to shape narratives of the pandemic. For example, former President Donald Trump tweeted on January 24, 2020: "China has been working very hard to contain the Coronavirus. The United States greatly appreciates their efforts and transparency. It will all work out well."[6] However, U.S. leaders quickly pivoted to blaming China, with Trump and then Secretary of State Mike Pompeo repeatedly using the stigmatizing terms "China virus" and "Wuhan virus" to refer to COVID-19.[7] Throughout 2020, U.S. media and government officials issued a flood of tweets alleging China's responsibility for the global pandemic. Some claimed that COVID-19 was a man-made virus traceable to the Wuhan Virology Lab.[8] Others argued that China was culpable for COVID-19's global spread because local government health officials repressed and delayed the release of information about the initial outbreak in Hubei Province.[9] At the state and local levels, U.S. officials also used Twitter to publicize their achievements fighting the virus or, in some cases, to shame those who failed to comply with pandemic-related regulations.[10]

In this chapter, we examine China's Twitter diplomacy about COVID-19 by analyzing an original dataset of Chinese ambassador tweet activity between June 2019 and July 2020. For the twenty-nine Chinese ambassador accounts active during this period, we find that 13,116 out of 32,707 of their tweets (40 percent) were related to COVID-19. Ambassadors primarily used Twitter to describe China's domestic response to the pandemic, stress the importance of international cooperation, highlight the provision of international medical aid to countries worldwide, and affirm the leadership role of the World Health Organization (WHO). At the same time, however, Chinese ambassadors sharply criticized U.S. statements about China and the U.S. COVID-19 response. Building on previous research about different countries' pandemic responses and health diplomacy, this chapter asks: what is the purpose and content of China's Twitter diplomacy about COVID-19?

We argue that Chinese ambassadors have used Twitter diplomacy as a key strategy to shape global and domestic narratives about China and COVID-19. By combining positive messaging with digital displays of anger, diplomats presented China as a responsible international leader while also fostering favorable public opinion at home. Criticism of the Chinese government's initial response to the first reported cases of COVID-19 in Wuhan made reshaping narratives of the pandemic an urgent priority for Beijing. Using an established Western social media platform like Twitter was attractive because it enabled Chinese diplomats to push back directly on unfavorable narratives and craft more positive depictions of China's actions using the very same forum in which content critical of China was generated and shared. Twitter diplomacy reflects the pluralization of global narratives on key issues involving China and its government's use of Western social media platforms to pursue discourse power on a global scale.

This chapter proceeds as follows: The following section situates China's Twitter diplomacy about COVID-19 within the context of China's domestic social media strategies and public diplomacy efforts. Next, we introduce the study's methods and data. In the subsequent section, we present key findings from empirical analysis of Chinese ambassadors' tweets about COVID-19 between June 2019 and July 2020. Finally, we conclude by discussing the specific implications of China's Twitter diplomacy for narratives of COVID-19 and outlining questions for further research.

Twitter Diplomacy in Domestic and International Contexts

"Twitter diplomacy" refers to a concerted, deliberate effort by government officials to use the popular social media platform to engage and influence foreign and domestic audiences. Twitter diplomacy can burnish a country's international image by directly engaging individuals worldwide with multilingual content on a familiar platform. Postings may blend information about official positions on key policy issues with more personalized, informal messages. Twitter diplomacy is a unique tool for official messaging because it ostensibly takes the form of direct, individual-to-individual rather than organization-to-individual communication. Diplomats can use Twitter as a flexible platform to disseminate news, advance official policy positions, promote positive coverage of their country, or engage with members of the public. They can also spar virtually across national borders without any real-world interaction—or even the need to get up from their desks. Social media platforms like Twitter can also help to disseminate traditional foreign policy staples, like policy speeches or statements from diplomatic meetings, to larger global audiences. Such individual and official expressions help craft larger, evolving narratives linking domestic and international scales.[11]

Before the social media era, the Chinese government used regulatory centralization and Chinese Communist Party (CCP) discipline to govern information flows between the state, traditional media, and the public. Commercialization of media in the 1980s generated more liberalized content reflective of audience preferences, which at the time included desire for critical commentary about politics and society and greater political participation.[12] However, domestic media coverage perceived as favorable to protests and violent repression of protests in Beijing's Tiananmen Square and across China in 1989 prompted re-centralization and restructuring of the media's regulatory apparatus.[13] A multilayered bureaucracy emerged as the CCP Central Committee tightened regulation of the entire media supply chain, from production to licensing to distribution.[14] Throughout the 1990s, the Chinese government introduced new licensing regulations for online content, organized industry associations like the Internet Society of China, and increased the liability of internet service providers (ISPs) and internet content providers (ICP) for newly defined online crimes.[15]

Regulating individual expression online became a top priority as Internet and social media use in China exploded. In 2000, estimates put the number of Internet users in China at approximately 22 million.[16] This figure soared to an estimated 710 million users as of 2018.[17] The rapid adoption of social media platforms like Weibo, established in 2009, and WeChat, established in 2010, enabled individual users to generate content and disseminate it rapidly to a large number of people. In 2012, the National People's Congress passed a provision requiring real-name registration for individual Internet and telephone users.[18] It also introduced increased monitoring and criminal liability for users with large followings considered "opinion leaders."[19] More recently, individuals acting as "mediating agents" on the popular Chinese social media platform WeChat have also attracted greater scrutiny.[20]

Chinese officials apply core elements of the domestic social media strategy in China's Twitter diplomacy: agenda setting, blocking, and monitoring. For example, the government molds public opinion via agenda setting through individual influencers and members of the "50 Cent Army," who publish bursts of online commentary to social media and government websites to distract netizens with praise of the Chinese state and its governance.[21] State-supported platformization contributes to the depoliticization of online discourse by "occupying" digital space with feel-good or sensational content designed to capture netizens' attention.[22] The government also deploys social media to limit collective conscience and block potential collective action by erecting administrative barriers and legal disincentives to constrain opinion leaders, deleting politically sensitive comments, blocking targeted keywords and results from search engines, disabling push notifications for news stories, requiring Cyberspace Administration of China (CAC) workers to promote approved news stories on news sites and social media, dictating content and language for news agency use, and increasing liability for ISPs whose networks "allow for illegal activity."[23] This results in what Patrick Dodge terms a "cat-and-mouse" dynamic between the government and citizens characterized by interactive cycles of censorship and dissent.[24] In addition, the government uses social media in a top-down fashion to gather information about local official performance, respond directly to public outcry, monitor individual users, and solicit public feedback on draft policies. Use of social media to promote horizontal information flows within the Chinese bureaucracy remains very limited.[25]

However, some features of China's domestic social media strategy cannot be extended to Twitter. Routine practices of censorship are the most obvious example. Twitter permits all of its users to delete previously posted tweets and to block selected individuals from viewing and commenting on their posts. However, it appears that Chinese ambassadors have used these approaches extremely sparingly. For instance, they have only occasionally employed the hidden-comments function.[26] However, Chinese ambassadors cannot prevent Twitter users from posting content critical about China or from tagging them in those posts (also known as "mentioning," signaled with the "@" symbol). Even though ambassadors rarely responded to such users, the interactive nature of Twitter means that Chinese officials are nevertheless exposed to critical commentary.

Twitter diplomacy can be considered a type of public diplomacy: the process and practice by which governments and other international actors engage foreign publics to promote their interests.[27] Its content includes activities ranging from embassy press releases to state-funded international art and artist tours to academic and cultural exchanges.[28] Public diplomacy may target particular countries and sub-national actors, or it may be oriented toward international audiences more generally. States employ public diplomacy to serve varied interests like improving national reputation and status, attracting foreign direct investment through "nation branding," increasing the credibility of treaty or alliance commitments, and signaling resolve.[29] Public diplomacy frequently underpins soft-power strategies utilizing culture and values to promote particular national images.[30] While public diplomacy is often understood as a long-term strategic effort to promote particularistic state interests, some view it as a fundamentally relational activity of "relationship management" with the potential to confer mutual benefit.[31]

Public diplomacy may encompass multiple types of communication strategies.[32] The first is direct communication: a country providing or seeking to influence information about itself. One such example is Chinese state media companies expanding their operations overseas or buying shares in foreign media.[33] Another instance is Chinese diplomats on Twitter retweeting news and policy positions created and promoted by state media and government bodies that portray China as a generous world power committed to building a shared future for mankind. Another type is indirect communication, in which a government's communication about a country uses materials sourced from that country. This occurs, for instance, when Chinese ambassadors tweet about the U.S. COVID-19 response using U.S. news sources.[34] Another type of a public-diplomacy communication strategy is to encourage and amplify international media that use Chinese sources, such as localized media sources for Chinese diaspora communities.

Social media has become a key platform for China's public diplomacy. As early as 2013, He Yafei, deputy director of the Overseas Chinese Affairs Office, endorsed the adoption of Twitter, Facebook, and other international social media, writing: "We must use new media tools more and more skillfully, encourage more social forces to devote themselves to overseas Chinese public diplomacy, and invite more internationally renowned Chinese elites to use social media to speak out."[35] An official 2015 report on China's public diplomacy described the importance of social media for engaging foreign audiences, suggesting that China "seize the opportunity of digital diplomacy, make good use of new media platforms, and spark positive interactions with the international community." The report noted: "Social media is highly interactive, highly adherent, and less restrictive, so it can become an effective platform for international communication and public diplomacy." It concluded, however, with a note of caution: "It is worth noting that social media is not only an information release platform and a distribution center, but also a site of collision and escalation of opinions, and it may even become a starting point for action."[36]

COVID-19 has made public diplomacy using social media even more appealing to governments because the pandemic has accelerated the digitalization of communication. Pandemic-era media consumption increased across the board, with rising numbers of people accessing news online and through social media. According to a poll conducted by the Reuters Institute in partnership with Oxford University, 73 percent of U.S. respondents surveyed across age groups reported that they used websites or social media to access news in April 2020, a two-point increase from January 2020. During this same time frame, the number of individuals using only social media to access news rose by five points.[37] Such trends may persist well after the pandemic, as the next generation of media consumers relies more heavily on online portals and social media to access information.[38]

The goal of China's Twitter diplomacy is to improve the country's international image by destabilizing critical narratives. Chinese diplomats can exert "sharp power" by using distraction and manipulation to "pierce, penetrate, or perforate the political and information environments in the targeted countries."[39] At the same time, they selectively promote pro-China accounts of current affairs, politics, and culture that differ from—and at times openly push back against—more negative foreign coverage. Direct follows of Chinese ambassador accounts and views of their retweeted postings in user Twitter feeds both reflect and amplify China's discourse power. Twitter diplomacy may also appease Chinese netizens who desire a stronger official defense of China's image, values, and diaspora interests. Many such netizens are located inside China, where Twitter is blocked. However, they can view content from Chinese ambassador tweets when they are translated into Chinese and referenced in outlets like the *Global Times*.

In addition to ambassadors, other official Chinese actors also use foreign social media platforms. Numerous Chinese missions, embassies, and consulates have active Twitter accounts. Examples include the Mission of the People's Republic of China (PRC) to the European Union, the Chinese consulate in Chicago, and the Chinese embassies in Canada, the Philippines, and Zimbabwe.[40] Individual Chinese diplomats other than ambassadors also have Twitter accounts. The most prolific and famous is Zhao Lijian, former Ministry of Foreign Affairs Information Department deputy director and spokesperson, who amassed over 1.9 million followers before pausing his tweets in January 2023. Chinese diplomatic actors also have accounts on other Western social media platforms like Facebook and Instagram. For example, the Chinese embassy in Washington, DC, has a Facebook page, and the Chinese Consulate General in New York City has an Instagram account.[41] Chinese official media, such as Xinhua News Agency and China Central Television (CCTV), maintain accounts with tens of millions of followers on Facebook as well as Twitter.[42] Despite this concerted social media push, however, China's government has struggled to promote an alternative vision of international order and moral appeals relative to the U.S.[43] Recent polling finds that views of China across advanced economies remain broadly negative.[44]

Data and Methods

This study analyzes an original database of Chinese ambassador Twitter activity between June 2019 and July 2020. We built this database by first compiling a list of all Chinese ambassadors and their respective country assignments as provided by China's Ministry of Foreign Affairs.[45] To identify each ambassador's Twitter handle, we next searched online for the ambassador's name, the name of the country where the ambassador is based, and the terms "Twitter" and "ambassador." We confirmed all ambassador accounts directly on Twitter. This process yielded a comprehensive list of all current Chinese ambassadors and their Twitter account information. We then used "Twitonomy," a third-party commercial analytics software, to download Chinese ambassadors' tweets and information about their tweet activity.[46]

Next, we analyzed the content of Chinese ambassadors' tweets. Using a sample drawn from all Chinese ambassador tweets during the study timeframe, we jointly developed a set of categories and keywords for coding. The authors then divided and manually coded each tweet based on its main topics. We then further subset all of the tweets about COVID-19 and repeated this procedure, switching the tweet decks that each author coded in the first round to provide an additional layer of review. Coding was not mutually exclusive: a tweet about COVID-19 in the U.S., for example, would be coded as containing the topics "COVID-19" and "U.S." However, tweets that fell into more than two categories were rare. Any instances in which the correct coding was not immediately apparent were highlighted and set aside for regular coding meetings in which the authors reviewed and discussed such tweets until agreement was reached. When tweets were in a foreign language that neither author was able to read, we used Google Translate to translate and code it.

Our data and methodological approach have several strengths. First, this study is the first to our knowledge to systematically collect and analyze the content of Chinese ambassador tweets between June 2019 and July 2020. This enables us to accurately identify patterns in the thematic content of Chinese ambassador tweets, as well as macro-level trends in Chinese ambassador Twitter activity like temporal clustering of account creation dates. This study assesses the content and purpose of China's Twitter diplomacy. We did not evaluate the veracity of individual tweets, nor did we attempt to measure their efficacy through user engagement statistics or the effects of ambassador messaging on public opinion.

Analysis of China's Twitter diplomacy is growing but remains limited. Journalistic accounts have examined individual Chinese ambassadors and specific tweets, but their findings may not be generalizable to the larger population of Chinese ambassadors active on Twitter.[47] Existing scholarly studies often consider Chinese ambassador tweets in the specific context of "Wolf Warrior" diplomacy,[48] only analyze the Twitter accounts of a small number of Chinese foreign policy entities,[49] or focus on earlier periods of Chinese social media diplomacy in which few ambassador Twitter accounts existed.[50]

Findings

Frequency

We find that tweets about COVID-19 accounted for a large proportion of Chinese ambassador Twitter activity between June 2019 and July 2020. During this period and for the accounts we studied, Chinese ambassadors issued 13,116 tweets related to COVID-19, 40 percent of the total number of tweets during this period. The first tweet mentioning COVID-19 was sent on January 20, 2020.[51] Chinese ambassadors' tweets about COVID-19 increased rapidly, peaking in March 2020, before declining gradually throughout summer 2020. This suggests that COVID-19 emerged as a crucial diplomatic issue for China in early 2020, especially during the early stages of the pandemic's emergence in China and its global spread. After China succeeded in controlling the early phases of its domestic outbreak, ambassadors continued to use their Twitter accounts to shape narratives about COVID-19, but they addressed the pandemic less frequently.

Key themes

The most common theme in Chinese ambassadors' tweets was China's domestic response to the virus outbreak. A total of 3,451 tweets addressed this topic, constituting 26 percent of all COVID-19-related tweets between June 2019 and July 2020. As reports emerged of a novel coronavirus in Wuhan, ambassadors retweeted official sources about the virus's appearance and top Chinese leaders' statements on it. As the scale and gravity of the COVID-19 outbreak grew, ambassadors kept up a steady tempo of Twitter postings, sharing statements from Chinese leaders and state media and urging strength and solidarity.[52] Diplomats also reported on domestic measures to limit virus spread, daily numbers of new cases in major Chinese cities and provinces beyond Hebei, and human-interest stories about survivors and life under lockdown. Although some tweets addressed the officially designated Day of National Remembrance on April 4, 2020, ambassador tweets typically did not share numbers of fatalities or stories about those who passed away or who had lost loved ones to the virus. Chinese ambassadors also tweeted regularly on their presentations of China's domestic virus response to foreign audiences through embassy press conferences, meetings with officials in the countries where they were posted, and other venues.[53]

International cooperation was the second most common theme in Chinese ambassadors' tweets about COVID-19. There were 2,394 tweets that addressed international cooperation, accounting for 18 percent of virus-related messages during this period. Ambassadors stressed in general terms that COVID-19 was "the enemy of the whole human race" and urged international solidarity.[54] Chinese ambassadors also expressed solidarity toward the people and governments of the countries in which they were stationed, using familiar Chinese diplomatic discourse of "long-standing friendship" and "brotherhood."[55] Ambassador tweets underscoring international cooperation also referenced China's participation in summits like the Extraordinary China-Africa Summit on Solidarity against COVID-19 in June 2020 and meetings of the G20 and other international groupings.[56]

Chinese ambassadors also tweeted frequently about international medical aid. There were 1,344 such tweets, accounting for 10 percent of all COVID-19-related tweets during the study period. These messages discussed the provision of free personal protective equipment (PPE), testing supplies, or medical expertise to other countries. In the earliest stages of the pandemic, medical aid across borders involved other countries' assistance to China. Ambassadors reported how neighboring countries like Japan and South Korea, as well as distant countries like Qatar, donated medical supplies to China. However, after China contained the virus and the pandemic spread worldwide, these tweets shifted accordingly to focus almost exclusively on the provision of medical supplies and expertise by the Chinese government, Chinese companies, and Alibaba founder Jack Ma to other countries and Chinese nationals overseas. Such tweets often included photographs of airplanes transporting medical supplies and stacks of boxes adorned with images of China's flag being received abroad. Chinese medical teams dispatched to assist other countries' emergency response also received close coverage.[57]

Chinese ambassador tweets about COVID-19 included criticisms and expressions of anger. There were 701 such tweets, accounting for a total of 5 percent of COVID-19-related messaging during the study period. The vast majority of them—649 out of 701 (93 percent)—expressed anger toward the U.S., accusing top U.S. officials of "lies and fake news" and of making statements that were "groundless and full of racism."[58] The most common form was ambassador retweets of critical commentary by various spokespersons of China's Ministry of Foreign Affairs, in particular Ministry of Foreign Affairs Information Department Director and spokesperson Hua Chunying. In this way, ambassadors amplified critical messaging that the ministry had already tacitly endorsed. However, numerous ambassadors also wrote their own tweets that were highly critical of the U.S. Another form was ambassador retweets of critical commentary by U.S. or other foreign commentators.[59] Although most digital displays of anger targeted the U.S., Chinese ambassadors also expressed antipathy toward Western media and even the West in general.[60] In rare cases, they also criticized local actors in the countries where they were stationed.[61]

Chinese ambassadors tweeted less frequently about other pandemic-related topics. At the start of the outbreak, ambassadors weighed in on the debate about the virus's origins and spoke out against discrimination and disinformation. They also shared information about the virus from Chinese media and WHO, primarily tips about preventing infection by washing hands or staying home. They constructed hero and heroine narratives by spotlighting Chinese frontline medical personnel's efforts to save patients and their selflessness and sacrifice.[62] In addition to coverage of international medical aid, Chinese ambassadors also tweeted about the supply and distribution of PPE sold to other countries. As China succeeded in containing the virus, ambassador tweets discussed sharing China's experience with other countries, for example through webinars with doctors abroad or presentations about key lessons for other countries. As vaccine development got underway, Chinese diplomats often tweeted "Good news!," followed by the latest updates about Chinese vaccine development and global distribution plans. Finally, ambassadors shared uniformly positive messages about China's economy and the international economy, stressing the resumption of work, economic recovery, and the prospect of future growth.

Chinese ambassadors also tweeted about other countries' responses to the pandemic. There were 1,429 such tweets, accounting for 10 percent of all COVID-19-related tweets in the study's timeframe. They ranged from the strong critiques discussed above to more descriptive reporting about the status of the virus's spread and sub-national responses to it. The small number of remaining tweets about other countries' responses to the pandemic centered primarily on the statements and actions of governments in countries where Chinese ambassadors were stationed. For example, Chinese diplomats retweeted updates from local officials about their pandemic preparations or specific actions taken, often adding their own brief commentary.[63] However, ambassadors' Twitter messaging contained minimal tailoring to particular national audiences. Although ambassadors did appear to sometimes highlight pandemic-related topics of high interest to local publics, the overall content and phrasing of their tweets addressing COVID-19 exhibited similar themes and did not routinely vary in response to specific country attributes.[64] Yet there was little evidence of the same tweets being reproduced verbatim across all ambassador accounts, which would suggest greater centralized coordination.

Ambassadors did not typically engage directly with other officials or users on Twitter. Diplomats rarely wrote or responded using the comments function, especially if they were based in places where the public was unreceptive—or even overtly opposed—to Chinese policies. Individual ambassadors' outreach to local publics varied widely. Both before and after the pandemic outbreak, some ambassadors tweeted frequently in the languages of their host states and shared country-specific holiday greetings, photos of themselves in traditional clothing, and images of local food and sights.[65] Despite minimal online engagement with other officials and users, however, ambassadors did interact often with the Chinese Ministry of Foreign Affairs Twitter account. Ambassadors routinely retweeted commentary by individuals like Hua Chunying and occasionally quoted tweets to which they added their own commentary.

Shaping Narratives of COVID-19 through Twitter Diplomacy

China's Twitter diplomacy is an evolving practice that exhibits dynamics of both centralization and decentralization. The concept of "improvisation" within hierarchical constraints evident in the fluid relationship between China's critical journalists and the state is also evident here.[66] In a few instances, the dissemination of specific content appeared to be coordinated across ambassadors. For example, numerous ambassadors tweeted in tandem about China's June 2020 white paper titled "Fighting COVID-19: China in Action," summarizing the country's domestic pandemic response.[67] Ambassadors also frequently retweeted the same tweets by the Ministry of Foreign Affairs spokespersons on COVID-19, suggesting that diplomats were encouraged if not formally directed or required to disseminate these official positions. For the most part, however, Chinese ambassadors enjoyed significant autonomy in their Twitter messaging on the common themes identified above. Some ambassadors tweeted often and embellished their tweets and retweets with emojis and more personal messaging, while others used the platform only occasionally and stuck primarily to tweets or retweets from official Chinese sources. However, Chinese ambassadors' use of Twitter has not always been smooth and successful. While many messages skillfully integrated punchy commentary with eye-catching photos and multimedia content, others appeared awkward and poorly suited to an international audience. Quotations from Xi Jinping's important speeches, for example, are unlikely to have the same resonance or appeal with foreign users as they might with a domestic audience.[68] We also identified examples of Chinese ambassador Twitter accounts being cancelled, although it is unclear if the account deletion was due to their online activity or to their switching of office.[69]

After China ultimately contained the virus outbreak in 2020, ambassadors lauded China's international contributions and stressed solidarity and shared humanity. Emphasis on international cooperation in Chinese ambassador tweets reoriented global discourse away from specific focus on China's virus outbreak, instead highlighting its unity with and contributions to other countries. Chinese ambassadors stressed the imperative of "working together to build a community for a shared future of mankind." They bolstered this position by interspersing their tweets on a variety of topics with calls for solidarity and international cooperation. One common pattern was praising other countries for helping China during its COVID-19 outbreak and then later stressing friendship and reciprocation when China subsequently aided other countries.[70]

In addition to feel-good positivity, ambassadors also used negativity to portray China as a responsible international leader. They did this by criticizing other countries—primarily the U.S.—for their pandemic response. Chinese diplomats also routinely condemned the U.S. and other countries for "pointing fingers" and "smearing China," contending that this detracted from a coordinated and thus more successful global approach to handling the COVID-19 pandemic. By pairing positive commentary about the strength of China's domestic response and its contributions to international cooperation with portrayals of faltering American handling of the crisis and Washington's alleged lack of material support to other countries, Chinese diplomats presented a world in which China—rather than the U.S.—was acting like a responsible great power.[71] Anti-U.S. rhetoric also characterizes highly coordinated PRC disinformation campaigns on other issues such as Taiwan.[72]

Chinese ambassador tweets emphasized China's contributions to international organizations and its commitment to global public-goods provision. They highlighted China's contributions to WHO, Xi's speeches there, and commentary by WHO Director-General Tedros Adhanom Ghebreyesus.[73] Such messages were almost uniformly positive: they endorsed the WHO's leadership role in coordinating the global pandemic response, while also admonishing those who chose to ignore the organization's directives.[74] Chinese officials also stressed China's commitment to providing global public goods like free vaccines to developing countries. Despite the suboptimal efficacy of Sinovac's vaccine at preventing symptomatic COVID infection, Chinese diplomats continued to stress its provision abroad as evidence of China's leadership in global medical aid and the fight against COVID-19.[75] Tweets about China's support for international organizations and global vaccine provision portrayed China as a country with both the capacity and the intent to aid other countries and play a positive global role as a great power.

Chinese ambassadors used Twitter to amplify their voices in global discourse and craft their own narratives of COVID-19 while pushing back on international criticism. Ambassadors' entry into the Twitter-sphere can be understood as part of a larger strategy to attain greater discourse power in shaping global narratives about China across multiple forms of media. Lu Wei, former director of the Cyberspace Administration of China, once defined "discourse power" as "the influence of a country's 'speech' in the world."[76] However, dramatic increases in China's economic, military, political, and cultural influence and the global expansion of Chinese state media have yet to generate a commensurate ability to fundamentally challenge Western-dominated international discourse. According to media analyst Wang Lv: "Associated Press, Agence France Press, United Press International and Reuters supply more than 80% of the news reported around the world, and about 50 top media [companies] in the West own 95% of the share of the global media market."[77] However, online media, particularly social media, offer a new entry point to global-discourse participation with much lower barriers to entry. By joining Twitter, Chinese officials can share favorable narratives of China and engage directly with foreign audiences on the same platforms where unfavorable narratives of China are being created and circulated.

Chinese diplomats further shaped narratives about COVID-19 by citing or even directly retweeting international organization and expert commentaries. Most of the time, Chinese ambassadors disseminated news and narratives generated by Chinese state media and government sources like Xinhua News Agency, CCTV, and Ministry of Foreign Affairs spokespersons. However, they also actively wove in authoritative voices of trusted international sources, ranging from *The Lancet*, a highly-respected peer-reviewed medical journal, to statements by officials from international organizations like WHO. China's efforts to shape global narratives of COVID-19 thus involve not only promoting content from Chinese state media and directly attacking those who criticize China, but also incorporating and elevating credible international voices that support China's preferred account. This strategy aims to engage overseas audiences with established frames of reference and trusted sources, while also providing familiar content to Chinese netizens.

China's Twitter diplomacy also aimed to recast critical foreign narratives about China's COVID-19 handling for a domestic audience. Repeated Chinese ambassador tweets about China's correct handling of the pandemic and pushback against foreign criticism promoted a domestic narrative of the virus centered on success through sacrifice. Digital displays of anger, frequently singling out the U.S., further signaled China's resolve to a domestic audience. Chinese diplomats' use of military language, including terms like battle, defense, and sacrifice, suggest that pandemic narratives of COVID-19 also simultaneously referenced the deteriorating state of U.S.-China relations.[78] State-owned media outlets like the *Global Times* and non-state-owned media like the Observer Network (*Guanchazhe Wang*) routinely translated ambassador tweets into Chinese, frequently highlighting their more combative messages to circulate for domestic consumption.[79] Ambassador tweets were also sometimes posted on Weibo, a platform in China akin to Twitter.

Some have suggested that Chinese ambassadors' critical tweets are part of an emerging "Wolf Warrior" phenomenon that has intensified during the global pandemic. Wolf Warrior diplomacy can be understood as "a new approach among the Chinese diplomatic corps to more aggressively defend their home country online."[80] In 2019, Xi reportedly issued a memo to Chinese diplomats urging them to show more "fighting spirit."[81] A year later, widespread critiques of China's disastrous early handling of the COVID-19 outbreak gave Chinese diplomats ample opportunity to display such mettle. As Peter Martin notes, China's highly centralized political system incentivizes its diplomats to use combative rhetoric to avoid any suspicion of political disloyalty—even if such behavior incurs foreign pushback and reputational damage.[82] Min Ye agrees: "The current regime's emphasis on political loyalty, not professional performance, has driven up the intensity of wolf-warrior diplomacy during Covid-19."[83]

While Wolf Warrior diplomacy has drawn international attention, it is intended primarily for a domestic audience. For ambassadors, such messages show their bureaucratic superiors and citizens at large their commitment to securing China's interests and reputation. Chinese ambassador to France Liu Shaye deemed the popular term "Wolf Warriors" as a term of praise, stating: "I am honored to be awarded the title. We are fighters who stand in front of the motherland and fight for her, and we want to stand in the way of 'mad dogs' that attack China."[84] Provocative messages like this help ambassadors accrue followers and notoriety by fanning public discontent with Western officials and media. Outspoken ambassadors can even parlay such attention for personal and professional benefit, as the promotion of provocative Twitter critic Zhao Lijian from counselor in China's Embassy in Pakistan to the Chinese Ministry of Foreign Affairs Information Department deputy director and spokesperson suggested.[85]

For the Xi administration, the domestic circulation of critical tweets aims to support its continued legitimacy by reacting to perceived foreign pressures and linking nationalist sentiment with the party-led state. Even as COVID-19's threat became global, the responses envisioned to it remained national and framed in terms of the state.[86] Bolstering legitimacy was an especially urgent priority for the CCP because many citizens were angry about government missteps after the initial outbreak. As the pandemic continued, circulation of critical ambassador tweets and commentary critiquing foreign actors facilitated a shift in public attention from domestic to international pandemic conditions.[87] On a larger scale, the amplification of individual Chinese ambassador tweets via state-owned media can be understood as part of broader institutionalized efforts to legitimate Chinese leaders' governance through nationalist appeals to the public.

For Chinese netizens, expressions of popular nationalism are generally permitted by the state and can provide opportunities for both "self-performance" and online community formation.[88] As Guobin Yang writes: "One of the social functions of nationalism is that it provides strong emotional resources for personal identity and a sense of belonging."[89] Online outlets which translate ambassador tweets into Chinese and analyze them for domestic readers, like the Observer Network, commonly feature a "comments" section at the bottom of the articles. These comments sections are active spaces of individual expression and public discussion, even if their content is routinely monitored and curated to include only messages aligned with official positions. In this way, even those in China without access to Twitter or foreign-language ability can also participate indirectly in Twitter diplomacy to some extent. By sharing comments and reading others' views, individual netizens can express their emotions and gain a genuine even if superficial sense of solidarity with fellow citizens. More broadly, the comments sections also function as rare domestic spaces where non-state and state actors simultaneously contest and construct both individual and national identity.[90]

Conclusion

This chapter analyzed the role of China's Twitter diplomacy in crafting global and domestic narratives about COVID-19. Using an original dataset of all Chinese ambassador tweets between June 2019 and July 2020, it finds that Chinese ambassadors used original posts and retweets to address topics including Beijing's self-professed defeat of the virus, the importance of international cooperation, China's experiences and lessons, domestic economic recovery, provision of medical supplies and other aid abroad, vaccine development, virus origins, anti-discrimination, and disinformation. By combining positive messaging with digital displays of anger, most commonly targeting the U.S., ambassadors sought to construct narratives about COVID-19 that promoted China as a responsible international leader while simultaneously fostering favorable public opinion at home.

Several conclusions can be drawn from this analysis. First, China's Twitter diplomacy seeks to destabilize critical narratives about China and COVID-19. Its objective is not to persuade or establish a coherent alternative order, but rather to promote an informational "counter-order" on Western social media platforms by fostering skepticism toward China's critics at home and abroad. Twitter diplomacy's promotion of skepticism by selectively criticizing foreign actors and by elevating credible international voices favorable to China distinguish this from earlier Chinese official media efforts to simply project positive images about China abroad.[91] Second, China's Twitter diplomacy targets both foreign and domestic audiences. Chinese diplomats' tweets engage varied international stakeholders—including officials and citizens in their posting locations, other countries' diplomats and officials, and diaspora communities—as well as Chinese citizens using Twitter or accessing ambassador tweets via domestic platforms. Finally, Twitter diplomacy provides additional evidence of the pluralization of global narratives on key issues involving China and its government's embrace of Western social media platforms to pursue discourse power on a global scale vis-à-vis other countries—especially the U.S. At the micro-level, we find significant variation among individual ambassadors' tweet content, tone, and frequency, even though the strategy of Twitter diplomacy itself is centrally initiated and directed.

How China's government crafts narratives of COVID-19 through Twitter diplomacy is of vital concern today. In November 2022, a rare wave of nationwide popular protests emerged in China against the Xi administration's zero-COVID policies. Even though China's pandemic response prevented mass casualties between 2020 and 2022, its mounting economic and social costs ultimately rendered it a domestic political liability rather than attractive international exemplar. Beginning in December 2022, the government rapidly dismantled key elements of the zero-COVID approach, including lockdowns, quarantines, daily testing, and digital health codes. Chinese diplomats will need to leverage all of the tools at their disposal, including Twitter, to create a positive narrative of China's later-stage response to COVID-19 while pushing back on criticism from home and abroad. As praise and blame contend in contemporary Chinese nationalist discourse, new narratives are emerging about pandemic recovery, resilience, renewal, and resistance.[92]

China's Twitter diplomacy provides important new insight into Beijing's social media and public diplomacy strategies. China's Twitter diplomacy is not limited only—or even primarily—to the pandemic. Out of all tweets by Chinese ambassadors between June 2019 and July 2020, 60 percent addressed topics other than COVID-19. Chinese diplomats are similarly using Twitter diplomacy to craft and contest international and domestic narratives about repression in Xinjiang, protests in Hong Kong, the Belt and Road Initiative, China's space program, and Huawei and

TABLE 1. Chinese ambassadors' COVID-19-related Tweets, by topic (June 2019–July 2020)

TOPIC	# OF TWEETS
International medical aid	1,344
COVID-19 information	170
China's response	3,451
Sharing China's experience	329
Other countries' response	1,429
China's economy	495
International economy	445
Vaccine	423
International cooperation/multilateralism	2,394
Anger referencing the U.S.	649
U.S.	704
Heroes and heroines	530
Virus origins	429
Disinformation	450
Anti-discrimination	383
Anger referencing non-U.S./unspecified countries	52
Other aid	146
Sale of personal protective equipment, medical equipment, medicine	163
Other	51

5G technology. China's Twitter diplomacy about COVID-19 is thus only one part of a broader, ongoing effort to pursue global discourse power on a range of issues.

NOTES

1. Shortly after this chapter's completion, the platform Twitter's name was changed to X; references to Twitter have been retained. Zhao Yanbo (@AmbZhaoYanbo [*account no longer exists]), "I'm pleased to join Twitter and look forward to engaging with more Batswana. Feel free to follow me and stay looped in," Twitter, February 27, 2020.
2. Authors' database, December 2022.
3. Burson Cohn & Wolfe, "Twiplomacy 2020," BCW Twiplomacy, July 20, 2020.

4. Justin Trudeau (@JustinTrudeau), "To deal with COVID-19, we need everyone to do their part - this needs to be a Team Canada effort. That's why we're helping businesses right across the country produce supplies that will keep you safe. Watch this video and click this link for more info: https://bit.ly/2UoQBUP," Twitter, March 20, 2020.
5. For a summary of these instances, see Tommy Beer, "All The Times Trump Compared Covid-19 to the Flu, Even after He Knew Covid-19 Was Far More Deadly," *Forbes*, September 10.
6. Donald Trump (@realDonaldTrump), "China has been working very hard to contain the Coronavirus. The United States greatly appreciates their efforts and transparency. It will all work out well. In particular, on behalf of the American People, I want to thank President Xi!," Twitter, January 25, 2020.
7. See, for example, Secretary Pompeo (@SecPompeo), "Disinformation is not only coming from random actors around the world - but also from the Chinese Communist Party, Russia, and the Iranian regime. We must not permit these efforts to undermine our democracy, our freedom, and how we're responding to the Wuhan Virus," Twitter, March 20, 2020.
8. Tom Cotton, "We still don't know where coronavirus originated. Could have been a market, a farm, a food processing company. I would note that Wuhan has China's only biosafety level-four super laboratory that works with the world's most deadly pathogens to include, yes, coronavirus," Twitter, January 30, 2020. The U.S. government has continued to advance the claim that COVID-19 originated in the Wuhan Virology Lab. See, for instance, the Senate Committee on Health Education, Labor and Pensions report, "An Analysis of the Origins of the COVID-19 Pandemic: Interim Report," October 2022, https://www.help.senate.gov.
9. Thom Tillis, "The Chinese government engaged in one of the biggest cover-ups in modern history, lying to the world and allowing the spread of #COVID19. I introduced legislation with @LindseyGrahamSC to allow @realDonaldTrump to sanction China for its actions," Twitter, May 12, 2020.
10. Andrew Cuomo, "New Yorkers rose to the occasion and together we bent the curve. I'm so proud to be a New Yorker," Twitter, June 8, 2020.
11. On Twitter's use as a tool to shape narratives within and beyond national borders, see for example Burson Cohn & Wolfe, "Twiplomacy 2020," BCW Twiplomacy, July 20, 2020.
12. Michel Oksenberg, Lawrence R. Sullivan, and Marc Lambert, eds., *Beijing Spring, 1989: Confrontation and Conflict: The Basic Documents* (Armonk, NY: ME Sharpe, 1990).
13. Stephen J. Hartnett and Patrick Shaou-Whea Dodge. "Memory Activism and the Rhetorical Politics of Public Secrets, Forced Forgetting, and Dangerous Remembering,"

Rhetoric & Public Affairs 24, no. 4 (2021): 685–725.

14. For example, companies were only licensed to produce content for a specific category of news. Government licensing was also required to operate media-production equipment, like a printing press, and to produce and distribute news materials. Furthermore, distribution was limited to a specific locality to control information flows. See Rogier Creemers, "The Privilege of Speech and New Media: Conceptualizing China's Communications Law in the Internet Age," in *The Internet, Social Media, and a Changing China*, eds. Avery Goldstein, Jacques deLisle, and Guobin Yang (Philadelphia: University of Pennsylvania Press, 2016), 86–105.
15. Creemers, "The Privilege of Speech," 95.
16. Statista Research Department, "Internet Users and Online Shoppers in China 2000–2009," January 15, 2010.
17. Mike Kent, Katie Ellis, and Jian Xu, "Chinese Social Media Today," in *Chinese Social Media: Social, Cultural, and Political Implications*, ed. Mike Kent, Katie Ellis, and Jian Xu (New York: Routledge, 2018), 1.
18. Tania Branigan, "China to Expand Real-Name Registration of Microbloggers," *The Guardian*, January 18, 2012.
19. Creemers, "The Privilege of Speech," 99–100.
20. Wei Wang, "Mediating Agents on WeChat: A Local Turn in the Personification of State-Society Intermediaries," in *Engaging Social Media in China: Platforms, Publics, and Production*, ed. Wei Wang and Guobin Yang (East Lansing: Michigan State University Press, 2021), 159–178.
21. The 50 Cent Army got its name from the fifty Chinese cents that individuals reportedly received for each post. Peter Warren Singer and Emerson T. Brooking, *LikeWar: The Weaponization of Social Media* (Boston: Eamon Dolan Books, 2018), 100. See also Rongbin Han, "Defending the Authoritarian Regime Online: China's 'Voluntary Fifty-cent Army,'" *China Quarterly* 224 (2015): 1006–25; Gary King, Jennifer Pan, and Margaret E. Roberts, "How the Chinese Government Fabricates Social Media Posts for Strategic Distraction, Not Engaged Argument," *American Political Science Review* 111 (2017): 484–501.
22. Guobin Yang and Wei Wang, *Engaging Social Media in China: Platforms, Publics, and Production* (East Lansing: Michigan State University Press, 2021), xix–xx.
23. Creemers, "The Privilege of Speech"; Jeff Kao et al., "No 'Negative' News: How China Censored the Coronavirus," *New York Times*, December 19, 2020.
24. Patrick Shaou-Whea Dodge, "Imagining Dissent: Contesting the Facade of Harmony through Art and the Internet in China," in *Imagining China: Rhetorics of Nationalism in an Age of Globalization*, ed. Stephen J. Hartnett, Lisa B. Keränen, and Donovan Conley (East

Lansing: Michigan State University Press, 2017), 311–338.
25. In one of the few such cases, officials in localities such as Chongqing and Gansu Province have used WeChat groups to informally exchange governance experiences. China News Network [*Zhongguo xinwen wang*], "Weixin wenzheng: Tianshui qingshui xian xiangzhen lingdao ganbu weixin gongzuo qun suxie" ['WeChat governance': Tianshui and Qingshui counties township leading officials WeChat work group sketches], May 16, 2016, https://www.chinanews.com.
26. One example is Yang Wanming (@WanmingYang), "Recomendável: meu artigo sobre a luta contra a pandemia e a segurança da saúde pública" [Recommended: my article about the fight against the pandemic and public health security], Twitter, May 25, 2020.
27. Nancy Snow, "Public Diplomacy," in *Oxford Research Encyclopedia of International Studies*, eds. 2020; Jian Wang, "Localising Public Diplomacy: The Role of Sub-National Actors in Nation Branding," *Place Branding* 2, no. 1 (2006), 32–42.
28. Nicholas J. Cull, "Public Diplomacy: Taxonomies and Histories," *Annals of the American Academy of Political and Social Science* 616, no. 1 (2008), 31–54.
29. Keith Dinnie, *Nation Branding: Concepts, Issues, Practice* (New York: Routledge, 2015).
30. Joseph S. Nye, "China's Soft and Sharp Power," *China-US Focus*, January 5, 2018.
31. Jami Ledingham, "Explicating Relationship Management as a General Theory of Public Relations," *Journal of Public Relations Research* 15, no. 2 (2003), 181–198.
32. Suzanne Xiao Yang, "Soft Power and the Strategic Context for China's 'Media Going Global' Policy," in *China's Media Go Global*, ed. Daya Kishan Thussu, Hugo De Burgh, and Anbin Shi (New York: Routledge, 2017), 90.
33. On the increased presence of Chinese media outlets in Africa in particular, see chapter 9 in this volume; Wasserman and Madrid-Morales, "What Motivated the Sharing of Disinformation about China and Covid-19? A Study of Social Media Users in Kenya and South Africa."
34. The hidden-comments function permits Twitter users to remove selected replies from immediate public view and instead make them accessible only with an additional click. See, for example: Yan Xiusheng (@YXiusheng), repost from CNN Breaking News (@cnnbrk), Twitter, April 22, 2020.
35. "*Guoqiaoban fuzhuren he yafei: shifang qiaowu gonggong waijiao ju nengliang*" [He Yafei, deputy director of the Office of Overseas Chinese Affairs: Unleashing the huge power of public diplomacy for overseas Chinese affairs], October 16, 2013, http://www.gov.cn.
36. All quotations from Zhao Qizheng, Lei Weizhen: "*Gonggong waijiao fazhan baogao (2015)*," [Public Diplomacy Development report (2015)] (Beijing: Shehui kexue wenxian chubanshe, 2015), 192.

37. Nic Newman et al., *Reuters Institute Digital News Report 2020*, https://reutersinstitute.politics.ox.ac.uk.
38. The same poll found that respondents aged eighteen to twenty-four were twice as likely to access news through social media. Newman et al, *Reuters Institute Digital News Report 2020*.
39. Christopher Walker and Jessica Ludwig, "From 'Soft Power' to 'Sharp Power': Rising Authoritarian Influence in the Democratic World," in *Sharp Power: Rising Authoritarian Influence*, ed. Christopher Walker and Jessica Ludwig (National Endowment for Democracy, 2017), as cited in Sarah Hoffman, "Double-Edged Sword: China's Sharp Power Exploitation of Emerging Technologies (National Endowment for Democracy, Forum for Democratic Studies, 2021).
40. Twitter accounts of the PRC Mission to the EU (@ChinaEUMission); the Chinese Consulate in Chicago (@ChineseConsulate); the Chinese Embassy in Canada (@ChinaEmbOttawa); the Chinese Embassy in the Philippines (@Chinaembmanila); and the Chinese Embassy in Zimbabwe (@ChineseZimbabwe).
41. See the Facebook page of the Chinese Embassy in Washington, D.C. (www.facebook.com/ChineseEmbassyinUS/), and the Instagram account of the Chinese Consulate General in New York City (@chinacg_nyc).
42. Qingjiang (Q. J.) Yao, "The News as International Soft Power: An Analysis of the Posting Techniques of China's News Media on Facebook and Twitter," in *Engaging Social Media in China: Platforms, Publics, and Production*, ed. Guobin Yang and Wang Wei (East Lansing: Michigan State University Press, 2021), 133–156.
43. Mingjiang Li and Suisheng Zhao. "The Prospect of China's Soft Power: How Sustainable?," in *Soft Power: China's Emerging Strategy in International Politics*, ed. Mingjiang Li (Lanham, MD: Lexington Books, 2011), 247–266.
44. Laura Silver, "China's International Image Remains Broadly Negative as Views of the U.S. Rebound," Pew Research Center, June 30, 2021.
45. China Ministry of Foreign Affairs Embassy and Ambassador List: https://www.fmprc.gov.cn/mfa_eng/wjb_663304/zwjg_665342/2490_665344/.
46. For information about Twitonomy, see https://www.twitonomy.com/.
47. See, for example, Zhaoyin Feng, "China and Twitter: The Year China Got Louder on Social Media," BBC, December 29, 2019; Jevans Nyabiage, "China's African Envoys Take Twitter Tips from Trump in PR Offensive," *South China Morning Post*, December 14, 2019.
48. Daniel Mattingly and James Sundquist, "When Does Public Diplomacy Succeed? Evidence from China's 'Wolf Warrior' Diplomats," *Political Science Research and Methods* (2022); Min Ye, "Wolf Warriors Blow Hot before Cooling Down," *Global Asia* 15, no. 3

(2020).

49. Chris Alden and Kenddrick Chan, "Twitter and Digital Diplomacy: China and COVID-19," LSE IDEAS Strategic Update, June 2021.

50. Zhao Alexandre Huang and Rui Wang, "Building a Network to 'Tell China Stories Well': Chinese Diplomatic Communication Strategies on Twitter," *International Journal of Communication* 13 (2019): 2984–3007.

51. Chinese ambassador to India, Sun Weidong (@China_Amb_India), retweeted a tweet by CCTV stating: "President Xi Jinping has ordered resolute efforts to curb the spread of the novel coronavirus (2019-nCoV) that caused cases of pneumonia. #XiJinping," Sun Weidong, Twitter, January 21, 2020.

52. For example, the Chinese ambassador to Zimbabwe retweeted a tweet by *China Daily*: "President Xi Jinping on Sunday said the positive trend of containing the novel #coronavirus disease outbreak is expanding. #XiJinping #COVID19," Guo Shaochun (@ChineseZimbabwe), Twitter, February 23, 2020. "Stay strong Wuhan!," the Chinese ambassador to Barbados tweeted, Yan Xiusheng (@YXiusheng), Twitter, April 6, 2020.

53. For instance, the Chinese ambassador to Namibia tweeted: "Today I briefed about current situation of coronavirus epidemic in China. For now, there is no coronavirus cases among Namibians in China. We are confident to get the epidemic contained in shortest time, and will try our best to prevent spreading of the virus into Nambia," Zhang Yiming (@Amb_Yiming), Twitter, January 30, 2020.

54. For example, the Chinese ambassador to Namibia tweeted: "Virus does not respect borders and is the enemy of the whole human race. To defeat the virus, the mankind needs to choose confidence over panic, solidarity over division, and cooperation over scapegoating," Zhang Yiming (@Amb_Yiming), Twitter, May 14, 2020.

55. For instance, the Chinese ambassador to Qatar tweeted: "We are all brothers as a community of shared future. We can only defeat the epidemic by joining hands together," Zhou Jian (@AmbZhouJian), Twitter, March 16, 2020.

56. "Xi Chairs China-Africa Summit, Calls for Solidarity to Defeat COVID-19," Xinhua, June 18, 2020..

57. In Zimbabwe, for example, the Chinese ambassador retweeted a multi-message Twitter thread by a doctor on a Chinese medical team documenting the team's activities in-country, Guo Shaochun (@ChineseZimbabwe), Twitter, May 28, 2020.

58. Zhou Jian (@AmbZhouJian), "Lies and fake news from Mr. Pompeo," Twitter, May 15, 2020; Ambassador Xu Hong (@PRCAmbNL), "What Trump said is groundless and full of racism, totally ignored the great effort and sacrifice made by Chinese people!," Twitter,

March 17, 2020.
59. Zhou Jian (@AmbZhouJian), repost from T-House (@thouse_opinions), Twitter, June 2, 2020.
60. Zhou Jian (@AmbZhouJian), "If they don't shift the blame to China, 'what does that make the West look like?,'" Twitter, May 4, 2020.
61. Yang Wanming (@WanmingYang), "1-As suas palavras são extremamente irresponsáveis e nos soam familiares. Não deixam de ser uma imitação dos seus queridos amigos. Ao voltar de Miami, contraiu, infelizmente, vírus mental, que está infectando a amizades entre os nossos povos," [1-Your words are extremely irresponsible and sound familiar. They are an imitation of your dear friends. Upon returning from Miami, you unfortunately contracted a mental virus, which is infecting the friendship between our peoples], Twitter, March 19, 2020.
62. The construction of hero and heroine narratives about Chinese medical personnel also occurred during China's response to earlier epidemics. See Huiling Ding, *Rhetoric of a Global Epidemic: Transcultural Communication about SARS* (Carbondale: Southern Illinois University Press, 2014), 9–10; Xing Lu, "Construction of Nationalism and Political Legitimacy through Rhetoric of the Anti-SARS Campaign," in *The Social Construction of SARS: Studies of a Health Communication Crisis*, ed. John H. Powers and Xiaosui Xiao (Philadelphia: John Benjamins Publishing, 2008), 109–124.
63. Take for instance Chinese ambassador to Qatar Zhou Jian's retweet of a message by the Qatari Ministry of Public Health asking members of the public to stay home, adding the personal note "Stay at home, for one and for all. #StayHome" and an emoji of a home with a heart. Zhou Jian (@AmbZhouJian), Twitter, April 28, 2020.
64. For example, former Chinese ambassador to Brazil, Yang Wanming, tweeted significantly more often about achievements in vaccine development than diplomats based in other countries. See Yang Wanming (@WanmingYang), Twitter. Since the Chinese company Sinovac was conducting clinical trials for its vaccine in Brazil, this emphasis was likely intentional. Overall, ambassadors to developing countries tweeted more frequently about international medical aid; however, this might also have been because those countries received more of the aid given their economic circumstances.
65. For instance, former Chinese Ambassador to the Maldives Zhang Lizhong fostered a close relationship with the local public on Twitter by frequently engaging other users' tweets, answering questions, and sharing his discoveries about the Maldives and its culture. See Zhang Lizhong (@PRC_Amb_Uganda), Twitter.
66. Maria Repnikova, *Media Politics in China: Improvising Power under Authoritarianism* (New

York: Cambridge University Press, 2017).

67. "China Publishes White Paper on Fight against COVID-19 (Full Text)," Xinhua News Agency, June 7, 2020.
68. For example, see Zhou Jian (@AmbZhouJian), repost from China SCIO (@chinascio), Twitter, March 27, 2020.
69. For example, the Twitter account of Chinese ambassador to South Africa, Lin Songtian (@AmbLINSongtian [*account no longer exists]), was deleted after he departed his post in South Africa, and his Twitter account was replaced by a new one for his successor, current Chinese ambassador to South Africa, Chen Xiaodong (@ChinaAmbSA). For a news report confirming the departure of Lin Songtian and deletion of his Twitter account, see Carien du Plessis, "China's Former Ambassador in New Job," news24, April 16, 2020. An example of an account deletion which occurred during the study's timeframe involved Chinese ambassador to Somalia Qin Jian; however, the circumstances under which his account was deleted remain unclear.
70. "'You throw a peach to me, and I give you a white jade for friendship.' It is China's traditional virtue to repay goodwill with greater kindness," the Chinese ambassador to Botswana, Zhao Yanbo (@AmbZhaoYanbo [*account no longer exists], shared in one such tweet. Zhao Yanbo, March 30, 2020.
71. For example, multiple ambassadors retweeted a post by a Ministry of Foreign Affairs spokesperson stating: "US officials said they offered $100 million to China and other countries. We thank the American people for their kind help. But as a matter of fact, we haven't received $1 from the US government. By the way, has the US paid its dues to WHO?" Hua Chunying (@SpokespersonCHN), Twitter, March 20, 2020.
72. Stephen J. Hartnett, and Chiaoning Su, "Hacking, Debating, and Renewing Democracy in Taiwan in the Age of 'Post-Truth' Communication," *Taiwan Journal of Democracy* 17, no. 1 (2021), 21–43.
73. Examples include: Guo Shaochun (@ChineseZimbabwe), repost from Tedros Adhanom Ghebreyesus (@DrTedros), Twitter, March 7, 2020; Yan Xiusheng (@YXiusheng), "President Xi Jinping addressed the 73rd WHA: China will establish a cooperation mechanism for its hospitals to pair up with 30 African hospitals and accelerate the building of the Africa CDC headquarters to help the continent ramp up its disease preparedness and control capacity," Twitter, May 18, 2020.
74. For example, the Chinese ambassador to the Netherlands tweeted: "Support WHO is support saving lives. Those heeding its advice are more successful controlling [the] virus, while those ignoring its advice are paying a price." Xu Hong (@PRCAmbNL), Twitter, May 24, 2020.

75. A large phase-3 trial in Brazil found that two doses of Sinovac administered fourteen days apart were only 51 percent effective in preventing symptomatic COVID infection; they were 100 percent effective in preventing severe COVID as well as hospitalization after fourteen days from the second dose. WHO, "The Sinovac-CoronaVac COVID-19 Vaccine: What You Need to Know," June 10, 2022.
76. Lu Wei, "National Discourse Power and Information Security against the Background of Economic Globalization," *Qiu Shi Magazine*, July 18, 2010.
77. Suzanne Xiao Yang, "Soft Power and the Strategic Context for China's 'Media Going Global' Policy," in *China's Media Go Global*, ed. Daya Kishan Thussu, Hugo De Burgh, and Anbin Shi (New York: Routledge, 2017), 83.
78. Mika Aaltola, "Avian Flu and Embodied Global Imagery: A Study of Pandemic Geopolitics in the Media," *Globalizations*, 9, no. 5 (2021), 667–680.
79. See for example: "*Meiguo wuqing jujue moxige yimiao qingqiu, wo dashi: 4 zhang tu gaosu ni shei cai shi zhen pengyou*" [The U.S. mercilessly rejects Mexico's vaccine requests, Chinese ambassador: 4 pictures tell you who is the real friend], *Guancha wang* [Observer Network], March 2, 2021.
80. Jessica Brandt and Bret Schafer, "How China's 'Wolf Warrior' Diplomats Use and Abuse Twitter," Brookings Institution, October 28, 2020. In contrast to existing analysis, we find that the "wolf warrior" designation does not accurately capture the full range of variation in individual official messaging. All ambassadors, including those who had the most critical tweets, had messaging that varied widely in its content and tone. See Nick Atkinson, "China's Wolf Warriors Aren't the Majority of the Pack," *The Diplomat*, March 23, 2022.
81. Keith Zhai and Yew Lun Tian, "In China, A Young Diplomat Rises as Aggressive Foreign Policy Takes Root," Reuters, March 31, 2020; "China Demands 'Fighting Spirit' from Diplomats as Trade War, Hong Kong Protests Simmer," Reuters, December 4, 2019.
82. Peter Martin, *China's Civilian Army: The Making of Wolf Warrior Diplomacy* (New York: Oxford University Press, 2021).
83. Ye Min, "Wolf Warriors Blow Hot before Cooling Down," *Global Asia* 15, no. 3 (2020): 102–106.
84. Zhao Yusha, "Chinese Envoy Proud of 'Wolf Warrior' Title to Safeguard National Interest, as China Presents Respectable Image," *Global Times*, June 18, 2021.
85. Yue Hairong, "Zhao Lijian churen waijiao bu xinwen si fu sizhang" [Zhao Lijian appointed as deputy-director of the Information Department of the Ministry of Foreign Affairs], *Pengpai xinwen* [The Paper], August 23, 2019.
86. Priscilla Wald, *Contagious: Cultures, Carriers, and the Outbreak Narrative* (Durham, NC:

Duke University Press, 2008).

87. Guobin Yang, *The Wuhan Lockdown* (New York: Columbia University Press, 2022), 160.
88. Such "self-performance" by individual netizens may involve the use of dramatic and sensationalizing visual memes in addition to written commentary online. Guobin Yang, "Performing Cyber-Nationalism in Twenty-First-Century China: The Case of Diba Expedition," *From Cyber-Nationalism to Fandom Nationalism: The Case of Diba Expedition in China*, ed. in Hailong Liu (New York: Routledge, 2019), 1–12. See also Guobin Yang, *The Power of the Internet in China: Citizen Activism Online* (New York: Columbia University Press, 2009).
89. Yang, "Performing Cyber-Nationalism in Twenty-First-Century China," 5.
90. Kecheng Fang and Maria Repnikova, "Demystifying 'Little Pink': The Creation and Evolution of a Gendered Label for Nationalistic Activists in China," *New Media & Society* 20, no. 6 (2018), 2162–2185.
91. On China's global media strategy and efforts to project positive images of China, see Yang, *The Wuhan Lockdown*, chapter 8.
92. On the 2015 Tianjin explosions, another crisis in China during which epideictic rhetoric of praise and blame interacted with national identity narratives to generate discourses of recovery, resilience, and renewal, see Lisa B. Keränen and Yimeng Li, "Rebuilding in Unity: The 2015 Tianjin Explosions and Renewal Discourses in Chinese Social Media" in *Communication Convergence in Contemporary China: International Perspectives on Politics, Platforms, and Participation*, ed. Patrick Shaou-Whea Dodge (East Lansing: Michigan State University Press, 2021), 149–174.

Contributors

Ji-Hyun Ahn is an associate professor of communication in the School of Interdisciplinary Arts and Sciences at the University of Washington Tacoma. She is the author of *Mixed-Race Politics and Neoliberal Multiculturalism in South Korean Media* (2018). She has published many articles on race and transnational media in East Asian popular culture in journals such as *Media, Culture & Society*, *International Communication Gazette*, *Cultural Studies*, and the *Asian Journal of Communication*. Her most recent project studies anti-Korean sentiment and the rise of (new) nationalism in East Asia.

Nicholas Atkinson is a graduate of the Hamilton Lugar School of Global and International Studies at Indiana University. His current work addresses the evolution of China's media engagement and public diplomacy strategies during the COVID-19 era. Other areas of his research include China's efforts to reduce global poverty and build stronger trade ties with Europe.

Zifeng Chen is a PhD student in the Department of Media and Communications at the London School of Economics and Political Science and also holds a PhD in literature at Peking University. She works as a media commentator for various newspapers. Her research interests include popular culture, cybernationalism, and political ideologies in China. She has published on these topics in many Chinese and English journals, and her dissertation, "The Discourse Field of Contemporaneity: The Construction of 'Traditional Culture' Imagination since the 1980s," has received the Outstanding Dissertation Award from Peking University.

Wendy Leutert is an assistant professor and GLP-Ming Z. Mei Chair of Chinese Economics and Trade at Indiana University's Hamilton Lugar School of Global and International Studies. Her research focuses primarily on Chinese state-owned enterprises, overseas investment, and international development. Her recent publications include articles in *Studies in Comparative and International Development*, *Business and Politics*, *World Development*, *New Political Economy*, *Pacific Affairs*, and *The China Quarterly*.

Zihao Lin is a hearing, sighted doctoral student (he/his/him) in the Department of Comparative Human Development at the University of Chicago. Trained in communication in China and Germany, Lin uses social network analysis, critical discourse analysis, and ethnographic methods to understand human practices and meaning-making processes in the increasingly digitalized world. Lin's current research interest includes the politics of disability and deafness, access intimacy, and the technical and affective labor of "information barrier-free" projects in contemporary China.

Yingyi Ma is professor of sociology and the director of Asian/Asian American studies at Syracuse University. In 2019, she was selected as a Public Intellectual Fellow at the National Committee on U.S.-China Relations. Ma is a sociologist of education and migration. She has published extensively in the areas of college major choices, international student mobility, and higher education in China. Her book, *Ambitious and Anxious: How Chinese Undergraduates Succeed and Struggle in American Higher Education* (2020) by Columbia University Press, has since been featured in various national and international media outlets such as the *Washington Post* and *Times Higher Education*.

Dani Madrid-Morales is a lecturer in journalism and global communication at University of Sheffield, United Kingdom. He has published extensively on global communication flows, the impact of digital media in Kenyan and South African societies, and the influence that foreign countries (e.g., China and Russia) have on sub-Saharan African media markets. In his most recent work on misinformation in sub-Saharan Africa, he has measured the prevalence of inaccurate information on the continent (with results appearing in *African Journalism Studies*) and described users' motivations for sharing misinformation (with results appearing in *International Journal of Communication*). He is co-editor of *Disinformation in the Global South* (2022) with Herman Wasserman.

Bingchun Meng is a professor in the Department for Media and Communications at the London School of Economics and Political Science (LSE), where she directs the LSE PhD Academy and co-directs LSE-Fudan Global Public Policy Research Centre. Her research interests include gender and the media, political economy of media industries, communication governance, and comparative media studies. She has published widely on these topic areas in leading academic journals. From 2020 to 2021, she served as a Senior Fellow of Global Governance Futures 2035 organized by the Global Public Policy Institute in Berlin under the sponsorship of the Bosch Foundation. Her book *The Politics of Chinese Media: Consensus and Contestation* was published by Palgrave in early 2018.

Veronica Jingyi Wang is currently a PhD candidate of cultural studies at Cambridge University. Her PhD research looks on queer culture and youth space in China, and she has previously written works on folk culture, media representation, and subaltern literature of China. Before joining Cambridge, Veronica studied international relations (receiving a BS) and anthropology (receiving a MS) at the London School of Economic and Political Science. While being an academic, she is also active in putting her research into public impacts through managing her own social media video platforms in China, writing for public magazines, and introducing Sino-U.K. cultural exchange. Her most recent public engagement project is on representation of Asian women on screen.

Yan Wang is a research fellow in the School of Public Policy at the London School of Economics and Political Science (LSE) and a former LSE fellow in LSE's Department of Methodology. She received a BS in sociology and an MA in management from Tsinghua University and a PhD in sociology from LSE. Her research focuses on state legitimacy and public opinion. She is especially interested in how actors' agency shapes authoritarian governmentality and the realization of the public's social rights, and how and why public opinion changes during the state-society interactions. Wang has won several research grants, including a Research Infrastructure and Investment Fund grant at LSE and a British Academy Small Grant. She is the author of the book *Pension Policy and Governmentality in China: Manufacturing Public Compliance* (2022). Her recent publications include articles in the *Information, Communication, & Society*, *Journal of Chinese Political Science*, and *The China Quarterly*.

Herman Wasserman is a professor of journalism at Stellenbosch University, South Africa. He has published widely on media in sub-Saharan Africa; the intersection of geopolitics, media, and power; and disinformation in Africa. His latest monograph is *The Ethics of Engagement: Media, Conflict and Democracy in Africa* and he is co-editor of *Disinformation in the Global South* (2022) with Dani Madrid-Morales. He is editor in chief of the journals *Annals of the International Communication Association* and *African Journalism Studies*. He is a fellow of the International Communication Association.

Yizhou Xu is an assistant professor of media studies at Old Dominion University. His research interest deals with the mobile technology industry in China, particularly at the intersections of platforms, labor, and state policy. Xu was a postdoctoral fellow at University of Michigan's Digital Studies Institute, and he obtained his PhD in Media & Cultural Studies from the University of Wisconsin, Madison. Prior to completing his PhD, Xu was a documentarian and broadcast journalist based in Beijing, working for news agencies including CBS News, NPR, and Swiss TV. His work has been published in *Social Media + Society*, *Journal of Cultural Economy*, and *Communication and the Public*.

Guobin Yang is the Grace Lee Boggs Professor of Communication and Sociology at the Annenberg School for Communication and the Department of Sociology at the University of Pennsylvania, where he directs the Center on Digital Culture and Society and serves as deputy director of the Center for the Study of Contemporary China. He is the author of *The Wuhan Lockdown* (2022), *The Red Guard Generation and Political Activism in China* (2016), and *The Power of the Internet in China: Citizen Activism Online* (2009). He is also the editor or co-editor of six books, including *Engaging Social Media in China: Platforms, Publics and Production* (2021).

Elaine J. Yuan is an associate professor in the communication department at the University of Illinois at Chicago (UIC). Her research focuses on how digital technology and new forms of communication mediate various social institutions and cultural practices. Her award-winning book, *The Web of Meaning: The Internet in a Changing Chinese Society* (2021), examines the role of the Internet as a symbolic space for the changing cultural practices of privacy, nationalism, and the network market in China. Her research has been funded by the U.S. Social Science Research Council, Chiang Ching-kuo Foundation, Kaifeng Foundation, UIC Institute for Public Civic Engagement, and UIC Institute for the Humanities, and UIC Institute for Research on Race and Public Policy.

Ning Zhan is currently an associate professor of communication at Shanghai International Studies University and a PhD candidate in sociology at Syracuse University. Ning Zhan's research focuses on examining mental health issues among individuals in contemporary China.

Yang Zhan is an assistant professor of cultural anthropology in the Department of Applied Social Sciences and a committee member of the China and Global Development Network at the Hong Kong Polytechnic University. She was a research fellow of China India Institute at New School for Social Research in 2021. Zhan's research interests include infrastructure of development, urbanization and migration, mobility and temporality, and voluntarism and anthropological theory. Her articles have appeared in *Urban Studies, Cities, Positions, Dialectical Anthropology, Urban Anthropology, Anthropological Forum, China Information*, and *Pacific Affairs*, among others. She also writes in Chinese and publishes in Chinese journals and media outlets. Zhan is the winner of the 2020 Eduard B. Vermeer Prize for the Best Article and was shortlisted for the Holland Prize in 2022. Her research projects have been supported by the Association for Asian Studies and Hong Kong Research Council.

Yuxi Zhang is a research fellow at the LSE–Fudan Global Public Policy Hub of the School of Public Policy at the London School of Economics and Political Science. Zhang received a PhD in social policy from the University of Oxford. Her research seeks to understand the healthcare universalization reform in China and, more broadly, social-policy developments in emerging market economies. Before joining LSE, she was a post-doctoral research fellow at the Oxford Blavatnik School of

Government. During the pandemic, she led a team to research China's public policy responses to COVID-19 and developed an interest in studying government and society resilience during turbulent times. She is the winner of the UKRI Strategic Priorities Fund grant. Her academic research and policy-engagement contributions have appeared in *Governance, PLOS One, Journal of the Royal Society Interface, Parliamentary Affairs*, the *WHO Global Preparedness Monitoring Board*, the *World Economic Forum*, and *Bloomberg*.

Index

A

AFP, 170, 200
Africa Check, 199
African attitudes toward China, 189–208
African migrants in China, 115–16
Agamben, Giorgio, 167, 174
Agence France Press, 227
AI captioning software, 82–85
AIDS epidemic, xii
Alibaba, xvii, 46, 50, 51, 54, 61. *See also* DingTalk
Alipay, 34, 54, 57
Aliyun, 54, 61
American Sign Language (ASL), 72
Americans with Disabilities Act (ADA), 70
Anand, Nikhil, 6
anger, 86, 106, 107, 139, 148, 150, 223, *231*
anti-African racism, 115

anti-Asian hate incidents, xxii (n.3), 115–16, 150
anti-Asian hate speech, 193
anti-Asian racism, 94, 127–28
anti-foreigner hate incidents, 115–16
anxiety, 53, 96, 108, 119, 123, 139, 147, 157–58
Appel, Hannah, 6
Asian exceptionalism, 172–73, 179
Asia Times (publication), 170
Associated Press, 227
attendance system (DingTalk), 53–54, 56, 59–61
avian flu outbreak (2013), xii, 140

B

barrier-free communication, 68–87
Basu, Rashmita, 10

248 | Index

BBC, 170
Beck, Ulrich, 98, 116, 117, 121, 124
Beijing, China, 25, 31, 97, 98
Beijing Xicheng Grandpa case, 151–54
Bethel House, 74–75
Biden administration (U.S.), 7
biopolitical nationalism, xiv–xv, 167–68, 174–79. *See also* K-quarantine model; nationalism
Biosewoom, 176
Black Lives Matter movement, 115–16
BosonNLP, 144, 162 (n.40)
Bowles, Samuel, 140
Bristow, Nancy, xi
Brown, Wendy, 15

C

Canada, 10, 199, 213–14, 219, 232 (n.4)
captioning practices, 81–85
care work, 34, 39
CCTV (China Central Television), 168, 220, 227
Cellular Broadcasting Service (CBS), 177
Center for Disease Control (KCDC, South Korea), 171
Centers for Disease Control and Prevention (CDC, U.S.), 7
chat box, 78–81
Chen, Julie, 51
Chengdu, China, 34
Chengdu Girl case, 149, 154–58, 159
China: avian flu outbreak and, xii, 140; Beijing Xicheng Grandpa case in, 151–54; CCP, 216, 228; Chengdu Girl case in, 149, 154–58, 159; college entrance exam (*gaokao*) in, 96, 101, 102–3; contact tracing in, 3, 4–5, 33–34, 45, 138; disability studies reading group in, 67–87; disinformation about, 191–208; "going out" strategy of, 189–91; government-grassroots system in, 10; lockdowns in, ix, 25–26, 38, 42 (n.27), 45, 141–42, 147–48; media perceptions of, xv; mediascape of, 191–95, 216, 233 (n.14); SARS epidemic in, xii–xiii, 33; sociality and context in, 141–43; Twitter diplomacy by, 213–31; Wolf Warrior diplomacy of, 190, 221, 228, 239 (n.80); zero-tolerance policy in, ix, x, 99, 230. *See also names of specific cities and companies*
Chinafrica (publication), 191
China Global Television Network (CGTN), 191
China Radio International (CRI), 191
Chinese Communist Party (CCP), 216, 228
Chinese disability reading group, 67–87
Chinese international students: on freedom, as concept, 93–111; mediated experiences of, 115–34
Chinese mediascape, 191–95, 216, 233 (n.14). *See also* China; social media
Chinese phase, as concept, 169
Chinese Sign Language (CSL), 69, 77–78, 89 (n.22), 90 (n.26)
Chinese Students for BLM (Facebook group), 115–16
choice, 101–3
Choli, Marilena, 140
Chow Yiu Fai, 167
Chun, Wendy, 50, 52
Chung Sye-kyun, 170
class politics, ix, 125–29
clock-in/clock-out attendance system, 53–54, 56, 59–61
CNN, 170
collectivism *vs.* individualism, 95–111

community, 30–32

community councils, 31

Confucianism, 95, 172, 173–74

conspiracy theories, xi, 193, *196,* 197, *198,* 199–200, 202, 205. *See also* disinformation

contact-tracing apps, 3, 4–5, 33–34, 45, 138. *See also* surveillance

control/resistance, 27. *See also* modes of control

cooperation. *See* solidarity

cosmopolitan capital, 97

cosmopolitanism, 97–99, 117, 133

Cotton, Tom, 232 (n.8)

counterveillance, 58–60. *See also* surveillance

COVID-19 pandemic (2020–), overview, ix–xv. *See also* pandemic crossings, as concept

Crenson, Matthew A., 11

crisis of disinformation, 189. *See also* disinformation

Crooks, Roderic, 50

CSL (Chinese sign language), 69, 77–78, 89 (n.22), 90 (n.26)

Cultural Foundations of Learning (Li), 95

Cultures and Organizations (Hofstede et al.), 95

Cuomo, Andrew, 232 (n.10)

Cyberspace Administration of China (CAC), 217, 226–27

D

Dahl, Adam, 12

Dai Ruikai, 68

danwei, 30

dataveillance, 50. *See also* surveillance

Day of National Remembrance, 222

deaf people and digital communication, 67–87, 89 (n.22)

death statistics, 6

de Kloet, Jeroen, 167, 174

Deng Xiaoping administration, 93

Ding, Huiling, xii

DingTalk, xiv, xvii, 46–62

disability studies reading group, 67–87. *See also* sign interpreters

Disability without Borders (DwB), 70

discourse power, 227

disinformation, 191–208, 209 (n.1)

Djokovic, Novak, 137

Dodge, Patrick, 217

Dong Ensheng, 143

Drug Utilization Review (DUR) system, 177

Du Hongru, 143

E

East Asian explosion, as phase, 169, 172

East-West dichotomy, 172–74

e-commerce, 28, 34–38

educations systems, 95–97

Edwards, Terra, 68

El País (publication), 170

English, Alexander S., 140

epistemic crisis, 14

ethics of care, 26

European explosion, as phase, 169

exceptionalism, 172–73, 179

Extraordinary China-Africa Summit on Solidarity against COVID-19, 222

F

Facebook, 14, 100, 116, 123, 201, 218, 220. *See also* social media

fake news. *See* disinformation

fear, 105–6, 139

federal health systems, 10
fengbishi guanli, 31–32
fengcheng, as term, 26
50 Cent Army, 217, 233 (n.21)
5G technology and COVID-19, 200, 201–2, *203,* 205, 230–31
Five One policy (China), 93–94
floating populations, 28
Floyd, George, 115
Fong, Vanessa, 97–98
Foucault, Michel, 167, 174
freedom and Chinese international students, 93–111
Friedner, Michele, 86

G

gaokao, 96, 101, 102–3
Gardner, Lauren, 143
geolocative tracking, 53–60. *See also* surveillance
Germany, 10
germ theory, 9
Ghebreyesus, Tedros Adhanom, 226
Ginsberg, Benjamin, 11
Global Health Security Index, 6
Global Times (publication), 219, 227
"going out" strategy, 189–91
Google Meet, 61
Gottweis, Herbert, 175, 177
government-grassroots system in China, 10
grid management, 32
Gries, Peter Hayes, 98
Grutter v. Bollinger, 96
guankongqu, 30
Guo, Shaochun, 236 (n.57), 238 (n.73)
Guardian (publication), 170
Gupta, Akhil, 6

H

H-1B visa program, 94
H1N1 influenza, 143
Hall, Stuart, 116
Han, Byung-Chul, 172
Hartblay, Cassandra, 68
hate incidents, xxii (n.3), 94, 115–16, 150. *See also* racism; xenophobia
hate speech, ix, 15, 150, 193. *See also* racism; xenophobia
healthcare industry (U.S.), 6–9
Health Code app (Tencent), 33–34, 54
health-code system, xv–xvi, 27, 33–35, 43 (n.42), 54–57
hegemonic order, 129–33
Hell Chosŏn, 178
hero and heroine narratives, xii, 175, 185 (n.41), 223, 237 (n.62)
He Yafei, 218
historical documentation as moral action, x–xi
hoaxes about China and COVID-19, 199–202. *See also* disinformation
Hong Xu, 236–37 (n.58), 238 (n.74)
household registration system, 33
Hua Chunying, 223, 225
Huang Shixin, 71
Hu Luanjiao, 68
Hwang Woo-suk, 175, 185 (n.41)
hypermobility, 29

I

iFlytek, 82
iMessage, 52
im/mobility, 27, 29. *See also* mobility restrictions
individualism, 9–10, 95–111. *See also* personal

freedoms vs. public security
individualized consideration, as concept, 96
Infectious Disease Control and Prevention Act (South Korea, 2015), 177, 181
influenza pandemic (1918), xi
Information Accessibility Design Guidelines to Information Terminal Equipment for Persons with Physical Disabilities, 71
infrastructures. *See* public infrastructures and pandemic crossings
Instagram, 220. *See also* social media
Institute of Medicine, 16
institutional contexts of digital technology infrastructures, 3–18
International Fact-Checking Network (IFCN), 199
International Health Regulations (WHO), 16
international medical aid, 222–23, 237 (n.64)
International Standard Organization (ISO), 171
International Traveler Information System (ITS), 177
Internet Society of China, 216
itinerary-code system, 27

J

Japan, 25, 74–75
jiankangma. *See* health-code system
Jin, Peter, 140
Johnson administration (UK), 8, 137

K

Kang, Jaeho, 183
Keating, Elizabeth, 68
k'ei pangyŏk. *See* K-quarantine model
keju, 96
Kenya, xv, xx, 190–208

Keränen, Lisa B., 140
Kim Byoungsoo, 177
King, Nicholas B., xiii
KI-Pass, 177
KogeneBiotech, 176
Korea and quarantine. *See* K-quarantine model
Korea International Exhibition Center (KINTEX), 176
Korean Broadcasting System (KBS), 173
Korean Center for Disease Control (KCDC), 171
Korea Trade Promotion Corporation (KOTRA), 176
K-drama, 182
K-pop, 182
K-quarantine model, xix–xx, 168–83
Kuss, Daria J., 140
Kwon Jun-wook, 178

L

labor migration, 28
Larkin, Brian, 5–6
Lee Sung-yoon, 172
LGBTQ communities, 104, 180–81
life-expectancy rate, 6
Li Jin, 95
Lindholm, Kirsten N., 140
Lin Jian, 167
Lin, Zihao, 61
lockdowns: in China, ix, 25–26, 38, 42 (n.27), 45, 141–42, 147–48; in South Korea, 168–83. *See also* mobility restrictions
loyalty, 228. *See also* nationalism
Lu, Jackson G., 140
Lu Wei, 226–27
Lu Yingdan, 147

M

Ma, Jack, 223
Ma, Zhiying, 32
Madrid-Morales, Dani, 191
Malle, Bertram F., 141
Martin, Peter, 228
Marxism, 131
Mason, Katherine, xii
mediascape statistics, 227. *See also* Chinese mediascape
medical aid, 222–23, 237 (n.64)
Microsoft Teams, 61
Ministry of Culture, Sports, and Tourism (South Korea), 170
Mirus, Gene, 68
mobility restrictions, 26–27, 28–32, 34–38, 93–95. *See also* lockdowns; risk control and society; surveillance
modes of control, 51–53, 54–57. *See also* contact-tracing apps; surveillance
Mok, Jonathan, 115
Monroe, Andrew E., 141
Moore, Phoebe, 49
moral action, research as, x–xi
moralization, xix, 137–40, 148, 151, 153–54, 158–59

N

Naive Bayes system, 144
Nakamura, Karen, 74–75
nationalism, xiv, 97–99. *See also* biopolitical nationalism; Twitter diplomacy
National People's Congress (China), 216
Nemorin, Selena, 50
neo-Taylorism, 49
NetEase, 46
networked governance, 11–12
New Genetics and Society (publication), 175
Northern Sign Language, 90 (n.26)

O

Observer Network (*Guanchazhe Wang*), 227–28
Olympic Games (Beijing, 2008), 97, 98
One Belt Road Initiative (China), 29
12345 hotline, 35, 43–44 (n.44)
online collaborative software (OCS), 51
online crimes, 216
othering, 149. *See also* racism; xenophobia
outsourced labor, 27, 34–38, 51

P

Pan, Jennifer, 147
pandemic crossings, as concept, xiii–xiv. *See also* COVID-19 pandemic (2020–), overview
pandemic individualism, 9–10. *See also* individualism
panopticon, 50
Pei, Minxin, 93
People's Republic of China (PRC). *See* China
personal freedoms *vs.* public security, 16, 106–8. *See also* individualism
personal identity, 104, 119, 125–29
personal is political, 125–29
PesaCheck, 199
platform economy, 34–38
Pokémon GO, 60
Pompeo, Mike, 214, 232 (n.7)
population control, 33
populism, 14–15
PRC Law on the Protection of Disabled Persons (rev. 2018), 71
privacy advocates, 4–5

public administration system, 10–13
public diplomacy, 217–18. *See also* Twitter diplomacy
public infrastructures and pandemic crossings, 3–18, 27–29
public security *vs.* personal freedoms, 16, 106–8. *See also* individualism
public sphere, 13–15
public-value model, 12

Q

quantified self, 50
queer communities, 104, 180–81

R

race and identity politics, 125–29
racial violence, ix, xiv, xxii (n.3), 115–16, 150
racism, xi, xxi, 94, 115, 127–28, 131–32, 173, 197–204, 208, 223. *See also* hate incidents; hate speech; stigmatization; xenophobia
reading group, online disability studies, 67–87
read receipts (of DingTalk), 52–53
Regulations on the Construction of Barrier-Free Environment (China, 2012), 71
remote sign interpretation services, 74–78
research and inquiry, x–xi, 48
Reuters Institute, 219, 227
ride-hailing services, 51
right-wing populism, 15
risk control and society, 30, 33–35, 115–18, 121, 124, 155–58, 180. *See also* mobility restrictions; surveillance
Robinson, Andrew, 49
Rogers, Emily Lim, 68
Roy, Melissa, 141
rumors. *See* disinformation
rural-urban migration, 28
Ryan, Michael, 33

S

Salazar, Noel B., 25
SARS (Severe Acute Respiratory Syndrome) epidemic (2003), xii–xiii, 33
Schmelz, Katrin, 140
Science (publication), 3
Scott, James C., 59
SD Bio-sensor, 176
sealed management, 31–32
Seegene, 176
selfishness, 106–7
self-quarantine app, 168
sentiment research, 143–51, 162 (nn.40–41)
Seoul National University, 173, 181, 186 (n.57)
sexuality, 104
Shanghai, China, 10, 25–26, 28, 110, 163 (n.48)
Shanghai Sign Language, 90 (n.26)
shequ, 30–32
Shew, Ashley, 68
Shijiazhuang, China, 25
Shinch'ŏnji, 169, 180
Sichuan Chengdu Girl case, 149, 154–58, 159
signed exact Chinese (*shoushi hanyu*), 77–78. *See also* Chinese Sign Language (CSL)
sign interpreters, 73–78, 89 (n.22). *See also* disability studies reading group
Sina Weibo, 143, 158
Singapore, 25
Sinovac, 237 (n.64), 239 (n.75)
SisaIN (publication), 173, 174
Slack, 46, 51
Slack, J. D., 120
smartphones, xiv

sociality and digital technologies, 137–59
social media: China's Twitter diplomacy, 213–31; Facebook, 14, 100, 116, 123, 201, 218, 220; Instagram, 220; as news source, 122, 219, 235 (n.38); WeChat, xiv, 34, 38, 58, 78–81, 216; Weibo, xiv, 122, 138, 143, 155, 158, 216, 227. *See also* Chinese mediascape
soft power, 192, 201
Sogou, 82
Solgent, 176
solidarity, 139–41, 225–26
Sorman, Guy, 172
Soss, Joe, 12
South Africa, xv, 190–208
South Korea, xiv–xv, 25, 167–83
standardized testing, 96, 101
state-led infrastructure, 28–29
static developmentalism, 131–32
Stevens, Mitchell, 96
stigmatization, ix, xii, 110, 139, 141, 155–56, 181, 197. *See also* racism; xenophobia
Stop AAPI Hate, xxii (n.3). *See also* anti-Asian hate incidents; anti-Asian hate speech
Sung Yoonmo, 178
supervised learning method, 143
surveillance, xvii, 28–33, 49–51, 54–60. *See also* counterveillance; mobility restrictions; risk control and society
suzhi, 106, 108
synchronized data set, 143

T

Taiwan, 25, 226
Tencent (company), 33, 46
Thailand, 25

think otherwise, as concept, 69
three-tier system (China), 28
3T model, 170–71, 177
Tiananmen Square incident (1989), 216
Tianjin, China, 28, 73, 240 (n.92)
Tibet, 98
Tibetan Sign Language, 90 (n.26)
Tillis, Thom, 232 (n.9)
time-space companionship, 34
Tomb Sweeping Day event, 145
Tooze, Adam, 121
travel and visa restrictions, 93–95. *See also* mobility restrictions
Treichler, Paula, xii
triumphalism, 110–11
Trudeau, Justin, 213–14, 232 (n.4)
Trump administration (U.S.), 7, 94, 99, 107, 197, 214, 232 (n.6)
tuanzhang, 38
Twitonomy software, 220
Twitter diplomacy, xiv, xxi, 213–31. *See also* nationalism; social media

U

ubuntu, 205
UN Convention on the Rights of Persons with Disabilities (UNCRPD), 70–71, 73
United Kingdom, 115–34
United Press International, 227
United States: African attitudes toward, *196*, 197; Chinese international students and, 93–111, 120, 125–26, 129–32; on Global Health Security Index, 6; hate speech and racial violence in, ix; public administration in, 10–13; visa programs of, 94. *See also names of specific leaders*

Updahya, Carol, 51
urban spatial zones, 30
U.S. explosion, as phase, 169

V

vaccination programs, x; in Africa, 193; in Brazil, 237 (n.64), 239 (n.75); in China, 94, 226; conspiracy theories on, 200, 201; in Singapore, 25; in South Korea, 25, 183 (n.5); in Taiwan, 25; in U.S., 6, 176
Van Assche, Jasper, 140
van Dijck, José, 50
Voibook, 82
Voice of America, 170

W

Wald, Priscilla, xii
wanggehua guanli, 32
Wang Lv, 227
WeChat, xiv, 34, 38, 58, 78–81, 216. *See also* social media
Weenink, Don, 97
Weibo, xiv, 122, 138, 143, 155, 158, 216, 227. *See also* social media
WhatsApp, 52
witnessing, xix, 94, 118, 133
Wolf Warrior diplomacy, 190, 221, 228, 239 (n.80)
Woolly, Jared, 140
workplace surveillance, 49–51
work visa programs, 94
World Health Organization (WHO), 3, 16, 33, 107, 169, 178, 197, 214, 226
World Trade Organization (WTO), 97
Wray, Christopher, 99
Wuhan, China, 25, 26, 141, 147–48, 232 (n.8)

wuliu, 28
wu zhang'ai shehui, 71

X

xenophobia, 116, 140, 193, *198,* 202, 207–8. *See also* hate speech; racism; stigmatization
Xi administration, 225, 226, 228, 230, 236 (nn.51–52), 238 (n.73)
Xi'an, China, 25
Xiang, Biao, 29, 36
Xingtai, China, 25
Xinhua News Agency, 220, 227
Xinjiang, China, 26
xinxi wu zhang'ai, 71
Xu, Daniel H., 10
Xu Yiqing, 147

Y

Yang, Guobin, 229, 233 (n.14, n.20, n.22), 240 (n.87, n.88)
Yang Wangming, 213, 234 (n.26), 237 (n.61), 237 (n.64)
Yong, Ed, 6
Yuan, Elaine J., 55

Z

zero-tolerance policy (China), ix, x, 99, 230
Zhang Yiming, 236 (nn.53–54)
Zhao Lijian, 213, 219–20, 228
Zhao, Xin, 140
Zhao Yanbo, 213
Zoom, xiv, 61, 67–87
Zuboff, Shoshana, 49